T0246302

VINTAGE CRIME

The publisher and the University of California Press Foundation gratefully acknowledge the generous support of the Richard and Harriett Gold Endowment Fund in Arts and Humanities.

VINTAGE CRIME

A SHORT HISTORY OF WINE FRAUD

REBECCA GIBB

UNIVERSITY OF CALIFORNIA PRESS

University of California Press
Oakland, California

© 2023 by Rebecca Gibb

Library of Congress Cataloging-in-Publication Data

Names: Gibb, Rebecca, 1981- author.
Title: Vintage crime : a short history of wine fraud / Rebecca Gibb.
Description: Oakland, California : University of California Press, [2023] |
    Includes bibliographical references and index.
Identifiers: LCCN 2023005933 (print) | LCCN 2023005934 (ebook) |
    ISBN 9780520385931 (cloth) | ISBN 9780520385948 (ebook)
Subjects: LCSH: Wine adulteration—History. | Wine fraud.
Classification: LCC TP548.5.A38 G53 2023 (print) | LCC TP548.5.A38 (ebook) |
    DDC 641.2/209—dc23/eng/20230301
LC record available at https://lccn.loc.gov/2023005933
LC ebook record available at https://lccn.loc.gov/2023005934

Manufactured in the United States of America

32 31 30 29 28 27 26 25 24
10 9 8 7 6 5 4 3 2

This book is dedicated to the inspirational boys and families living with Duchenne muscular dystrophy, and to those working unceasingly to find a cure.

Contents

Introduction: A Story as Old as Wine Itself   1

1. When in Rome   10

2. Dying for a Drink   30

3. An Enlightened Drinker?   50

4. I Predict a Riot   73

5. Appellation Nation   94

6. Winegate   118

7. You Say "Prost," I Say "Frost"!   138

8. Indiana Jones and the Glass Crusade   163

9. A Message to You, Rudy   185

10. The Last Drop   203

Acknowledgments   211

Notes   215

Selected Bibliography   233

Index   251

Introduction

A STORY AS OLD AS WINE ITSELF

THIS IS A FAKE WINE BOOK.

Readers looking to learn about the wine regions of France or the grape varieties of Italy will find slim pickings. Neither will you find a catalogue of every wine fraud committed, but you have not been duped: *Vintage Crime* is an abridged history of wine told through some of the most high-profile wine scams and some of the lesser-known duplicitous behaviors that have plagued wine for as long as it has been traded.

This is a book about people as much as wine, and people generally prove more interesting than fermented grape juice. There would be no wine without man—or woman—and there would be no drinkers to deceive, and thus this is a tale of people's relationships not only with wine, but with each other. At all stages, from the harvesting of the grapes to the last drops in the bottle, the trust of wine drinkers has been violated by grape growers and vintners, wine merchants and collectors. Even the wine cognoscenti have had the wool pulled over their eyes by men (and it is almost always men) seeking to mislead others for their own financial gain, as well as a boost to their ego and social standing. A splash of narcissism blended with greed makes for a toxic combination.

Yet victims of wine tinkering do not see themselves as losing out if they are unaware of the fraud. The guilty parties throughout history have generally been wine producers or merchants, and "as long as counterfeit wine goes undetected, the victims (excluding the honest wine producers who may lose market share to the false wines) may not really be victimized at all," suggests Copenhagen University law professor Lars Holmberg. "With the exception of wines adulterated with substances hazardous to the drinker's health, consumers are not necessarily hurt by wine fraud. As long as they believe the wine in their glass to be of satisfactory quality they may also perceive it to be so."[1] If a wine fulfills its purpose, does it matter that it is not what it claims to be? Does the deception invalidate the drinking experience? Granted, there is no forgiving those who knowingly adulterate wine and endanger the health of the final consumer, but throughout history, wine amelioration has often been accepted as a means of improving the wine-drinking experience. Instead of incarcerating these mixologists, perhaps we should thank them for saving us from a mouthful of sour, insipid wine.

Most wine misdemeanors can be categorized as amelioration rather than health-endangering adulteration. Ameliorated wines have given pleasure to drinkers for thousands of years, and ultimately, wine is about pleasure—not forgetting its intoxicating effect. Since Roman times, makers and vendors have been adjusting fermented grape juice to make it taste better, often in the hope of achieving a higher price. Whether it was the culturally acceptable addition of herbs and spices to mask the vinegary tendencies of wine in the first century AD, or bolstering weedy wines from northern France with riper, richer reds from Algeria in the early 1900s, ameliorating what nature failed to provide has been commonplace in a bid to make a nice glass of wine within the customer's budget. Even the wealthy have preferred their wines with a bit of something: a little over a century ago, supposedly purist Burgundy drinkers preferred that wine when it was enriched with a generous splash of rich Châteauneuf-du-Pape. Blending has always been a tool for wine producers and merchants, and the practice continues today in some of the most revered wine regions, including Bordeaux. Indeed, the likes of Châteaux Latour, Mouton Rothschild, or Haut-Brion typically make tens of thousands of bottles a year of their flagship wines, and these are typically composed of three varieties: Cabernet Sauvignon, Merlot, and Cabernet Franc, with the occasional splash of Malbec or Petit Verdot sometimes sneaking into the final blend. Each of the varieties within the classic trio brings qualities and characteristics that the others don't possess, and it could be argued this is amelioration with the law on its side. This form of blending has been legitimized by makers, vendors, and wine experts who corroborate the practices of a place, and appellation laws created in 1936 that cemented and validated the then practices of French wine regions. Their goal? To make wine that provided the greatest pleasure possible.

Why do we drink wine? For Christians, wine has religious symbolism: a sip of red from the communion cup during the Eucharist embodies the blood of Jesus Christ. Throughout history, wine has also been prized for its medicinal purposes, whether it was used for cleaning wounds or easing pain. While its health benefits are a source of heated debate today, it has long been viewed as a healthy and civilizing beverage rather than the route to alcoholic ruin.

Beyond its holy and healthy purposes, we drink wine because it gives us joy. Pleasure is "the end result of drinking a good wine" for most wine drinkers.[2] Pleasure can be derived from wine in different ways. Primarily, it is sensory pleasure: putting the glass to your lips and drinking in its heady scent and succulent texture before it gently warms your throat. This experience is available to anyone who wishes to indulge. For example, my mother doesn't know much about wine, but she can discern an outstanding wine from a bottle of plonk. That's why there is an empty magnum of 1986 Château Palmer holding open her kitchen door. It is a reminder of a wonderful birthday dinner in 2009, enhanced by a silken, sumptuous red wine that she can still conjure the taste of to this day. Did she enjoy it less than a Bordeaux aficionado who knows the soil types in the village of Margaux, home to Château Palmer, or the grape varieties that created the blend, or the season's weather conditions? You don't need to be a Master of Wine to be able to take pleasure from a great wine. However, to wine lovers, the beverage is much more than just a glass of alcohol—it is the people, the places, and the history that seize them and lead to an expensive habit. A trained palate helps identify components within the wine, the origin of flavors and textures, and such stimulation may bring greater joy; it may also detract from the pure, hedonistic pleasure of drinking wine. What's more, experience can also create a sense of expectation and lead to disappointment when a wine is compared with bottles or vintages that have been enjoyed previously. Ultimately, knowledge may improve your experience of what's in the glass, but it won't change the taste, as a former professor of philosophy at San Francisco State University explains: "Most wine knowledge does not directly enhance the pleasures to be had in wine, but rather, enhances one's ability to discover such pleasures. But the pleasures it gives you are not sensory but cognitive."[3]

This book should also leave you asking: What is an authentic wine? It's a slippery question. The notion of authenticity has morphed throughout time as cultural norms have evolved; it continues to mean different things to different people. As far back as imperial Rome, authenticity was desired by those who could afford it: the wealthy enjoyed rare wines from specific origins that reflected their wealth and good taste. Wine, as well as food, became a status symbol rather than simply fuel. Two thousand years later, many individuals still use wine as a means to gain kudos in their social circles. Ego is surely one of the driving forces behind the slew of pictures of the rarest and oldest bottles that a small bunch of elite wine drinkers post on their social media feeds, leaving the humbler drinker with a severe case of missing out. As the demand for fine wine from finite vineyards has grown globally, the world's wealthiest have seen price as no barrier to having these bottles in their cellars. The rewards for selling fake fine wines labeled as Burgundy and Bordeaux's best have become greater, while the risks of being caught in the rather chummy world of wine collecting have until recently been relatively low.

In this context of high reward and low risk, it is unsurprising that enterprising albeit dishonest individuals have been a driving force in a growing counterfeit culture. Wine shares similarities with the art world: talented artists-turned-forgers have embarrassed many dealers and galleries by convincing these so-called experts that their fake masterpieces are genuine. One of the problems that fine art shares with wine is that "the art world still relies, to a great extent, on the word of individual experts, connoisseurs whose personal opinion can change an artwork's value by millions."[4] It is the same with wine. "If the world believes that a work is authentic, then its value is that of an authentic work, whatever the truth may be."[5] In the most high-profile wine fraud cases in the past forty years, expert individuals have mistakenly given dubious bottles the thumbs-up, lending the fraudsters and their wine collections an aura of authenticity.

While fine-wine collectors are concerned that the contents of their bottle match the label, the notion of authentic wine has become more loaded in recent years. Head into a hip wine bar in a cosmopolitan city and the word *authenticity* often relates to the way in which a wine is made, rather than whether the wine is verifiably from vineyard A or château B. The natural-wine movement, which attracts some evangelical supporters, has positioned natural wine as the most authentic form of the beverage. The movement started in the 1980s as a backlash against chemical farming and mass-produced wines. Most producers of natural wine farm their vineyards organically, shunning synthetic pesticides, herbicides, and fertilizers, while others go a step further, adopting biodynamic farming methods based on the tenets of Austrian philosopher, spiritualist, and writer Rudolf Steiner. Followers work according to the lunar calendar and create esoteric concoctions to put in their compost, such as oak bark fermented in an animal's skull. Natural winemaking is a case of intervening as little as possible in the cellar, which means allowing natural yeasts to get the fermentation process going, rather than adding purchased yeast, and making no adjustments to the grape juice with commercially bought additives, other than perhaps a dash of sulfur dioxide, a naturally occurring antimicrobial and antioxidant, at bottling. While the French introduced a certification system for natural wine in 2020, there is no universal definition of it, which leads to wide interpretations. Unfortunately, positioning natural wine as authentic or "real" wine suggests that other wines are less natural or less genuine, which inevitably aggravates the non-naturalist majority. There is also the matter of different palates— one drinker might consider wine that is cloudy and smells like a farmyard to be faulty, while another might claim the same liquid is truly authentic to its roots.

Wine, at least, has a definition, making it easier to define what is and what isn't real wine in the eyes of the law. But it was a long time coming. In 1889, the French finally came up with a definition, one prompted by financial concerns: beverages that purported to be wine were undercutting the real thing. This was a time of shortage for the nation's winemakers, who were battling the vine louse phylloxera, which was laying waste to vineyards and wine communities. In a bid to quench the country's thirst, many drinks marketed as wine were created using rehydrated raisins or secondhand grape skins mixed with sugar, water, and coloring, rather than fresh grapes; wine producers trying to eke out a living in the midst of the continent's most devastating vine pandemic needed to differentiate themselves from these cheaper look-alikes. The *loi Griffe,* or Griffe law, stated that "no one may ship, sell or put up for sale under the name of wine a product other than that coming from the fermentation of fresh grapes or fresh grape juice."[6] For the grape growers of late nineteenth-century France and the politicians trying to protect the livelihoods of the people in their local regions, the Griffe law was a partial victory: artificial wines could still be sold, but they could no longer be marketed as "natural" wine after 1889.

The Griffe law marked the beginning of greater political involvement in the wine industry, which played a pivotal role in fighting fakes in the late nineteenth and early twentieth centuries. Fraud—in its many guises—was an economic threat to a large section of the rural community, and without laws to protect it, it faced financial ruin. There were no rules preventing a wine merchant from buying white grapes from the Loire or the Languedoc, for example, and turning them into a bottle of sparkling wine labeled Champagne. Legally, the perpetrators of this creative labeling were doing nothing wrong, and some customers didn't notice the difference in taste—some even preferring what would now be considered a counterfeit. Was a given wine authentic? Few French drinkers cared. But grape growers did: farmers could not attain the prices they needed to pay the bills because the arrival of wines from other parts of France and overseas depressed local grape prices. Out of economic hardship arose mass protests and violent riots. Those who are struggling to protect their livelihood will naturally have a different relationship with wine than those who quaff it without a second thought. That relationship affects our perceptions of what is authentic and whether we are victims of fraud.

In France, decades of pressure from wine producer groups led to the birth of an appellation system, which created borders around regions and villages to ensure that only Champagne could come from Champagne, Châteauneuf-du-Pape from Châteauneuf-du-Pape, and Chablis from Chablis. It was a protectionist move rather than a firm belief in a winemaker's ability to craft a wine with a sense of place from a set of specific grape varieties with a defined flavor. The concept of creating boundaries to protect local wines against the misuse of their name by rival wine producers and the perils of blend-and-bottle wine merchants hung on the concept of *terroir* (pronounced terr-wah). This French term—which doesn't translate directly into English, so has generally been adopted by English speakers—describes a place where a wine has been grown. This includes the soil and the climate, as well as the human choices involved in tending that piece of dirt. Entire books have been dedicated to discussing the concept of terroir, and the wine world has swallowed the term whole. The concept has spread its roots across the globe—a sign of France's revered status in wine circles—and it is the basis of the appellation system, which has been copied many times over.

Wine that comes from somewhere is by its nature finite. Terroir implies a specific piece of land that gives a wine a specific taste or texture that cannot be replicated elsewhere on planet Earth. In a world of multinational winemaking corporations, the idea of a small vineyard and artisanal wine taps into modern notions of authentic wine with provenance at its heart. However, the word *terroir* is now applied liberally and haphazardly. It has been appropriated by wine regions, winemakers, and marketing teams to lend gravitas to their places. And yet all wine comes from somewhere, so every wine has a terroir—good, bad, or indifferent. It's also subject to change: famous appellations—whether Chablis or Sancerre—have grown far beyond their original size, in no small part due to demand for their dry, crisp white wines rather than the suitability of the land. Similarly, the world's most revered Bordeaux estates are not classified by their land and can acquire vineyards from lesser-ranked producers, incorporating into their more expensive wines grapes that were previously destined for cheaper, less coveted wines. The late Paul Pontallier, managing director of Bordeaux's Château Margaux, tried to explain why this was permitted:

"Terroir is like genetics: you get what you're given but it takes education and nurturing. It's nurturing nature."[7] Terroir, it seems, is subject to interpretation by the grower, the winemaker, and the drinker; it cannot be measured or quantified, and yet we have imbibed the concept as if it were ancient and holy, which it is not. As social anthropologist Marion Demossier, who has studied the Burgundy wine region for more than twenty-five years, notes, "The concept originated in the codification of the AOC in the Burgundy wine region in France as recently as the early twentieth century yet in the early twenty-first century has come to be considered as a natural law of the quality of wine and some other consumer products."[8] What's more, the taste of a wine and its link to a place is a very modern phenomenon.

The coming chapters will whisk you back to the Roman empire and then lead you, via England, France, Germany, Austria, Italy, and more, to a twenty-first-century courthouse in New York City. This is a chronological history of wine, one told through some of the most well-known cases of fraud in addition to less well-documented incidents that have intrigued me personally. This is not a history of every wine fraud that has taken place—there are far too many to count—but each of the instances chosen takes place within a seminal period of change for the world of wine, allowing us to better understand that period of social and cultural history. Some chapters do not rest on a single instance of fraud but on general wheeling and dealing across an extended period (such as imperial Rome), while a chapter devoted to lead in wine traces its use from the 1600s to the present day. There are dark alleys to navigate and unsavory characters to meet along the way, so buckle up for this juicy journey.

1

WHEN IN ROME

||||||||||||||||||||||||||||||||||||||||||||||||||||||||||||||||||||||||||||||||||||||||||||||||||||||||||||||||||||||||||||||||||||||||||||||||||||||||||||||||||||||||||||||||||||||||

IT'S A SCORCHING SEPTEMBER MORNING in Provence and several families are crammed into a storage room swapping their perfectly good twenty-first-century clothes for rough togas. Nike Airs are ditched for bare feet; baseball caps swapped for leafy wreaths. This group of friends and family give up one precious weekend each year to do a job once reserved for Roman slaves: treading the grapes. On this same piece of dusty dirt more than two thousand years ago, it would have been hard to imagine that vines would still be grown on this piece of land and that its modern-day owner would attempt to re-create the wines of the first century.

The Mediterranean sun has not received the memo that autumn is approaching, and the picking team rises early to avoid the sweltering afternoon heat. The machine harvesters, which normally straddle the rows of vines, extracting bunches with a vigorous shake, remain in the shed. The sound of revving tractor engines and shuddering vines is replaced by voices singing. Rather than modern-day secateurs, Roman-style knives slice the stems of the whole bunches of sweet white grapes, which fall softly into baskets below. The vines are trained high on Roman-style pergolas, making it an infuriating task for the vertically challenged, but even the smallest of children help turn the harvest into wine, squashing the grapes under their tiny feet in the Roman cellar.

When local vigneron Hervé Durand took over the wine estate Mas des Tourelles in the early 1970s, he had a strong inkling that this was not just a place to grow grapes. The surface of the vineyard was strewn with pieces of pottery, Roman tiles, and small vases. Sixty years earlier, a local archaeologist and caver had spotted that there was something below the surface of the vineyard. It wasn't until Durand returned home after a stint teaching winemaking in a remote part of Argentina that anyone would bother investigating what really lay beneath the vines. It turned out that there was quite a lot more than roots and soil. Trowels at the ready, teams of archaeologists discovered that this was not only a modern-day place to make wine but had been home to a prolific amphora factory. They unearthed furnaces that had the capacity to produce between 1,500 and 2,000 amphoras a day. The clay-fired jars were used to transport the region's wine and olive oil. They might have gone on a cart along the Via Domitia, the first highway in France, which ran close to Mas des Tourelles. Romans literally paved their way over the Alps to connect Italy with France and didn't stop laying the road until they reached Spain. Remnants of the Via Domitia show it would have been a bumpy ride; it would be another two millennia before the French built their wide, smooth autoroutes. Most of the wine-filled amphoras, however, would have been sent to Beaucaire, then known as Ugernum, just four miles away. There, the wines would be loaded onto ships that sailed down the Rhône River to the Mediterranean Sea and beyond.

The amphoras found at Mas des Tourelles weren't just any old terra-cotta vases. Their makers had created a remarkably lightweight model for ease of shipping. Archaeologists painstakingly pieced together an amphora from the many fragments found on the site and found that these amphoras weighed just ten kilos, rather than the usual thirty, making it far easier to transport the local wines. The amphoras from Mas des Tourelles had some impressive journeys: remnants of these clay wine jars bearing the factory's stamp have been found in Ostia, close to Rome, as well as in Germany and England.

The discovery of the amphora factory was just the beginning of Durand's Roman adventure. He wanted to know more about the people who had lived in the area and worked the land back when Julius Caesar was busy conquering Gaul, so he called in the world's leading experts on Roman wine. They were only too happy to help when he told them he wanted to do what no one had done before: re-create a Roman cellar to make wines that the empire's citizens would have recognized. Durand consulted the texts of all the major writers on agriculture during Roman times, particularly Cato,[1] and the winery took shape: he installed a concrete trough where toga-clad children and their parents now tread the grapes annually, the khaki-green juices running into a channel below. Durand's teenaged grandson, an inauthentic twenty-first-century plastic bucket in hand, scoops up the liquid and pours it into *dolia*, large earthenware jars that can hold up to 450 liters of fermenting wine or a small child, as the younger members of the harvesting gang eagerly demonstrate before Durand's exasperated wife scolds them. Despite the enthusiastic treading of the many sticky-calved volunteers, there's more juice waiting to be liberated from the grapes, and that's where the Roman press comes in, which involves a winch and a 2,500-kilogram oak beam and requires four strapping men to operate. It's inevitably slow going, but boy does it draw a crowd.

Indeed, hundreds of visitors come to Mas des Tourelles to watch the Roman harvest in action, and on that day, the winery grounds resemble a trailer park. A flock of RV-driving holidaymakers turn up with their tour guide Jacky, a septuagenarian with a bushy mustache that would be the envy of any East London hipster. The tour group has already visited the Pont du Gard, a three-tiered aqueduct built in the same century in which the amphora factory at Mas des Tourelles hit peak production. On the eve of the Roman harvest, the RV drivers park, unload their fold-out tables and camping chairs, and dine off plastic plates. The next morning, they desperately seek shade from the ceaseless sun under the olive trees until the winery opens the doors to its Roman cellar.

It's inevitable that the winery tour concludes with corks being pulled, and the estate's three Roman wines are poured for the visitors: a red wine sweetened with honey, a dry white infused with seawater, fenugreek, and orris root, and finally a wine with a healthy dollop of *defrutum*—grape juice reduction—which imparts a flavor of hard candy. These wines are a historical novelty, the styles so unfamiliar to the modern drinker that few are likely to buy a case. It is all a question of taste, and there's no doubt the Romans liked their wines—and food—heavily flavored, often to disguise what was beneath. The practice of adding a generous splash of seawater—preferably sourced a decent distance from the fetid waters near the shore—as well as herbs, and exotic spices for the wealthy drinker, wasn't seen as adulterating but as improving on what nature had failed to provide. Romans did not raise their eyebrows when herbs and spices were found swimming around in their amphoras; all they needed was a strainer to make the wine free of floaters. It would take chemists two millennia to come to grips with the science of turning grape juice into wine and to learn how to prevent it from souring; in the meantime, Romans used these additions to disguise wine's vinegar-like characteristics and gradually developed a liking for the flavors imparted by the camouflaging agents.

Given the growing taste for pepped-up wines, producers often added spices, herbs, and floral essences after fermentation, or hosts might add a dash of pepper or cumin to perk up a wine before serving it to their guests. Meanwhile, Romans on the road were known to carry a packet of their favorite herbal blend to infuse any wine they bought from the local tavern, in the same way that Brits take their favorite tea bags on foreign holidays. Taking it a step further, Apicius, the author of the most famous Roman cookbook, offered his own spiced wine recipe, which required heating more than 650 grams of honey with a little over a liter of wine, stirring the two with a stick, and periodically skimming off any scum. Once cooled, a little pepper, mastic, saffron, and five mushed-up dates were added before pouring the mixture into nearly 10 liters of already-sweet wine.[2] Charcoal was often used to clarify the wine. Roman epicureans were clearly not purists when it came to their wine and food, unlike present-day gastronomes, who emphasize the provenance and purity of ingredients, but Apicius's sweet-wine recipe isn't far away from a cup of mulled wine today, which usually involves sugar, cinnamon, star anise, cloves, bay leaves, and orange peel. Today, there are few complaints at Christmas markets or on a cold ski slope that the *Glühwein* or *vin chaud* is not the truest reflection of the grape and the place it was grown. Drinkers are not deceived: they imbibe it with a clear understanding that it is an ameliorated wine-based drink that is perfectly suited to the context and enjoyed accordingly.

Likewise, many wines were consumed during Roman times in full awareness that they were not the product of grapes alone. A common aperitif at dinner parties was mulsum, a wine blended with impressive levels of honey. Today, Mas de Tourelles makes and sells its own mulsum, but it is a red wine made from the Grenache grape and blended with honey, thyme, and pink pepper. The honey flavor is hardly subtle, but the drink is not too sweet—otherwise no one would want a second sip. For the Romans, mulsum not only whetted the appetite for the meal ahead but was also considered a healthy beverage: in his thirty-seven-volume *Natural History*, an encyclopedic compilation on everything from the universe and the human body to the animal kingdom and philosophy, Pliny the Elder mentions Pollio Romilius, a man who had defied the average life expectancy and reached the age of 100.[3] When asked his secret to a long life, he replied that it was thanks to mulsum on the inside and oil on the outside.

Simplicity was not the order of the day when it came to Roman food either. Rather than allowing the quality of a freshly caught fish to shine or the tenderness of a piece of meat to impress, Roman cuisine was heavy on herbs, spices, and sauces. It was sometimes difficult to identify what was on the plate—and on occasion, that was the intention. Apicius delighted in dishing up "salt fish" that had neither salt nor fish in it but was instead a liver pâté served in the shape of a fish, to play with his guests' senses. Written in the first century AD, some of his recipes wouldn't be out of place in a celebrity chef's cookbook more than two thousand years later. There are sausages, rissoles, and vegetable broths, but also a host of dishes that leave the modern cook aghast: poached flamingo—or parrot, if there wasn't a flamingo on hand— peacock burgers, dormice dipped in honey, and stuffed sows' wombs were all on the menu. How about picking up a pig's stomach from the butcher for one of Apicius's gourmet recipes? It simply required a cleaning with vinegar and salt before being stuffed with minced pork, brains, raw eggs, pine nuts, and peppercorns, as well as a plethora of herbs and spices, including lovage, anise, and ginger, before boiling.

HERBS AND HALLUCINOGENS

Wine producers in Rome had a cornucopia of ingredients at their disposal to make wines that were pleasurable and would remain so for more than a few months. In the lead-up to the harvest, winemakers would use seawater to wash out their clay fermentation vessels and line them with pitch to make them both water- and airtight. Winemakers might then sprinkle their just-fermenting wines with pitch, a thick, sticky substance derived from pine trees that is still used in Greece to make retsina. It was thought that pitch made the wines both fuller bodied and more pleasant aromatically (although who really likes retsina?).

One of the key writers on wine and all things farming in the Republican period was Marcus Porcius Cato. He spent his childhood on the family farm close to Rome before embarking on a long military career, and he provides us with plenty of winemaking information in his wide-ranging book *De agri cultura* (ca. 160 BC). In between battles against the Carthaginians, he'd return to the farm and get his hands dirty, gaining the experience that enabled him to pen his practical guide to all things agricultural. If a farmer needed to know how many spades or rakes to buy, what offerings to make to the gods before harvest, or how many slaves were required to work the farm, Cato was the man. He created the Roman equivalent of *Farming for Dummies*, detailing the exact equipment and labor required for a vineyard of 100 *iugera* (about 62 acres) and a winery, including instructions on how to establish the vineyard and manage the winemaking process.

It's clear from Cato's guide that winemaking was far more than just allowing nature's yeasts to ferment some sweet grape juice. There are many possible additions for Cato's wines: marble dust (a source of lime, which increased stability by reducing the wine's pH), resin, old seawater, and boiled-down wine or must, the wine world's term for unfermented grape juice. His recipe for a Greek wine can be distilled into three parts: pick ripe grapes, add some old seawater, then add a small amount of old boiled wine. For those living far from Italy's shores, he amended his recipe to include must boiled in a copper or lead pot mixed with a faux seawater made from salt and fresh water to produce a brine, which may have helped to give the wine a longer life. The last ingredient added was ground calamus (sweet flag), a plant whose root can cause hallucinations, and then the wine was left to age in the sun for two years. The Greeks and the Romans were fans of leaving their best wines out in the sun, maturing them for long periods despite lacking the technology to preserve them, whether by using the antioxidant and antibacterial compound sulfur dioxide or using sealed bottles to keep out oxygen. The wines would inevitably oxidize and become more deeply colored but retain their sweet unctuosity, perhaps resembling something like the fortified wines from the island of Madeira, which are deliberately oxidized and heated.

While modern wine producers might be aghast at the slew of ingredients in Roman wine, these additions weren't generally seen as a form of adulteration. These techniques were seen as both legitimate and necessary, with the period's most influential writers, including Cato, and later, Pliny the Elder and Columella, legitimizing these practices in their writing. A native of the Spanish city of Cadiz, Columella moved to Rome and owned several farms, which informed his bestseller, *De re rustica*.[4] The tome covers all aspects of working the land, from ploughing to the cultivation of fruit trees, vines, and olives, the breeding and rearing of cattle, the keeping of domestic animals, beekeeping, and fish-pond management. When it comes to wine, we learn that fenugreek, dates, myrrh, cinnamon, and saffron are some of the many common ingredients. Yet there is a contradictory approach to meddling with wine: despite advocating the use of herbs, spices, seawater, and sweeteners, Columella and his contemporaries also claimed that the finest and rarest wines should definitely not be adulterated. "We regard as the best wine any kind which can keep without any preservative, nor should anything at all be mixed with it by which its natural savor would be obscured; for that wine is most excellent, which has given pleasure by its own natural quality."[5] The finest—and purest—wines were imbibed by the rich, who could afford to value provenance and authenticity and use them as a means to display their wealth and good taste.

The average Roman would have had a different relationship with wine; purity and its origins would have been of little concern. For the masses, the wine in their jugs was probably not far from becoming vinegar, and a sprinkle of this and a dash of that generally improved the drinking experience. For the most well-traveled members of the Roman empire—the army—wine was the official drink. However, the wine that soldiers were given as part of their rations was more like vinegar and was blended with water to produce a drink called *posca*. It is no wonder that entrepreneurial wine merchants with substandard wines would make a beeline for army encampments, where they could also sell some of their better—and more expensive—wines to the generals; *posca* was not a drink for high-ranking military officials.

It wasn't just lowly soldiers who had to be content with a poor excuse for wine. Slaves would be given *lora,* which was made using secondhand grapes. The skins of already-trodden grapes would be pressed to eke out any remaining juice. In a case of waste not, want not, the Romans would add water to these grape skins, hoping to induce another fermentation. The resulting low-alcohol wine, known today as *piquette* in France, was destined for quenching the thirst of slaves and, according to Cato, each would receive close to a bottle's worth a day. However, Pliny admitted there was no pretending that these drinks were genuine wine: "These liquors made from grape-skins soaked in water, called by the Greeks seconds and by Cato and ourselves afterwine, cannot rightly be styled wines but nevertheless are counted among the wines of the working classes."[6]

The definition of wine as a drink made solely from the fermentation of fresh grapes was not ushered into law until 1889 in France, but Pliny was of a similar opinion in 77 AD. Wine was made from grapes and "artificial wine" from millet seeds; fruit, including dates and figs; herbs; or watered-down grape juice that was boiled and left to evaporate in the sun.[7] While there was a swath of additions made to wines of the day, Pliny was rather a purist: "So many poisons are employed to force wine to suit our taste," he wrote, "and we are surprised that it is not wholesome!"[8] Like Columella, Pliny seemed to have a sliding scale of what he deemed acceptable and authentic. There were levels of amelioration that could be condoned and other additives and processes that were negatively perceived. While many producers aged their wines in the sun or in smoky rooms (similar to the way in which the modern peaty whiskies of Islay are infused with their smoky taste), Pliny denounced the use of such practices when it came to the wines from France's Mediterranean coast, particularly those of Narbonne: "No positive statement can be made, in as much as the dealers have set up a regular factory for the purpose and color them by means of smoke, and I regret to say also by employing noxious herbs and drugs—in as much as a dealer uses aloe for adulterating the flavours and the colour of his wines."[9]

LET ME ENTERTAIN YOU

In Roman high society, the dinner party was an important part of public life where alliances were cemented and deals made. While both rich and poor ate a Mediterranean diet of olives, cheese, and vegetables during the Republican period (509 BC–27 BC), that began to change as Rome expanded and as it encountered older civilizations, like that of the Greeks, who had established important trade routes. New and exotic foodstuffs arrived in Rome, including garum, a fermented fish sauce; spices; and fine wines. Only the wealthiest could afford these imported luxuries, making them a marker of class. In imperial Rome, the nouveaux riches and upwardly mobile members of society wanted to eat and live like the wealthiest, and food and wine became a way of showing one's cultural sophistication. But money doesn't buy class, as is demonstrated in *Trimalchio's Feast*, a fictional account of a dinner party written by Petronius, the official arbiter of good taste in Emperor Nero's court. The feast is held by self-made man and former slave Trimalchio. He and his wife serve only the rarest foods—twelve courses of them—and 180-year-old Falernian wine, which the guests believe not to be genuine. Despite the expense and extravagance, Petronius portrays the whole evening as cringeworthy: good taste, it seemed, could not be bought.

Wine flowed throughout the *cena,* the Romans' main daily meal, in contrast with the ancient Greeks, who waited until a meal was finished before uncorking the wine (along with post-dinner entertainment, which often included a naked flautist). In Rome, a slave known as a *cellarius* played the role of sommelier and was charged with decanting the wines from the amphora in the cellar to a jug, ensuring that any residue or sediment didn't make it into the diners' cups. There were various ways of clarifying wine, including using egg whites, a non-vegan technique still in use today, but more often it would be poured through a sieve-like strainer to separate the liquid from the floaters—which included the dead yeast gunk known as lees, as well as any herbs and spices that the winemaker had added. The *cellarius* might also heat the wine or chill it, sometimes adding snow to make a slushy type of drink, as desired by the guests. But at a fancy dinner party, the hopefully superlative quality of the wine served wouldn't need any amelioration. No sophistication points were awarded for adding honey or herbs to a top Roman wine, but this was a rare luxury that only the wealthiest could afford.

While the hefty wine lists of Michelin-starred restaurants are now awash with Bordeaux, Burgundy, and Champagne, the wine producers of Greece and southern Italy had cornered the fine-wine market of imperial Rome. To impress your peers in the first century AD, when Apicius, Pliny, and Columella were putting pen to papyrus, Campania's best, Falernian, was the drink to choose. Hailing from the slopes of Monte Massico, about thirty miles north of Naples, there were several styles of Falernian wine. It was most commonly a sweet white wine, as were most fine wines of the day, but some dry styles were produced too, according to Pliny. Discerning types claimed that the characteristics of Falernian differed according to site: the vines' position on the hillside was the key to quality, and the middle of the slope was the most prized, as it remains today in Burgundy's famed Côte d'Or. Falernian also had its own sambuca-like party trick: it could be set on fire, according to Pliny, which was likely a reflection of its high alcohol content. Its lofty reputation was soon in danger, however. A number of Falernian producers, eager to make the most money they could, began prioritizing quantity over quality. In addition, there were plenty of untrustworthy traders who had never set eyes on those hallowed vineyard slopes but who were happy to profit from the prices that fake Falernian wine fetched. There's hard evidence of the Falernian price premium on the wall of a bar in Pompeii: a wine list there reads, "For one *as* [a unit of currency] you can drink wine, for two you can drink the best, for four you can drink Falernian." While the bar owner was certainly charging extra for the Falernian—four *as* would have been a hefty chunk of the average Pompeii citizen's daily wage—it's been argued that at just four times the price of the house pour, this Falernian was unlikely to be the real deal. There's also a distinct possibility that what was originally in the amphoras marked Falernian could have been genuine, and once empty, the amphoras were refilled with something far cheaper. Today, the makers of some of world's most expensive wines smash their bottles after emptying them to thwart fraudsters from using this refilling trick.

Around two hundred years earlier, when Cato was having his say on wine, it was not Falernian but Greek wines that were the A-listers' drink of choice. The Aegean islands of Lesbos and Chios were among the most popular sources of sweet, alcoholic white in ancient Greece as well as the later stages of the Roman Republic. Homer, author of the epic Greek poems the *Iliad* and the *Odyssey,* name-checked Pramnian wine as one of the finest available, although it isn't clear whether Pramnian was a grape, place, or style. The question is still up for debate, but this unctuous wine, which would have been deeply colored due to ageing in Greece's hot climate, is thought to have been made on Lesbos and several other islands. The Italians were playing catch-up and it took them a while to compete with the Greeks' best. But by 49 BC, when Julius Caesar crossed the Rubicon, an unimpressive river just to the north of modern-day San Marino, which was then the northern entry point to Italy, the finest Italian wines were worthy of the top table. The wines of Falernian, along with the Sicilian wine Mamertine, had staked their claim as the must-have pour in Rome, and Caesar served up amphora after amphora at a victory banquet.

Unlike Apicius and other members of Roman high society, the average Roman didn't host swish dinner parties or jump on a boat to Libya simply because the prawns there were reputed to be super-sized (they weren't, and Apicius returned empty handed and out of pocket). Most of Rome's inhabitants didn't have a kitchen, let alone a private chef and a horde of slaves to cook, clean, and attend to their every need. Everyday dining was a little less ostentatious and so was the wine, as Iliaria Gozzini Giacosa explains in *A Taste of Ancient Rome*. Breakfast would generally be leftovers from the day before—bread, cheese, honey—and lunch would be an impromptu affair.[10] In the same way that office workers might pop out for a sandwich or head to a café for their midday meal, Romans would pick up something from a stall in the street or go to a tavern. After a siesta and some exercise, Romans loved to go for a soak in the local baths, whether to work up an appetite for dinner or to do some naked networking. If they got peckish, there were always street vendors selling snacks to tide locals over until dinner. While the rich would use dinner as an opportunity to cement business relationships, for most families, the evening meal was bread, cheese, and olives again, with soup or some meat. Dishes that are now considered quintessentially Italian had not yet been invented: pizza, pasta, and polenta were not on the menu, as many of the key ingredients, like corn and tomatoes, would not make their way to Italian shores for another 1,500 years. And while the Italians might be known for their love of espresso, the sugar to take the edge off its bitterness wasn't available until at least the 1400s, and even then, there was no way the poor could afford such luxuries.

For the everyman in imperial Rome, the choice of wine was as humble as the choice of food. Forget expensive imported wines from

Greece, shipped in amphoras and stamped with their place of origin and vintage; the average Roman would take a jug down to the local tavern and drink a very ordinary wine that would make the worst Pinot Grigio today seem intensely flavored by comparison. That's perhaps due to the fact that grape growers loved to coax as many bunches from their vines as possible, sacrificing quality for quantity. Yields were huge by today's standards. Cato wrote about a vineyard that yielded 20,000 liters of wine per hectare of vines, while a little over a century later, Varro's agriculture tome *De re rustica* mentioned vineyards in the Faventia area (now known as Faenza, a city southeast of Bologna) that were producing as much as 30,000 liters per hectare. Columella suggested farmers could obtain a more moderate 17,000 liters out of every hectare of vines planted, but that figure is still very high in the context of modern grape growing: high-yielding flatlands of Veneto's Prosecco-producing area offer growers around 13,500 liters per hectare, while the finest vineyards of Burgundy, known as *grands crus*, aren't allowed to produce more than 3,500 liters, according to appellation limits. While a complex debate rages on in wine circles about yields and their effect on quality, it doesn't take a wine expert to work out that a vine can't be expected to produce wines with any intensity of flavor when it is asked to ripen so many grapes at once.

Despite the likely lack of flavor, the empire thirsted for wine. It's been calculated that in the first and second centuries AD, the population of Rome was one million, and estimates suggest that every adult consumed the equivalent of a bottle of wine a day. One of the world's leading experts on Roman wine, André Tchernia, has suggested in his seminal work *Le vin de l'Italie romaine* that the city's inhabitants might have consumed between 145 million and 180 million liters of wine every year. This might sound like a lot, but as Tchernia points out, it was rather restrained compared to fourteenth-century Florentines, who each knocked back about 100 liters more a year than the average Roman.[11] Those heady days are long gone. Italians have really dried up their act in the past century and now consume fewer than 40 liters per head annually, but they're also no longer diluting their Barolo or Chianti.

WATERING DOWN

Wine snobs might turn their noses up at a white wine spritzer or the addition of a few cubes of ice to a glass of lukewarm rosé, but in the whisky world, adding water is the norm, reducing the heat of the alcohol as well as helping to liberate some of its otherwise locked-up aromas. The reasons behind cutting wine in ancient Rome weren't dissimilar to the reasons for cutting whisky today. Romans had a taste for sweet white wines and those tended to be high in alcohol. The period's writers mentioned ways of concentrating the sugar in the grapes, including leaving them to shrivel on the vine or picking them and allowing them to raisin in the sun, increasing their potential alcohol level. But drinking wine neat was considered barbaric, and if Romans wanted to go about their daily business with a clear head, slaking their thirst with full-strength wine was a bad idea. Weak beer was a possibility, but it was generally considered a drink for the plebs. The sweet wines of the empire acted as the cordial to Rome's water. Ratios of wine to water varied, from two parts wine to one part water to the highly dilute ratio of one part wine to twenty parts water mentioned in Homer's *Odyssey*.

While diluting wine was common, it didn't prevent inebriation. Both Pliny and the poet Juvenal clearly disapproved of the wave of binge drinking that occurred during their lifetimes, as well as the overt displays of luxury and excess. Columella also lamented the "licentiousness and drunkenness" of the first century AD. The wealthy seem to have relished their feasts and after-dinner drinking games, known as *commissatio*. In a ritual that wouldn't be alien to many of today's university students, participants would scull entire goblets of wine in a bid to keep up with their peers. However, there were no tequila slammers; the game was played with watered-down wine taken from a mixing bowl known as a *cratera*. Participants would have to hope the ratio of water to wine was sufficiently high that they did not stagger home.

Although it was prudent to water down your own wine, thinning wine with water, known as stretching, was perceived to be dishonest if it occurred behind closed doors. The difference between watering your own wine and diluting a customer's wine was the intent to deceive another for profit. Dilution by merchants and bar owners with the intent to maximize profits at the expense of their customers was easy to do and difficult to prove. In his *Epigrams,* the poet Martial mentions a man called Coranus who managed to make a lot of "wine" despite a poor harvest, thanks to his liberal use of water.[12] What's more, before Vesuvius erupted, one of the many graffiti artists in Pompeii had a very public say on the practices of one bar owner who was thought to be heavy-handed with his dilution of wine. More than 5,000 pieces of graffiti have been uncovered by archaeologists in Pompeii, ranging from tags to drawings, obscenities, and the outing of people's bad behavior. The complainant in this instance scrawled, "What a lot of tricks you use to deceive, innkeeper. You sell water but drink unmixed wine."

Regardless of its strength, wine's acidity and alcohol might have had some antibacterial effect on the water with which it was mixed, but it would hardly prevent an outbreak of cholera, typhoid, or dysentery, which were common. The Romans were pretty good when it came to clean-ish water. The imposing three-tiered arch of the Pont du Gard, looming over the glassy River Gard some 450 meters below, provides a solid and imposing reminder of the Roman empire's might and resourcefulness. In its heyday, it delivered 40,000 cubic meters (roughly 10.6 million gallons) of fresh water daily to the people of Nîmes. Unless you were filthy rich, you got your water from a public fountain. According to a translation of Plutarch, who wrote a series of biographies of illustrious Greeks and Romans, Cato drank only water "on his campaigns, except that once in a while, in a raging thirst, he would call for vinegar, or, when his strength was failing, would add a little wine."[13] If one of Rome's top dogs was happy to drink undiluted water straight from the source, one would assume it must have been healthy, but there are plenty of historians who aren't convinced. Some argue that the water was contaminated and that's why so much wine was consumed, although that's been countered by the claim that few would have been able to afford to drink wine all day every day.[14]

Whether or not the water was clean when it was drawn from the fountain, there were plenty of opportunities for it to be contaminated in the crowded, dirty streets of Rome. Residents threw the contents of their chamber pots out into the streets despite the availability of public latrines; they washed their bottoms with a wet sponge on a stick, but handwashing facilities were nonexistent. It wasn't uncommon for a dead animal or the occasional human corpse to be lying around, which was hardly conducive to disease prevention. What's more, a daily trip to the unchlorinated baths might have been relaxing, but the water was hardly pure. One leading doctor working in the early years of the empire suggested that those with bowel trouble should bathe their anuses in the hot pools, which runs contrary to modern-day warnings not to enter communal baths or swimming pools following a bout of tummy trouble. Conversely, Rome's medicine men suggested that anyone with an open wound ought not to go in the water, as it was so unclean. As a result of the perils of life in the city in the Roman empire, life expectancy was low: as many as half of all children died before reaching the age of ten, and according to some convoluted mathematical extrapolations, adults could expect to live for somewhere between twenty and thirty years.

WINE AS MEDICINE

Romans were commonly advised by their doctors to drink alcohol because of its reputed health-giving benefits. With the medical world's endorsement, wine became more virtuous and honest than beer. From the second century BC to the first century AD, doctors prescribed different wines for a wide range of ailments. Upset bowels could be settled with Signine from the modern-day town of Segni, forty-five miles southeast of Rome. About an hour's drive further south, the town of Setia, now known as Sezze, also enjoyed the favor of Rome's most powerful emperors, as its wine was thought to be easier on the stomach than all others. The poet Martial claimed it was sharp and tangy, with a fig-like flavor, and it would often be chilled (and diluted) with snow.[15] Meanwhile, the white wine from Sorrento divided opinion: both Galen and Pliny recommended it for convalescents, although others were less complimentary—the emperor Tiberius compared it with good vinegar. While Pliny was not always kind to wine, he said it could have "miraculous properties" ranging from inducing sleep to curing snakebites, preventing pregnancy, and, conversely, promoting conception, depending on one's choice of wine.[16]

Wine didn't just cure on the inside, either. Just as alcohol is used as an antiseptic and antibacterial today, in Roman times it was often administered topically, to relieve pain, and used for bathing wounds. In his *Use of Liquids*, Greek physician Hippocrates included an entire chapter on the type of wines to use to wash wounds, including surgical incisions, and to treat gynecological issues, sore rectums, and much, much more.[17] He had a major influence on Greek and Roman medics, including Galen, who bathed the wounds of gladiators in wine-soaked bandages and prescribed wine as a pain reliever. Regardless of whether wine was truly effective in healing so many ailments, its alcohol content would have at least made those who were suffering feel a little better.

Despite the purported health benefits of wine, there was also a darker and potentially fatal side to drinking it: lead. In a bid to satisfy their taste for sweet wine, to disguise any flaws in the wine, and to increase its shelf life, the Romans added sapa or defrutum, which were created by reducing grape must to a thick syrup-like consistency, often in lead-lined pots. The lead would often leach into the syrup, adding a sweet yet toxic tang. Recipes for producing sapa are given by Roman authors, including Pliny and Columella, and it was used as an ingredient in many of Apicius's recipes. Pliny also suggested that wine producers should dip a lead sheet into a wine to check whether it was going bad, which surely would not have helped its toxicity. While these practices would today be considered illegal adulteration due to their potentially lethal consequences, adding sapa was considered a form of amelioration in Roman times, highlighting how perceptions of what is and isn't fraudulent have evolved over the course of history. In recent times, several scientists have doctored wine using the recipes in Roman texts and have made some startling discoveries. Columella's wines would have contained around 20 milligrams of lead per liter, but chronic lead poisoning could be induced with an intake of just 0.5 milligrams per day, according to Josef Eisinger, an expert on lead poisoning through the ages.[18]

In 1983, there was an almighty fuss in academic circles over the role of lead in the Roman empire, a controversy that spilled into the mainstream media. The front page of the *International Herald Tribune* on June 1 included the headlines "Reagan Predicts Improvement in US-Soviet Links" and "The Roman Empire: Victim of Poisoning." The latter story emerged after an American archaeologist, Sara C. Bisel, examined the bones of fifty-five victims of the Vesuvius eruption (AD 79) and found that their lead content averaged 84 parts per million, compared to 3 parts per million for prehistoric people. "Much has been written about lead as a factor in the decline of the Roman empire," Bisel stated. "But this is the first time we have had actual Romans to test," since most Romans were cremated.[19] In the same year that Bisel's findings were published, a Canadian scientist, Jerome O. Nriagu, published *Lead and Lead Poisoning in Antiquity,* in which he claimed that lead, including lead-laced wine, could have been responsible for lead poisoning as well as the reproductive failure of the Roman ruling classes. Nriagu claimed that the "psychological profiles of the emperors and usurpers who reigned between 50 BC and 250 AD suggest that the majority of them probably suffered from lead poisoning."[20]

The pair's findings so infuriated Alan Cameron, professor of Latin at Columbia University, that he sent a letter to the editor of the *Tribune* several weeks later. Cameron was angry that the "hoary theory" of lead poisoning bringing down the Roman empire had reared its head again. He admitted, "No doubt some Romans did suffer lead poisoning, whether from their water, from lead-glazed pots or from lead-based paint . . . [but] it is simply preposterous to suppose that lead poisoning can have had any bearing on the collapse of the Roman empire." Cameron argued that the empire "was not maintained for more than half a millennium by anaemic and colic-ridden men staggering around in an advanced stage of lead poisoning of which they were ignorant and about which they certainly said nothing."[21] Since then, many academics have sought to disprove Nriagu's argument.

Whether or not lead-infused wine was a contributing factor to the fall of the empire, there has never been a greater appetite for all things Roman, whether it's visiting Pompeii, taking a tour of the Colosseum, or re-creating Roman recipes and wines. And as the Roman harvest ends at Mas des Tourelles, it's time to buy a few bottles. The glass bottles are perhaps the only nod to modern times. I ask Durand why he doesn't sell the wine in amphoras if he is aiming to be truly authentic. "Well, can you imagine trying to lift an amphora full of wine into the back of your car?" he asks. It's a Fiat 500. I opt for the half bottles.

2

DYING FOR A DRINK

THE ROMANS FELT THE FULL force of the sweetening effects of lead and yet, a thousand years after the sacking of Rome, lead poisoning had not gone away: in 1498, the city's Catholic clergy issued a papal bull to address the issue. This official decree from the pope made it illegal to add lead salt to wine, but the message didn't travel well: almost 200 years later and 600 miles north in the city of Ulm, Germany, monks started to keel over inexplicably. By the late eighteenth century, one of the most famous composers of all time seemed to have succumbed to the fatal effects of lead in wine, and even in the late twentieth century, crystal decanters continued to leach toxic levels of lead into the wine and spirits residing within them. Once thought to be harmless, lead in wine has been proven to constitute harmful adulteration. The painfully slow acceptance of evidence that was presented by a doctor in Ulm in the late seventeenth century might have been due to poor communications at the time, but there were certainly many wine merchants who placed their own financial interests before the health of others, allowing the practice to continue.

The case of the poisoned monks took place in 1696, the end of a tough century for Germany. The Thirty Years' War (1618–1648) had laid waste to the country's villages, people, and vineyards. What started as a conflict between the Catholic and Protestant states of the Holy Roman Empire in Germany became a European war, embroiling troops from as far afield as Spain and Russia. The country became a series of battlefields: it has been estimated that 18,000 villages, 1,500 towns, and 2,000 castles were razed. Inevitably, many vineyards were destroyed or abandoned, particularly along the course of the Rhine and Mosel Rivers, which played host to deadly battles. Marauding armies raided wine cellars and demanded wine, not to quench their own thirst but to sell to fund their war expenses. Swedish troops led by King Gustavus Adolphus advanced across Germany and settled in Mainz in 1631, where they forced the locals to cover their sovereign's expenses of 46,000 thalers (silver coins). The wine producers of the Rheingau, to the west of Mainz, did their bit to settle the region's debts, handing over 1.6 million liters of wine over the next three years.

As if a three-decade-long war weren't enough to contend with, famine and plague finished off many of those who hadn't fled their villages: seven million people died during the first half of the seventeenth century. The stoic wine producers who opted to replant their vineyards were to endure yet more misery: Louis XIV, the Sun King, was thirsty for land and in the late 1680s, towns and vineyards along the Rhine were destroyed yet again as Louis pushed his forces eastward in a devastating but doomed onslaught. German wine production would not return to pre–Thirty Years' War levels until 1970.

However, at the end of the seventeenth century it was Mother Nature, not bloodthirsty men, that became the grape grower's worst enemy, leading to a renewed period of wine "improvement" as producers and merchants sought to make their products more attractive. The

Little Ice Age, a period of cooler temperatures spanning the fourteenth to the mid-nineteenth centuries, brought freezing winters and cold, wet summers across Europe. Crops failed to ripen and famines were common; fish migrated south in search of warmer waters. Vines are particularly sensitive to the elements and in the grip of this cold snap, ripening grapes in Germany was even tougher than usual. The resulting crop levels were lower and what few grapes there were tended to produce sour wine that no one wanted to drink. Wine provided essential calories and intoxicated the drinker, but it also had to be pleasurable, and the sweetening effect of lead was often the way to achieve this.

It was around this time that Riesling became Germany's signature grape. The variety was first documented in the Rheingau in the fifteenth century by a local cellar master, and it became the grape of choice for replanting vineyards after the Thirty Years' War. Riesling has a lot going for it, and the Germans were sensible to choose it back then: it is a hardy vine that withstands cold winters and buds late, mitigating the problem of spring frosts. It isn't particularly sensitive to fungal diseases and can yield a relatively large number of bunches without compromising quality, something that cannot be said about many varieties. Although Riesling has recently fallen out of favor with wine drinkers, who mistakenly think that it only produces sweet wine, growers in the late 1600s would have given their right arm to have been able to make something naturally sweet and luscious. Instead, they harvested under-ripe grapes that made tart wines. At the time, wine producers along the Neckar Valley in the warmer climes of southwest Germany had more success at ripening grapes than those based in cooler, more northerly regions. The wines would be shipped along the Neckar River to northern Europe and along the Danube River from Ulm, a key wine port, to Austria and beyond. But the cold, wet summers of the 1690s and the struggling economy of the area enticed dodgy dealers to add lead-laced sweetening mixtures to their wines, with fatal results.

A THEORY OF RELATIVITY

Sitting on the banks of the Danube about an hour's drive from Stuttgart, Ulm is now best known as the birthplace of Albert Einstein. Founded in 850 AD, more than a thousand years before the German physicist changed the world with his theory of relativity, Ulm was forever altered by the British bombing raids of 1944 and 1945, which wiped out more than 80 percent of the city center, leaving little of its medieval heritage. The world's crookedest house and tallest church survived the World War II attacks, however, and remain popular visitor attractions. Ulm's history as a hotbed of wine adulteration in the late seventeenth century is less well known and is understandably not a fact that members of the local tourism board wish to promote. However, if they did, they would realize that Einstein wasn't the only highly intelligent man the city has produced.

Eberhard Gockel, the city's physician in the 1690s, was prolific in both his professional and personal life, writing papers on illnesses caused by spells, suggesting cures for witches and werewolves, and solving the mystery of an egg-laying rooster, as well as finding the time to father eighteen children. His mystical medical work had to be put to one side, however, when monks at two local monasteries began to fall seriously ill. The pious brothers were struck down with terrible stomach pains, fever, irritable bowels, nausea, insanity, paralysis, and in some cases, deafness and death. Initially, the monasteries' water sources were suspected to be the cause of their ills, but the wells were inspected and showed nothing untoward. Gockel noted that teetotalers among the brethren were not suffering and deduced, rightly, that something fishy was going on. He turned his attention to wine, the other major source of the monks' refreshment. At this time, the Catholic Church was the wine engine of Germany: monastic orders had acquired huge landholdings during the Middle Ages, thanks to donations from the nobility as well as smallholders, who bequeathed their land to the church in an attempt to wash themselves of their sins and receive a free pass to heaven. The monasteries planted vines primarily to make sacramental wine, but production went far beyond their needs for the Eucharist. Safe drinking water wasn't on tap, so monks received wine rations with their meals, and it would be served to pilgrims and guests. The monks were also shrewd businessmen: wine was a big earner for monasteries, and unlike secular wine producers, religious orders were exempt from burdensome taxes.

In Ulm, Gockel's investigation into the brethren's wine supply continued. Having ruled out the wells at the afflicted monasteries as the cause of contamination, he discovered that a few visiting fathers had developed the same symptoms as the resident monks after enjoying a glass or two of wine, yet recovered when they returned to their own monasteries. The doctor himself ended up with a nasty fever and colic pain after accepting glasses of wine on his visits; it took him six months to recover fully. The monks had not made the wine but purchased it from a local merchant, and suspicion was now mounting. Gockel's lightbulb moment came after reading about the symptoms of lead poisoning in a book by Samuel Stockhausen. Stockhausen had written of a chronic illness affecting lead miners and potters (who used lead-based glazes); exposed to lead fumes and dust, they had developed symptoms identical to those of the monks in Ulm.

On inspecting the monasteries' wine barrels, Gockel found a sweet, sticky substance, and he sniffed out the wine merchant who had sold this wine to the brothers. The man had been adding litharge, a lead monoxide solution, to make the tart wines of the day more palatable. The merchant gave Gockel his recipes. One resulted in a wine that contained 16 grams of lead per liter, according to lead poisoning expert Josef Eisinger: "Added to wine at the recommended dilution, the lead content of the wine would be about 70mg/l," he explains. When Gockel decided to try out these recipes, he found the "worst and sourest wine" available. After adding his lead-infused extract, the wine became "the best and loveliest."[1]

Gockel's findings were included in a report collated by the local duke's doctor, which led to a new law condemning to death those responsible for adding litharge to wine. However, it turns out that this wasn't the first law that had been created in Ulm forbidding lead in wine. In 1487, some two centuries earlier, the town's publicans had been given a long list of substances that were not permitted in wine, a list that included none other than lead oxide and lead carbonate. The message seemed to fall on deaf ears: adulteration or so-called correction of wine continued. A decade later, an imperial edict also outlawed adding lead, among other additives, to wine. Offenders who were caught were fined and had their wines poured into the river, but in the days before chemical analysis, these laws were difficult to enforce. To compound the issue, some medical experts of the day thought that a bit of lead in wine was no cause for concern. For the monks, the ill effects were quickly apparent, but for most, lead poisoning was a slow and gradual process. As a result, it was difficult to be certain that the cause of any illness was lead: absorbed into the bloodstream, it accumulates in the skeleton, and its symptoms only present when it reaches a critical level, by which time it's too late.

Unsurprisingly, Gockel's life-saving detective work was a public relations disaster for Ulm wine shippers—the sale of wines from the nearby Neckar Valley was banned by some neighboring states. However, the lessons learned from this unsavory episode were allegedly suppressed, according to the duke's doctor. The duke's report was intended to be circulated throughout other states but that failed to happen, perhaps due to fear of further damage to local wine sales. It was yet another opportunity missed in the long and fateful history of lead in wine.

AN UNFINISHED SYMPHONY

More than a century after Gockel discovered the toxic nature of lead in wine, unsuspecting individuals, including one of the world's greatest composers, were still dying for a glass of wine. As Ludwig van Beethoven neared the end of his days, he was more convinced than ever that wine would ease his pain, oblivious to the fact that it was probably the cause of his lifelong suffering. Clearly, he had not read Gockel's work or the duke's report. Hours before he took his final breath, a long-awaited wine delivery arrived, and his last words, "Pity!—pity!—too late!" were uttered in response to its tardy arrival.[2] It had been more than a month since Beethoven had written what would be one of his last letters to his music publisher, B. Schott & Sons, in the town of Mainz, requesting some "very good old Rhine wine" on doctors' orders.[3] Wary of paying over the odds for a fine wine, Beethoven asked his music publisher to source and send the wine from its headquarters 460 miles away. The bottles finally arrived at Beethoven's house in late March 1827. The four words expressing his disappointment about the unfortunate timing of the wine's arrival would be his last in what had become an increasingly silent world for one of the world's most celebrated composers.

Born in the German city of Bonn in December 1770, Beethoven moved to Vienna in his early twenties to pursue his musical career but began losing his hearing at the tender age of twenty-seven. He kept it a secret until 1801, when he finally admitted to a doctor friend, Franz Wegeler, that he was losing the sense most vital to his profession: "For the last three years, my hearing has grown weaker and weaker— I cannot hear the high notes of instruments or voices—I can hear sounds, but I cannot make out the words."[4]

Beethoven's hearing continued to deteriorate over the next decade. By 1816 he was totally deaf in one ear; by 1818 his friends and visitors had to resort to written communication. It is incredible to think that in 1812 he could barely hear yet managed to write his radical Eighth Symphony. Music journalist Tom Service has called it "one of the shortest, weirdest, but most compelling symphonies of the nineteenth century."[5] It shattered symphony-writing conventions, and its mood was far more upbeat than Beethoven's own; at the time, the composer was struggling with inner turmoil and tense relations with his two younger brothers. Despite the family rift and his deteriorating health, Beethoven went on to write a Ninth Symphony. In 1824, following the debut performance, he had to be turned to face the audience to watch the standing ovation.[6]

Beethoven would surely have been astonished at the sustained level of interest in his digestive system today, nearly 200 years after his death. An inordinate number of academic articles have been written about his gastrointestinal health—never have so many people been so interested in someone's internal movements. In 1801, Beethoven wrote to Wegeler about his frequent attacks of diarrhea, and he continued to have cramps and bad bowels for the rest of his life. He suffered from rheumatism, jaundice, constant eye pain, fever, "gouty headaches," and frequent nosebleeds. It was noted that he "often was irritable and erratic in his behaviour," but if you were losing your hearing and in almost constant pain, it might be hard not to come across as a little cantankerous.[7]

Doctors and historians continue to debate the cause of Beethoven's deafness, his other illnesses, and his ultimate demise on March 26, 1827, at the age of fifty-six. The autopsy recorded cirrhosis as the cause of death, but medical analysis back then was far from sophisticated. This was a period when a change of air was a recommended solution to ill health, and leeches were in high demand in the medical world. Other causes of Beethoven's death may have been overlooked because the tools to identify them simply didn't exist, giving rise to a number of divergent theories, from tuberculosis to syphilis to bowel disease. In the 1970s, theorists conjectured that Beethoven had suffered from a connective tissue disease. In 1992, British rheumatologist Thomas Palferman argued in the *Beethoven Journal* that the composer died of sarcoidosis, a disease that causes small patches of inflammatory cells to develop in and on the body, particularly on the skin and lungs. Just four years later, in the prestigious medical journal *The Lancet*, a doctor and a music historian claimed that Palferman was trying to put a square peg in a round hole: his conclusion didn't fit all of Beethoven's symptoms. "Though a good explanation for his eye conditions, sarcoidosis could not account for Beethoven's deafness," the pair concluded.[8]

The cause of Beethoven's deafness has sparked as much intense speculation as his cause of death. It's a conundrum that long intrigued American doctor Mike Stevens. Following his retirement, the Utah-based ear, nose, and throat specialist combined his loves of classical music and medicine, spending a year scrutinizing every article, book, and scrap of paper he could find about Beethoven's life and medical condition. While he admits to a preference for Chopin (who suffered from respiratory illness for most of his life), the piano-playing doctor has been known to perform Beethoven concertos. Stevens considered all purported diagnoses, from otosclerosis and autoimmune hearing loss to syphilis, but the evidence didn't stack up. It probably wasn't otosclerosis, a condition in which abnormal bone growth inside the ear results in gradual hearing loss, he argued, as it would have been detected in the ear examination conducted during the autopsy. It probably wasn't autoimmune hearing loss, since no blood was found in his stools. Although Beethoven believed his deafness and dodgy bowels were related, autoimmune hearing loss, explained Stevens, progresses over weeks or months, not years. And it probably wasn't syphilis: samples of Beethoven's hair and bone showed no sign of mercury, which was used to treat the disease in the early nineteenth century. What's more, a thorough reading of extensive medical records by his many physicians elicits no mention of syphilis, although some still argue that it was passed on to Beethoven by his alcoholic father.

The most likely cause of Beethoven's hearing loss was lead poisoning, Stevens concluded. He published his paper in 2013, gained a master's degree for his trouble, and remains convinced that lead was the culprit.[9] He was not alone. A lock of hair supposedly snipped from Beethoven's head on his deathbed by the promising young pianist Ferdinand Hiller and kept in a glass locket eventually found its way to a fishing village in northern Denmark. Carried by an unnamed Jew fleeing Germany in 1943 and left in the hands of a local doctor, it would remain with the physician's adopted daughter until 1994, when it was offered up for sale at auction house Sotheby's. The author of *Beethoven's Hair*, Russell Martin, tracked the progress of Lot 33, which was purchased by a consortium of Beethoven fanatics and analyzed by Walter McCrone, the man who "demonstrated conclusively that the Shroud of Turin had been painted in the fourteenth century and was not, therefore, the burial cloth of Jesus." What's more, McCrone had determined from a hair sample "that Napoleon had not died from arsenic poisoning," as previously suggested.[10] He was just the man for this job. Using techniques familiar to scientists but few others, McCrone determined that the owner of the hair had a high level of lead in their body when they died. Levels of other elements, like sodium and copper, were within expected ranges, but when it came to lead, the lock was off the charts—the hair contained forty-two times the amount of lead in the control samples, leading the team conducting the analysis to conclude that the maestro "had been massively toxic with lead at the time of his death and may have been for dozens of years before."[11]

A similar conclusion was reached when a bone fragment believed to be from Beethoven's skull was sent by California businessman Paul Kaufman to the US Department of Energy's Argonne National Laboratory in 2005 for testing. Kaufman had inherited the fragment from his great-great-uncle, an Austrian doctor. Kaufman wasn't sure if it was really part of Beethoven's skull or if that was an inventive family fable, but the scientists seemed pretty sure it was authentic. What was considered cutting-edge analysis and advanced X-ray technology supported McCrone's earlier finding that Beethoven's body contained massive amounts of lead and had for many years. So how did it get there?

The possible cause of the high level of lead was wine—the very stuff that Beethoven used throughout his life to ease his suffering. There are other possible sources of lead poisoning—lead glazes on earthenware, lead-soldered water pipes, lead crystal glasses—but a growing body of experts was convinced that Beethoven's love of wine, wine likely tainted with lead, was responsible for his lifelong health troubles. In short, he had plumbism, medical biographers concluded. Others suggested the lead could have come from treatments he received for a bout of pneumonia he suffered in late 1826.[12] Skeptics argue that he didn't show one of the common symptoms of lead poisoning—wrist drop—but the conclusion did go a long way toward explaining many of his ailments, and it was difficult to argue with the overwhelming scientific evidence gleaned from his hair and bone at that time.

But science moves on, and received wisdom can be repudiated. In 2015, it was revealed that those skull fragments might not have been Beethoven's after all, despite the music community and sections of the medical profession having been convinced of their authenticity since the mid-1980s.[13] What's more, huge advances in genetic research in the past two decades and continued intrigue regarding Beethoven's ill health and ultimate demise have prompted further investigation into his hair, and the results have left some scratching their heads. The lock of hair snipped by Ferdinand Hiller on Beethoven's deathbed was not Beethoven's but a Jewish woman's, according to genetic testing: "Accepted by many as authentic, the hairs have been subjected to a number of scientific tests, which have led some of Beethoven's medical biographers to conclude that Beethoven's health problems, hearing loss, and death may have been caused or compounded by plumbism," its authors reported. But there are five other sets of strands of Beethoven's hair that have ended up in the hands of universities, museums, and Beethoven appreciation societies around the globe that are considered to be genuine. Genetic testing on the quintet of authenticated locks suggests that Beethoven did have liver disease, likely cirrhosis, perhaps due to a combination of a genetic predisposition for developing liver problems, hepatitis B, and his consumption of wine, which was commonly laced with lead at the time.[14]

Beethoven eventually gave up the conducting baton when he became totally deaf, but he never gave up wine. As early as 1800, he told friends he had "begun to consume a substantial amount of wine with meals in the hope that it would stimulate his increasingly poor appetite, as well as ease his pain."[15] It is also thought that Beethoven might have drunk wine to numb not only his physical pain but also his emotional pain; some claim he hit the bottle as early as age seventeen, following the death of his mother. She had endured life with her alcoholic second husband, Johann van Beethoven, who had been a promising singer and music teacher but couldn't stay away from the bottle. When Johann died in 1792—Ludwig was just twenty-two and had recently embarked on a new life in Vienna—a local official drily remarked that his revenue from liquor taxes was about to take a hit.[16]

Beethoven's housekeeping records reveal that the composer spent a considerable amount on wine, though it wasn't necessarily money well spent. Rather than the fine, expensive stuff, he had a weakness for the wines of Buda (which merged with the city of Pest in 1873 to become Budapest), as well as a liking for macaroni and cheese, which surely can't have been good for his digestion. At that time, the hillsides of Buda were covered with vineyards growing red grapes, including the spicy Kadarka variety, the fresh and fruity Kékfrankos, and the intensely colored Csóka. The trio would be blended to make Budai Vörös—Buda red—and this characterful wine would often be sold to thirsty locals directly from the vineyard, as well as to wine merchants from Greece and Macedonia.

Beethoven's drinking wasn't confined to burly Hungarian reds; he also had a taste for the white wines of Germany, as the letter to his German publisher showed. When the wine finally arrived, it included two bottles from Rüdesheim, a winemaking village in the Rheingau region. The wine was probably made from the Riesling grape, which had found a home on the slopes rising above the Rhine near the spa town of Wiesbaden. While Riesling's birthplace is not certain, the first mention of the variety was made in the Rheingau in March 1435. Almost 300 years later, in 1720, the Benedictine-owned slopes of Schloss Johannisberg were replanted, and Riesling became its one and only variety. The noblest wine producers along the Rhine would soon follow suit.

These holy winemakers have another claim to fame: in the autumn of 1775, they discovered the benefits of harvesting their Riesling grapes late in the season. According to legend, a messenger carrying the document giving the monks of Johannisberg the green light to harvest the grapes in their vineyard was held up by two weeks. Why he and his horse took so long to deliver the message to start picking remains a mystery, but during that fortnight, the grapes started to shrivel, becoming sweeter, and tasted bloody good. The resulting wine was named Spätlese, or late harvest. The discovery of the deliciousness of late-picked, shriveled Riesling marked the beginning of a new era for German wine. For nearly two centuries, German Riesling was venerated. Its sweet nectar was prized by the European elite, including Hock-drinking Queen Victoria, and prices for the very finest German whites often exceeded those of Bordeaux's greatest.

When Beethoven's delivery of Rüdesheim wine arrived, the region was enjoying its newfound time in the sun. Unfortunately the composer would never fully enjoy its sweet nectar. His assistant Anton Schindler did write to the publisher to let him know that Beethoven took a few spoonfuls of the wine before he passed away at 5:45 pm on March 26, 1827. In a tragic case of historical irony, Beethoven was unaware that he was literally dying for a drink.

HEED NO WARNING

More than a decade after Beethoven's death, Schindler published a biography that detailed Beethoven's drinking habits and revealed more about his tastes, stating, "Unfortunately, he especially liked the flavour of fortified wines which were very bad for the weakened stomach. He would heed no warning."[17]

Fortified wine's combination of high alcohol and intense sweetness would be no good for anyone with a sensitive tummy, but we know that in Beethoven's time many ports—and other fortified wines—were also lead ridden. Today, port is made using the same fortification process employed in Beethoven's time: the fermentation that converts grape juice to wine is brought to an abrupt stop by the addition of potent brandy, which kills the wine yeasts. Raising the final alcohol level to 19 or 20 percent means there is no way back for the yeast and the fermentation is irreversibly halted, creating a sweet, spirity beverage. However, in the late eighteenth century, the fortifying brandy, which accounts for around one-fifth of a bottle of port, was often distilled in lead-lined vessels. As if that weren't bad enough, the fortified wine would be shipped in wooden barrels that were sometimes sealed with lead-lined lids or lead fasteners. An American doctor, Gene V. Ball, provided scientific proof that fortified wines of the late eighteenth and early nineteenth centuries were laced with extremely high amounts of lead.[18] In the early 1970s, Ball managed to source a bottle of "Old Canary Wine" produced between 1770 and 1820 and a bottle of 1805 port from a dusty cellar and analyzed them in his laboratory in Alabama. The wines had lead contents of 1,900 and 830 micrograms per liter respectively—between five and ten times the level found in port wines released in the early 1970s. Lead levels have happily fallen further since then: a 2003 study found less than 20 micrograms per liter in modern-day port production.[19]

If port had not been a popular drink when these toxic wines were produced, its deleterious effects might have not been so widely felt, but at the same time that lead was seeping into port's fortifying spirit, its star was rising. Wines hailing from the vertiginous vineyards of the Douro Valley, a two-hour drive inland from the city of Porto, weren't commonly exported in the sixteenth and early seventeenth centuries, but international politics was set to intervene. In 1654, in his new role as Lord Protector of England, Scotland, and Ireland, Oliver Cromwell signed a treaty with Portugal, opening opportunities for British merchants. With the royals reinstated in 1660, the country's links with Portugal were further strengthened. Charles II's marriage to Portuguese princess Catherine of Braganza in 1662, and the deterioration of relations with Louis XIV in France, paved the way for a Portuguese wine boom and a similarly dramatic slump in French wine sales in England. Portuguese wine expert Richard Mayson states that annual trade from Portugal to England increased from 120 tons (120,000 liters) to 6,880 tons (6.81 million liters) between 1650 and 1700.[20] Things kept on getting better for Portuguese trade: the 1703 Methuen Treaty lowered import duties on wines from Portugal, rubbing salt into the open wounds of French winemakers. By the second half of the eighteenth century, Portuguese wine represented seven in ten bottles of wine consumed in England.

It is no coincidence that the move away from drinking claret—red wine produced in Bordeaux in southwest France—to the fortified wines of Portugal correlated with a rise in the incidence of gout in high society. The nineteenth century's godfather of gout, British physician Alfred Baring Garrod, claimed that alcohol was the "most powerful of all the predisposing causes of gout,"[21] and fortified wines were the worst offenders. The aristocracy took delight in gorging on the richest foods and drinking to excess, and it is likely that the high levels of lead in the most popular wine of the time, port, compounded their health problems. Academics have spotlighted leading members of British society as having been afflicted with lead-related (saturnine) gout. Potential sufferers include physicist Isaac Newton, diarist Samuel Johnson, King George IV, and poet Alfred Lord Tennyson, while George Frideric Handel, the man behind the *Messiah* and its "Hallelujah Chorus," was a glutton by all accounts. His long list of medical complaints seems to suggest plumbism as a likely cause. The *Messiah*, now a Christmas classic, was originally performed in the not-so-festive month of April 1742, seventeen years before Handel's death at age seventy-four. Given the historical accounts of his diet and ever-increasing frame, it's somewhat surprising he lived that long. While it is far from certain that he died of lead poisoning, there are flashing neon signs pointing to the diagnosis: joint pain, loss of vision, paralysis of his right hand, confusion—the list goes on. David Hunter, a Handel expert and music librarian at the University of Texas, examined the competing causes of the composer's ailments and death and concluded that his demise was due to lead poisoning. His love of wine was a major factor.[22] However, we will never know conclusively unless Handel's body is exhumed from its resting place in Westminster Abbey, and having contacted the Abbey to find out if that could happen, the answer is a definite no.

Whether it was port or German Riesling, wine was certainly not the only source of lead contamination in the eighteenth and nineteenth centuries. It could be found in drinking water, food and the plate on which it was served, cosmetics (including face powder), and medicines. However, the sheer quantity of wine ingested by Handel and Beethoven over their lifetimes, and the widespread but illegal practice of adding lead to improve the flavor of cheap wine, make for a convincing argument.

LEAD-ING THE WAY

The chocolate-box villages of Alsace, framed by vineyards that cascade down hillsides in the shadow of the Vosges mountains, are an unlikely setting for discovering the effects of leaded gasoline. But at the side of a busy road leading west from the town of Colmar through the village of Wintzenheim, a famous winemaking family was testing its grapes for lead. The year was 1989 and Léonard Humbrecht was serving as president of a leading French wine organization, as well as running one of the region's most respected producers, Domaine Zind-Humbrecht.

His son, Olivier, who had become France's first Master of Wine that same year, had just returned home from a stint in London working for the French national food and wine marketing body, Sopexa, which counted as military service for those who didn't want to take up arms. At the time, the body of evidence demonstrating the deleterious effects of leaded gas on health and the environment was undeniable. Lead had long lubricated engines; the forward-thinking Japanese had banned leaded gas as early as 1986, and in 1989, it represented just 0.4 percent of all sales at UK gas stations. French policy makers, though, proved rather more reluctant than other European powers to introduce stringent laws on leaded gas, likely due to concerns it would lead to further emissions regulations and impact the country's car manufacturers.

However, suggesting that the national drink—and other important agricultural crops—could be affected by car emissions might have some sway on opinion. Studies had already demonstrated a direct link between raised levels of lead in children's blood and the occurrence of brain damage and learning disorders, and youngsters living near highways and town centers had a far higher likelihood of developing these illnesses. Could grapes grown near roads be toxic? "My father and I were asked by the national [wine] authorities to study lead and other metals, as we had a vineyard by the roadside," recalls Olivier Humbrecht.[23] Their Gewurztraminer grapes were analyzed as cars sped past en route to Colmar, and those from rows neighboring the road displayed much higher levels of lead than those distanced from the exhaust fumes. However, during the process of turning grapes into wine, lead levels drop far below the recommended safe levels. That's because lead is mostly contained in the skin of the grape, and when it comes to making white wines like Gewurztraminer, the skin is removed from the pulp as soon as possible, reducing the opportunity for lead to leach into the juicy pulp, which then ferments to make wine. What's more, since undertaking this experiment, the legal limits on lead in wine have been reduced several times and now stand at a historically low 0.2 milligrams (200 micrograms) per kilogram. In the 1993 study compiled from analysis by the Humbrechts and many other grape growers across the country, it was found that the average level of lead in French wines was a safe 64 micrograms per liter, compared with 150 micrograms in the 1960s.[24]

While lead is definitely not sloshing around in wine glasses in dangerous quantities, that doesn't mean that it isn't present in wine today. As recently as 2002, heavy wine drinkers in Argentina—those consuming two liters of wine a day—showed high levels of lead in their blood, which when added to the huge amounts of alcohol consumed, didn't do much good for their health.[25] In fact, alcoholics whose drink of choice was red wine showed similar symptoms to those who had worked in lead mines. Don't choke on that glass of Malbec quite yet: moderate drinkers need not be alarmed. It is estimated that humans ingest about 40–60 micrograms per liter of lead a day through breathing, eating, and drinking. The legal limit of lead in wine has been on lawmakers' minds since the 1950s, and it has been reduced and reduced again to a level that won't harm health. In fact, it's likelier that the recommended daily intake of water contains more lead than a couple of glasses of red at the end of a day's work: it's estimated that a person would need to drink eighty glasses of wine a day to exceed the safe daily limit.

At about the same time the Humbrechts were testing their roadside vineyard, lead capsules that traditionally protected wine-bottle corks were also causing widespread alarm. Sensational headlines had the public worried that the capsules were leaching lead into their wine; in fact, they were no more dangerous than canned tuna or fruit cocktail, which contained just as much lead as most of the wines analyzed at the time. Further investigation showed that even corroded capsules had no effect on wines with a sound cork, but that didn't stop the media and public from calling for a total ban. The US Food and Drug Administration obliged in 1996. However, many wine collectors have a horde of old bottles sporting lead capsules in their cellars. There is a simple way to avoid any harmful effects: open the bottle and wipe the top before pouring, and it should be fine.

It is wise, however, to avoid lead crystal decanters. They may sparkle brightly and look antique-chic on the sideboard, but they should remain empty, as they leach lead into wine and spirits. The history of lead in crystal glassware goes back to Christopher Merrett (1614–1695), the Englishman who is now believed to have put the fizz into sparkling wine. While the Champenois have long taken the credit for putting bubbles in wine, Merrett had written about adding sugar to wines "to make them drink brisk and sparkling and to give them spirit" thirty years before the monk Dom Pérignon was popping corks in the Marne Valley.[26] Merrett wasn't just busy with bubbles; he also translated *The Art of Glass* by Florentine priest Antonio Neri, thereby giving English businessman George Ravenscroft (1632–1683) the know-how to produce lead crystal glassware on a commercial scale. Lead imbued glass with better resistance to wear and tear and gave it a brilliant shine, thanks to its ability to refract light; no wonder glassmakers wanted to use it.

It took another three centuries to prove that lead crystal (or flint glass) was contaminating the alcohol poured into these beautiful glasses and ornate decanters. In 1991, scientists from Columbia University in New York City revealed the stark results from experiments on lead crystal wine decanters.[27] The research team poured a bottle of port, which contained a safe 89 micrograms per liter of lead, into three separate decanters and then, over the course of four months, recorded how lead levels soared to a mean of 3,318 micrograms per liter across the trio of vessels. They also analyzed wine and spirits taken from decanters in the homes of fellow faculty members. In one shocking instance, the lead level in a brandy stored in a decanter for more than five years had risen to an "extraordinary" 21,530 micrograms per liter— thought to be about the same level as the wines sweetened with lead salts by the Romans that caused untold damage to the peoples of its empire. It wasn't just long-term storage that had the researchers alarmed: leaching began within minutes of decanting white wines into lead crystal decanters, and at the four-hour mark, the lead levels had tripled. No wonder US authorities and lawmakers were stirred to action. Since then, the World Health Organization has reduced its recommended daily intake of lead, in 2010 advising that levels in drinking water shouldn't exceed 10 micrograms per liter. It seems that the message has finally gotten through. Modern science has substantiated the centuries-old suspicions that lead in wine can be fatal. Despite numerous attempts, it took a lengthy two millennia for lead to be given its marching orders and in that time, its victims have included the great and the godly. What's also certain is that Beethoven's Tenth shall forever be known as the "Unfinished Symphony." Do we have wine to blame?

3

AN ENLIGHTENED
DRINKER?

||||||||||||||||||||||||||||||||||||||||||||||||||||||||||||||||||||||||||||||||||||||||||||||||||||||||||||||||||||||||||||||||||||||||||||||||||||||||||||||

THE WORLD OF FOOD AND DRINK EXPERIENCED a revolution in the years after Louis XVI and his probably misquoted "let them eat cake" wife, Marie Antoinette, lost their heads to the guillotine in 1793. The final throes of the eighteenth century and the opening decades of the nineteenth gave birth to the first food critics, the first celebrity chef, and the first whiffs of wine connoisseurship. This new and modern era of gastronomy was paired with a delectable array of food writing; once the preserve of recipe books, gastronomic literature oozed out of the epicurean epicenter of Paris in the post-Revolutionary period. Food was no longer fuel, it was a measure of one's cultural standing, and woe betide anyone seen dining at the wrong restaurant.[1] It was only a matter of time before the intellectualization of food flowed into the country's favorite drink: wine. The publication of new wine books on both sides of the English Channel gave birth to a better understanding of what was good and what the upwardly mobile ought to be drinking to maintain or elevate their social standing. It also highlighted the importance of purity and provenance. The elite could afford to be picky at precisely the time wholesale adulteration of food was hitting new highs, affecting those who didn't have the means to be so choosy.

One of the unintended yet appetizing consequences of the French Revolution was the birth of the restaurant and the restaurant critic. Before the storming of the Bastille, the restaurant scene was embryonic at best, but in the years that followed, it mushroomed as the now unemployed chefs and waitstaff of the toppled nobility became restaurateurs. But the restaurant had initially started to take shape under the ancien régime. In a seminal work on the origins of the restaurant, historian Rebecca Spang flipped the starter-sized world of food historians like a pancake when she proposed that restaurants did not have their origins in the French Revolution but emerged in the 1760s.[2] Scouring the archives, it turned out that the original restaurant was not a dining venue but a broth that was designed to revive those with a sensitive or weak disposition (restaurer is the verb "to restore" in French). While broths or consommés were the first thing a Frenchman thought of when he referred to restaurant in the mid-1700s, wine was also included in several definitions for its ability to lift one's spirits. The makers of the nourishing broths—restaurateurs—extolled the medical benefits of their liquid meals, whether to ease a sore stomach or a weak chest, and they'd go as far as claiming their small cup of soup would improve people's state of mind. These restaurateurs dubbed their establishments maison de santé (literally, "house of health"), and they weren't the only ones wanting to jump on the wellness bandwagon. The phrase de santé began popping up in ads in local circulars, where it was appended to tea, mustard, chocolate, and more. While the thought of eating mustard to keep the doctor away may seem amusing, little has changed: more than two centuries later, the health food market continues to be big business and was recently valued at more than $800 billion—that's a lot of turmeric tea and quinoa.

It wasn't just what eighteenth-century restaurateurs were serving up but how they were serving it that shaped the blueprint for the modern restaurant. Yes, there have been places to have a drink and get a bite to eat for millennia, but this marked a new form of dining out that we would recognize today. Customers could turn up at a time of their choosing, take a seat at their own table, and choose what they wanted to eat from a menu, which displayed prices so there was no nasty shock when the bill arrived. This might not seem particularly novel today, but up until then, dining out in Paris had hardly been an experience to savor. Inns and cookshops for both locals and tourists would serve up the same fare at the same time every day, and there was a distinct possibility that dining in them would involve sharing a table with some inhospitable locals. A German visitor, Joachim Nemeitz, spent two years in the city and his 1727 book *Séjour de Paris* acted as a local guide for newcomers, offering advice on the best places to stay, visit, and dine, as well as providing cultural tips on fitting in. Of the dining scene, he wrote, "Almost everyone believes that you eat well in France, and especially in Paris; but they're wrong." While the city's wealthy ate well thanks to their private chefs, eating out was fraught with problems, Nemeitz complained: "The meat is poorly prepared, you eat the same thing every day and the menu very rarely changes."[3]

Unfortunately, things didn't change for some time. It was nigh on impossible to open what to us would be a recognizable eatery in the years before the Revolution due to the legal straitjacket regulating the sale of food. If you wanted to buy a loaf of bread, you went to the guild-approved *boulanger;* if you wanted a cured sausage, you visited the *charcutier;* for roasted meats, it was off to the *rôtisseur.* Entry into these specialized guilds was prized, and woe betide anyone who veered even slightly off course and toward someone else's territory—unless, of course, you belonged to two different guilds, which a few did. There were also the master cooks—the *traiteurs*—who had the stamp of approval to dish up full meals, and some of them became restaurateurs. Initially the restaurateurs offered the eighteenth-century equivalent of today's pop-up eating experience, but in 1786 a royal decree gave them the nod to have dining rooms with tables where customers could order and eat their food. The first of these was opened by Antoine Beauvilliers, who had trained in the kitchens of the future Louis XVIII and who became "the most famous restaurateur of Paris," according to the famed lawyer and gastronome Jean Anthelme Brillat-Savarin. "He was the first to have an elegant dining room, handsome well-trained waiters, a fine cellar, and a superior kitchen."[4] It seems the restaurant was starting to take shape, and its true form would be revealed in the years after the Revolution.

The guilds were on shaky soil as the ancien régime took its final breaths. While these trade associations were a barrier to entry for the many, they had provided a training ground for the next generation of artisans, and had regulated food quality at a time when there was plenty of opportunity to adulterate foodstuffs. However, they were finally given the boot in 1791 and their removal, along with the removal of the monarchy, opened up a whole world of freedoms for the cooking profession. The aristocracy's chefs and waitstaff moved from serving in the noblest private dining rooms to running restaurants for a wider society. The barrier to entry to these restaurants was not your lineage but how many *sous* you had for a meal, effectively preventing the majority from entering.

By the time Englishman Francis William Blagdon published his Paris musings in 1803, the city's restaurant scene was much changed, but Beauvilliers was still in the premier dining league. Situated on the first floor of a hotel and capable of feeding up to three hundred diners daily, his was an ornate and elegant restaurant with an ambiance and food that edged out its nearest rivals. Blagdon effused, "Good heaven! The bill of fare is a printed sheet of double folio, of the size of an English newspaper. It will require half an hour at least to con [sic] over this important catalogue."[5] Blagdon lists thirteen soups, twenty-two hors d'oeuvres, beef served eleven ways, thirty-two poultry and game dishes, twenty-three varieties of fish, and thirty-nine desserts, to name but a few of the menu items—and this wasn't unusual in the city's finest eateries. The wine list was equally lengthy, with fifty-two choices, and if diners ordered a bottle off the list but drank less than half of its contents, they'd only pay for a half bottle.

At the turn of the century, Beauvilliers was one of around a hundred restaurants in Paris offering everything from a fine dining experience to simpler fare for the common man (the latter would have included a soup, a main course, and perhaps even dessert at a fraction of the price of the fine dining menu). The number of restaurants in Paris increased sixfold during the First French Empire (1804–1814), rising to an estimated three thousand by 1820, but how did the public know where to go? In the absence of the guilds, the voice of authority had been silenced. Who could the public trust when it came to what they put in their mouths? Into the void stepped a new breed of food writer.

A WRITING REVOLUTION

Alexandre Balthazar Laurent Grimod de la Reynière has a reasonable claim to the crown of the world's first food and restaurant critic. Ambitious restaurateurs and food producers in Paris courted him in the opening years of the nineteenth century. Grimod was the force behind the annual food guide *Almanach des gourmands,* the equivalent of a Michelin guide to the city's best places to eat. He was a rather unusual character who, like many contemporary food writers, did not always please those he was writing about. His lack of popularity was proved in 1812, when he issued a public notice claiming that he had died. He put on a funeral banquet to see how many people would show up, and few did. Those who bothered to turn up didn't think it was particularly funny when he made an unexpected entrance—although by all accounts, he put on a good spread.

Being Grimod can't have been easy. The only surviving child of an aristocratic couple residing on the Champs-Élysées, he was born with deformed hands; this so shamed his parents that they claimed he'd been mauled by ravenous pigs in infancy. They kept him out of sight as much as possible, yet he sought out the limelight. When he was in his mid-twenties he hosted a macabre fourteen-course funeral-themed dinner, complete with spectators; it was the first of many. His unhappy parents eventually sent him to an abbey near Nancy for two years' confinement. After his incarceration, he resisted the temptation to return home, making the wise decision to stay away from a tumultuous Paris until 1794. Instead, he traveled the country learning about food and keeping his aristocratic head low, while all around him, the nobility was meeting a bloody end.

Following his return to a much-changed Paris, Grimod, who had previously dabbled in theater reviews, noted that the theaters as well as the growing number of restaurant tables were filled not with his cultured aristocratic friends of the old regime but with those who were less refined. What they needed, he decided, was a guide to fine dining and gastronomy and, in 1803, that's what he gave them. The first *Almanach des gourmands* provided not only reviews of the city's eateries and food sellers but guides to seasonal produce, advice on setting a table and being the perfect host, as well as a smattering of food-inspired poetry and advice on stain removal. Grimod was assisted by an elitist group of friends, whom he called his jurors, although he tended to have the final word. They would meet one evening a week to eat and pass judgement on what passed their lips. His first volume sold an estimated 12,000 copies, a success that secured his spot as a key figure in the development of gastronomic literature, one who could make or break local purveyors with his assessment of their wares in much the same way that food and wine critics do today.

The fact that his publication was called *Almanach des gourmands* marked a new era for the term *gourmand* as well as for *gastronome*, which had until this time more typically been associated with gluttonous behavior. While his critics considered him vulgar and self-indulgent, Grimod and his contemporaries redefined what it meant to be a food lover. The gourmand was a man (invariably a man) with a refined and sophisticated appreciation of fine food and wine, which was something that readers of this new form of writing were told was aspirational. Eating and drinking was no longer purely for the calories; where you dined, how you laid a table, and what you put in your mouth became barometers of your social status and cultural standing. French food historian Patrick Rambourg sums it up neatly: "The better you are at entertaining, in the 19th century, the more of a gastronome you are perceived to be, and the more you are perceived as a person who has had success in society."[6]

It might not come as a surprise that the now-bastardized phrase "Tell me what you eat, and I shall tell you what you are" was coined during this period by one of these self-titled gastronomes, Jean Anthelme Brillat-Savarin. A lawyer by trade, he spent the latter half of his life, unbeknown to most of his friends, penning *The Physiology of Taste*, which was published at his own cost in 1825. A few months after the first printing of five hundred copies hit the shelves, he attended a service to mark the thirty-third anniversary of Louis XVI's execution. He was by this time a seventy-year-old man, and sitting in a cold cathedral on a January day was not the wisest decision; he contracted pneumonia and died two weeks later. He would not witness success of his book, which is still in print today, nor the naming of a soft cheese in his honor.

His book is a semi-autobiographical work with a focus on the world of food. It details how to be a good host and the importance of food in everyday life, as well as personal anecdotes from the dining table. In parts, it is a cookbook with details on how to fry, as well as how to make a perfectly boiled egg, which is something that remains a risky business two hundred years later. Brillat-Savarin extols the virtues of everything in moderation: the book starts with his twenty "Aphorisms" or rules for those who want to be a gastronome, which include don't stuff your face, and do water down your wine so you don't get drunk. He later provides treatments on obesity: eating and sleeping in moderation and taking exercise on foot (or horse) are his prescriptions. He also gives unwitting insight into the period's attitudes toward women: the lady of the house was in charge of coffee but the man was in charge of the wine (which would not do in my house), while he compares a dinner that doesn't finish with cheese as being "like a beautiful woman with only one eye." However, he does get brownie points for his rigid insistence on punctuality: "A host who makes all his guests wait for one later comer is careless of their well-being."[7] According to Brillat-Savarin's translator, one nineteenth-century gourmet lived by this rule and set dinner for 5:00 pm. At 5:05 pm he locked the door, and latecomers were neither allowed in nor invited again.

The fact that the full title Brillat-Savarin bestowed on his book was *The Physiology of Taste; or, Meditations on Transcendental Gastronomy* gave further credibility to foodie culture and this new form of literature. He was born in 1755, and his life spanned the opening of the first simple restaurants in the 1760s, the fall of the monarchy (which led to a brief period in exile in New York, where he professed to enjoy Welsh rarebit—a fancy form of cheese on toast), the abolition of the guilds and the rise of new tastemakers, and the proliferation of Parisian restaurants under Napoleon I (1804–1815), which led to new ways of dining, including the à la carte menu as well as the prix fixe for the more budget-conscious customer. These were seminal moments in the history of food, and Brillat-Savarin was one of the few to record this changing of the guard. But democracy was not being served on a plate: refined tastes remained the preserve of the educated and affluent man. Brillat-Savarin may have differed from Grimod in that he said women could be gourmands, but you don't have to read between the lines to see connoisseurship wasn't available to all. "Animals feed themselves, men eat; but only wise men know the art of eating," he declared.[8]

Similarly, the eccentric Grimod also suggested that those with a refined palate were more likely to be wealthy and academically minded.

If Grimod was the first restaurant critic, Marie-Antoine Carême, known as Antonin, is thought of as the first celebrity chef, and he set a new standard for food writing from the perspective of the kitchen.[9] While Grimod reviewed food and Brillat-Savarin philosophized, Carême brought the culinary arts into the homes of both the wealthy and the common woman. He was chef to Europe's rich and famous, but in 1833, his five-volume, all-encompassing *L'art de la cuisine française* brought his trade secrets to the kitchen of anyone who could afford a copy. With the humble home cook in mind, his first recipe is the everyman dish pot-au-feu—beef stew—but he covered almost everything imaginable: hundreds of soups, fish, and meat dishes, as well as the showstopping cake designs and sugar towers that set him on a course to fame.

The author of *The Three Musketeers*, Alexandre Dumas, gave Carême the nickname "the king of chefs," but he was as far removed from royal stock as possible. Born in a shack in the Left Bank slums of Paris to poor but exceedingly virile parents—he was apparently the sixteenth of twenty-five children—he was left to fend for himself at the age of ten, during one of the bloodiest points in the history of Paris. In 1793, with the blade of the guillotine falling daily, including through the necks of Louis XVI and Marie Antoinette, he was rescued from the tumultuous streets by the owner of a chophouse who gave him room and board, and in return he spent five years working in the kitchen, learning the basics before moving on to an apprenticeship at a successful patisserie in a fashionable part of town. It was here that his artistic confectionery window displays attracted cooing crowds and offers of employment from the Parisian elite.

By the time he died in 1833—probably of carbon monoxide poisoning after a lifetime of breathing in the smoke of the kitchen fires—the chef and author had run the kitchens of an English prince and a Russian emperor, had catered for Napoleon's wedding, and had fed the Parisian elite. However, his book was not intended for the elite—he hoped it would attract a wider audience. He said that he hoped "every citizen in our beautiful France" would be able to read it and "eat delicious food."[10]

THE BIRTH OF WINE WRITING

The growing body of food writing aimed at the cultured diner and the ambitious at-home cook inevitably percolated into the world of wine, slaking a growing thirst for knowledge and expertise. However, the arrival of mass print production during the Enlightenment not only benefited scholarly wine writers; it also paved the way for fans of wine adulteration to disseminate their recipes. At the start of the nineteenth century, there were few works that resembled a modern wine book. Parisian wine merchant André Jullien came to the rescue in 1816, publishing *Topographie de tous les vignobles connus,* which was translated into English eight years later. Its publication was a marked departure for the wine world. In the period leading up to its release, writing about wine had focused on the medical benefits of particular wines, the wine-making processes in the author's particular corner of the world, or the virtues of the wines of ancient Greece and Rome as viewed through rose-tinted glasses.

In the mid-1790s Jullien moved from the wine region of Burgundy to Paris. He set up shop as a wine merchant on the rue Saint-Sauveur in the second arrondissement, a short walk from the city's new fine-dining restaurants in the Palais Royal. He would have needed to eat well to fuel his many pursuits—running his wine business, writing, revising his books, and inventing a pipe to transfer wine from one vessel to another without damaging the liquid, an invention that attracted the attention of Jean-Antoine Chaptal, one of France's most famous wine chemists.

But Jullien is best remembered for penning his *Topographie,* a book for aspiring wine nerds or, in his words, those "anxious to keep a good cellar." With it he guided not only keen drinkers but his fellow wine merchants on the other side of the Channel to the finest wines in France and beyond. For those eager to find out how Champagne was made and which villages made the finest examples, here was a man who had the answers. The text was published almost four decades before Bordeaux's 1855 classification, which ranked the most highly prized estates in five leagues known as *grands cru classés* for the Universal Exhibition in Paris, and Jullien had already gotten the measure of it: La Fitte (sic), Latour, Margaux, and Haut-Brion were the four châteaux in his top-ranked category, as they were in 1855, and as they remain two centuries later. That's not to say Jullien was some sort of oracle: the wines of these four estates came with a significantly higher price tag than those of their neighbors and had done so for more than a century before he set out his ranking. That said, his descriptions of the styles of wine produced by each are remarkably similar to the characteristics they display today—for example, the "fineness" of Château Margaux and the "substance" of Latour.[11] He identified the whites of Montrachet and Sauternes as the nation's best whites, and the vineyards of Burgundy that he called the best are still on a pedestal: Romanée-Conti, Richebourg, and La Tâche. But it is the sheer breadth and depth of this book that turned wine writing and wine knowledge on its head: Jullien also described the growing conditions and characteristics of wines in such far-flung locales as Russia, China, and Philadelphia, whose vines, taken from the Médoc region of Bordeaux, were as near an imitation of the French as he could find on the other side of the Atlantic. He created a new genre of wine writing that provided discerning readers with the equivalent of a buying guide, and it was such a success that he penned several more editions and saw it translated into English before dying of cholera in 1832.

In 1833, English journalist and newspaper editor Cyrus Redding published *A History and Description of Modern Wines,* which expanded on Jullien's work. He traveled throughout Europe describing how the vines were grown and the wines were made, and the main styles of wines across the continent, from Champagne to Cyprus. He showed a distinct preference for the wines of France; he didn't much admire the wines of Italy, calling those of Brescia "tolerable," which was hardly a compliment, while those made just outside of Rome were "as bad as any in Italy."[12] To be fair, he did praise Tuscany, as well as the sweet wine Lacryma Christi, made on the outskirts of Naples. Redding's book not only served as a reference—an early *Oxford Companion to Wine*—but was also a soapbox from which he lambasted the prevalence of fake wines, particularly concocted ports and sherries, that were widely sold on the English market. He promised that his book would "guide the reader in the search of good wine, and tend to confirm the preference for what is really excellent."[13] Although he complained that fashions rather than wine quality dictated drinking trends in England, his work and that of Jullien and others like them provided expert voices for those who wanted guidance, and that was typically the upper-class gentleman. It was he who could afford to buy these books, drink the finest wines, and store them in his cellar. However, it wasn't just the aristocracy that wanted to know more about wine as the nineteenth century progressed—extracts from Redding's book were printed in newspapers, and a second wave of wine books aimed at a wider public in the 1860s and 1870s suggested that there was a growing desire among the professional middle classes to know more about wine.

While it was generally men reading these wine books and buying wine, women were devouring copies of *The Physiology of Taste* and Mrs. Beeton's *Book of Household Management*, which referenced the works of Redding and Brillat-Savarin and provided guidance on how to be the hostess with the mostest. "Nothing spreads more rapidly in society than the reputation of a good wine-cellar, and all that is required is wines well-chosen and well cared for; and thus a little knowledge, carefully applied, will soon supply," advised Mrs. Beeton.[14] The proliferation of these wine and food books through the early and mid-nineteenth century meant more people could name and request the best vineyards, regions, and years, whether or not they could afford them or knew their true taste. These readers would have been unlikely to discern a real bottle of Bordeaux or Champagne from a pretender, but the idea that wine came from a particular place and some places were better than others was starting to trickle into the mainstream. Provenance and place of origin are the cornerstone of wine law around the world today, but in the nineteenth century, buying wine was akin to playing roulette. A reputable wine merchant was thought to be the only guarantee that what was being sold was the real deal, and even then, there was no way of easily testing it without access to a chemistry set or a trained palate—and those were as rare as a glass of real Romanée-Conti.

UNCORKING THE TRUTH

At the same time that food and wine were becoming intellectualized, leading to a growing awareness of what was good, it was becoming clear that a glass of Bordeaux or a tot of port might contain more than just fermented grapes, including ingredients that were not appetizing. In 1820, a German chemist living in central London, Friedrich Accum, lifted the lid on the adulteration of food and drink, opening the public's eyes to the scale of adulteration that was occurring in everyday products, from bread and ale to wine and even that most British of all dessert accompaniments, custard. The first print run of a thousand copies of Accum's *Treatise on Adulterations of Food, and Culinary Poisons* sold out in less than a month. Adulteration was now in the spotlight, but it was hardly new. A 1682 book published for London wine merchants described how to ameliorate wines and improve the unpalatable; it was republished five times over the course of the next century. Meanwhile, dodgy Parisian wine merchants had been the subject of an exposé, published anonymously in 1770, which claimed that in one year alone they had brought close to eight million liters, or 30,000 casks, of "vinegar" into the city before cleaning it up with potentially fatal but sweet-tasting lead acetate.[15] However, it wasn't until the publication of Accum's book that the mainstream press and its readers sat up and took note of the swollen underbelly of the food and drink world.

Accum was clearly aiming to rouse the British population from its laissez-faire slumber with his rhetoric. Subtlety was not his strong point: the book's cover featured a skull sitting in an urn and covered with a shroud; the urn is emblazoned with the statement "There is death in the pot." Although wine was just one drop in a much wider scandal, Accum claimed that few other products were "adulterated to a greater extent than wine."[16] In the wake of several cases involving fake foodstuffs, including tea leaves made from tree leaves, the British had so far been very British, adopting the "oh dear, how terribly dreadful" attitude before waving the problem to one side and going about their daily business with a nice cup of hopefully unadulterated tea. Accum was more fired up: he wanted action and the perpetrators brought to justice, and he detailed ways of detecting foreign substances in foods, although many of his methods required special equipment—which, conveniently, he sold from his shop in Soho. Bread was stretched with alum or potatoes, Double Gloucester cheese sometimes acquired its color from red lead, and the leaves of the cherry laurel tree apparently tasted like almonds and were used by a school cook to flavor custard, leading to several ill students.

Stamping down on the adulteration of wine wasn't a high priority compared with that of foodstuffs and beer, which was often consumed by children as well as adults due to poor water quality. What's more, most of the wine chicanery was unlikely to cause anyone to keel over: "The sophistication of wine with substances not absolutely noxious to health, is carried out to an enormous extent in this metropolis. Many thousand pipes [a pipe is a 550-liter barrel] of spoiled cyder are annually brought hither from the country, for the purpose of being converted into factitious Port wine."[17] For those looking to make their own port, Accum explained how: infuse four ounces of wood from the logwood tree (the heartwood of which is used for dyeing textiles) and half a pound of rhatany, a shrub whose powdered roots helped give color to red wines, in a pint of brandy and a gallon of cider. After a week-long infusion, strain the liquid and mix with three more gallons of cider and two pints of beetroot juice. Pop it in a barrel for a month and voilà! There are plenty of other recipes provided by Accum's contemporaries for making imitation port—both from those who lambasted the practice and those who thought it was a great-value alternative to the real thing—but there was usually cider and brandy involved, and some form of coloring agent, from sloes and bilberries to elderberries. Mature port was seen as superior to the just-shipped stuff, and there were creative techniques to make it seem older than it was by forging a crust on the port, soaking corks to give them the appearance of age, as well as warming up the wine either in the oven or in warm water to speed up the maturation process. It really was rather crafty.

At that time, port was Britain's most popular drink and due to its "spiritous strength and coarseness" it was an easy wine to fake without detection.[18] However, the finer wines of France were also imitated in the back streets of London: "They can squeeze Bourdeaux out of the sloe, and draw Champagne from an apple."[19] But at this time, there were few who knew the real taste of Champagne; those who could tell Champagne from sparkling gooseberry or apple wine were generally able to afford the genuine article. While Accum and many of his contemporaries felt this wine craft was underhanded, not everyone was so sniffy about a bit of mixing and blending to get something that was well priced and perfectly drinkable. In fact, several recipe books were printed encouraging publicans to make their own wines or to stretch the wines they had purchased. In a wine guide published in 1860, one wine-merchant-turned-author praised the blending creativity of his fellow British merchants, claiming the ability to mix one thing with another helped the country negotiate a supply crisis: in the mid-1850s, a fungal disease, oidium, had ravaged vineyards across western Europe, devastating crops and sending wine prices sky high. The interim solution was to stretch what little merchants had or substitute a vague lookalike for the real thing: "Made under the magical hand of the merchant we got a good pleasant wine for immediate use without any style or pretentions about it, it is true; but nevertheless wine which will serve us until a better sort gets cheaper."[20]

These widespread practices were driven by profiteering individuals and a thirsty audience. When the first wave of wine reference books had come into print, there were few people who had the knowledge to accurately identify the fakes, and even fewer who had access to scientific equipment that claimed—but may have not yet have been sophisticated enough—to detect the knock-off wines. What's more, the Wild West wine merchant business was able to operate without fear—few of the swindlers were caught or prosecuted. Sure, lead in wine was certainly detrimental to health, but many of the ingredients used to cook up phony wines, from cider and berries to beetroot, weren't harmful, and as a result, regulation was low on the priority list for lawmakers.

The perpetrators defended their businesses and their methods. A "practical liquor manufacturer" who claimed to have many years' experience as a distiller, maker, and chemist in both Bordeaux and New York authored an insider's guide to the "manufacture and adulteration of liquor" and wines in 1858. Aspiring "sherry" makers were advised to use cider, raisins, and almond oil, while mock Claret could be produced from South African "Cape" red. These trade secrets came at a price, however: the book cost $2.50, equivalent to approximately $80 today. The writer defended adulteration on several fronts: when it came to health concerns, he admitted there was an "objectionable part" of the trade that used toxic substances, but none of the recipes in the book, nor the finished products, contained anything harmful. What's more, he argued that adulteration was necessary to slake a thirst that would otherwise not be quenched, suggesting that the entire crop of Europe's vineyards, if exported, would not even furnish the needs of New York City: "The city of New York alone sells three times as many 'pure imported brandies' and four times as many 'pure imported wines' annually, as all the wine-producing countries export."[21] He also claimed that as many as twelve million bottles of so-called Champagne were sold each year in the United States alone, but official figures from the Champagne region show that in 1855, the total number of bottles leaving French ports was less than seven million. With such a shortfall, the four different recipes he provided for reproducing Champagne—all a theme on cider, sugar, water, and lemon juice—would have been well used. The author also engaged in some nationalistic finger pointing, claiming the French and the Brits were all faking wines too.

The upstanding Bristol wine merchant Charles Tovey suggested a swift but very British eviction policy for anyone trying to peddle adulterated wine: "Show them the door; and if they are not inclined to adopt the manners of a well-bred member of the canine species, then by the most forcible manner eject them summarily."[22] Tovey was one of several reputable wine merchants who drew on their insider knowledge to write wine books in the mid-nineteenth century, not only to educate their customers but also to expose the dodgy dealers who were damaging the industry, and consequently the earnings of honest merchants: "There can be no question that the Wine Trade is losing its position by the introduction into it of unscrupulous traders."[23] Tovey went on to quote an advertisement for "Essence of Sherry Wine," which claimed to be "a very superior preparation of improving the bouquet and flavor of inferior Sherries, and imparting the Sherry Wine bouquet to South African and other white wines."[24] There was also an "Essence of Port Wine" that promised to do similar things to South African wine.

While protectionist wine merchants attempted to uphold the reputation of their profession against the shiftier elements, there were plenty of good reasons to give wines a spit and polish: most of them weren't very good. In 1828, one French expert, B. A. Lenoir, gave his verdict on the state of the nation's wines: "I am sorry to say that in France barely a sixth of the wine we make here has desirable qualities; the other five-sixths is made up of mediocre to terrible wines."[25] Indeed, there was a lot of bad wine being made across the country, despite the improvements in scientific knowledge that had taken place during the Enlightenment and the Napoleonic era.

One of the Enlightenment chemists was Antoine Lavoisier, and he might have become a more familiar name in wine circles had his head not been chopped off in 1794. A leading chemist of his time, he came up with the idea of elements and identified both oxygen and sulfur, among other things, but he was a member of the nobility and worked within a much-despised group of the ancien régime, which would prove his undoing. However, in his short lifetime, he discovered that wine was not the result of a mystical process but a predictable reaction whereby yeast transformed sugar into alcohol and carbon dioxide. Lavoisier influenced many, including his fellow chemist Jean-Antoine Chaptal, who had the country's favorite drink on his mind.

France had nature on its side: its climate, soils, and free-draining hillsides were the perfect environment for making fine wines, but its farmers didn't know how to make the most of what nature had given them, lamented Chaptal in his influential *Traité sur la vigne*, a practical guide to growing grapes and making fault-free wine. It also acted as a personal soapbox: Chaptal questioned why so many renowned French wines had fallen into disrepute while others had managed to improve or maintain their reputations. He pointed his finger directly at careless and ignorant growers who followed the same practices blindly year after year. Too many grape growers chose to plant varieties that offered quantity over quality, producing coarse wine. And while there were plenty of established growers who were letting the side down, there were also many inexperienced vineyard owners who needed guidance following the shake-up of land ownership that occurred after the Revolution.

If wine was to remain an important part of the French economy, standards needed to be maintained, and Chaptal took on the role of standard bearer. He blended and distilled what had been learned in the vineyards, cellars, and laboratories over the past century and created the first practical guide for winemakers, which was subsequently translated into many languages, including English, Spanish, and Italian. While Chaptal's influence on wine production in the early nineteenth century stretched from grape to glass and from Sancerre to Sydney, his name is most associated with the addition of sugar to grape juice before it ferments, a process known as chaptalization.

Some sources claim that Chaptal invented the practice, but several winemakers had championed the method before he arrived on the wine scene. Whether they used pure sugar, honey, or molasses, the aim was to make a wine that was more stable and better balanced after fermentation, due to its higher alcohol content. When Chaptal ended up as interior minister for France under Napoleon between 1800 and 1804, he found himself in a stronger position to spread the word than those who had come before him. While some considered adding non-grape sugar to wine a form of adulteration—and today it is only permitted in cool regions in cold years, when grapes don't reach full ripeness—it was actively encouraged, having been given the French government's official stamp of approval when it distributed a manual to wine producers entitled *The Art of Making Wine*, which was effectively a reworked version of Chaptal's *Traité*.

It would have come as a disappointment to Chaptal that in 1828, four years before his death, just one-sixth of French wine was considered "desirable" despite his efforts to raise quality across France. Chaptalizing wines to increase the final alcohol level, or even fortifying them, gave them greater resilience on long journeys to market. Authorities and scientists had become more vigilant about the use of lead to both sweeten wines and disguise any vinegar-like characters. Chaptalization "offered a wholesome alternative."[26] Gradual improvements in scientific knowledge over the 1700s and early 1800s gave wine adulterers less reason to adulterate. Wine took an additional leap forward in the middle of the nineteenth century when another French scientist, Louis Pasteur, turned his attentions to wine. He began to unravel the mysteries of fermentation and helped clean up France's act when it came to wine faults, identifying the bacteria, acetobacter, that turned wine to vinegar while in transit. In the days before science shined its light on the microscopic bugs responsible for fermentation, wine had spoiled very quickly: in 1765, the French *Encyclopédie* (volume 17) defined wine as middle aged after just four months, and it reached old age after its first birthday. However, there were attempts to remedy this: in that same year, the records of one of the city's wine merchants, Nathaniel Johnston, showed that merchants were burning sulfur wicks in the freshly rinsed casks to disinfect them before they were filled with wine, a technique borrowed from the Dutch, according to Jean-Robert Pitte in *Bordeaux/Burgundy: A Vintage Rivalry*. By using sulfur, as well as keeping barrels filled to the brim, merchants were better able to get wines to their destination without them spoiling.

In a bid to give wine a longer shelf life there were also developments in glass bottles and well-fitting corks. Wine was shipped in barrels rather than bottles until as recently as the 1970s. Today, it's common to see "Estate Bottled" or the French equivalent, *Mis en bouteille à la proprieté*, on a wine label. While you might not give it a second thought, bottling wine just a few meters from the vineyard used to be a big deal. It was introduced to reassure customers that nothing untoward had occurred between the grape and the glass, although these days, shipping wine in heavy bottles over thousands of miles is severely criticized for its impact on the environment. Before estate bottling became the norm, wines were typically bottled by local merchants. They'd receive a cask of wine from France or South Africa and put it in bottles ready for sale. From time to time, they might have to use various tools at their disposal to clean up faults that had developed during the journey or tweak the blend to better suit the palates of their customers. Before the advent of paper wine labels, merchants might also stamp their names on wine bottles, not only to advertise their services but to stop their competitors from reusing their precious bottles.

Embossed bottles were also popular with wealthy customers who liked to flaunt their affluence by having their initials or coat of arms stamped on their bottles. But this fell out of favor in the mid-1800s as glass wine bottles went from being a rare item made by skilled glass blowers to a mass-produced product. Molds created the standard wine bottle shapes and sizes we know today, providing a uniform neck into which to jam a tight-fitting cork. Thankfully, corkscrews had been created in the late seventeenth century, although if you're ever short of a corkscrew, the internet can demonstrate how to dislodge a cork using just a shoe and a wall, or even car keys. Until bottle necks became a standard size, a cork was wedged unceremoniously into the top of the bottle or tied down with string or wire, which allowed for easy removal but hardly provided an airtight seal—nor did it guarantee that the liquid wouldn't leak out. But the stuff inside the bottle needed to be worth the glass.

By the mid-1800s, the scientific world seemed to be getting a better handle on what goes on in a bubbling vat of fermenting wine. Knowledge flowed from the French chemistry labs to humble cellars in Bordeaux, Burgundy, and beyond, giving even the most rural vignerons the information required to make fault-free wines. Improved quality and storage was slowly reducing the need for "adjustments" by winemakers and wine merchants, although that's not to say everyone had cleaned up their act. There was still plenty of gypsum being added to sherry half a century after Accum published his *Treatise*. While Britain passed its first law outlawing food adulteration in 1860, it did little to remedy the situation. Arthur Hill Hassall, one of the leading lights on food adulteration at the time, wrote a letter to the editor of *The Times* in 1874 revealing that he had taken samples of nineteen sherries on the market and subjected them to full chemical analysis. His results showed that two of the "wines" contained no wine at all, while seventeen, including some of the finest examples on the market, were "plastered." Gypsum or calcium sulphate, which is used to make plaster of Paris, is permitted for sherry production today (although it is rarely used) to improve its acid balance, which not only helps stop nasty bacteria from growing, but also helps fix its color and improve its taste, something that was clearly needed at the time.

The emergence of food writers like Grimod and Brillat-Savarin and wine writers like Jullien, Redding, and Tovey contributed to an intellectualization of what people put in their mouths, but it hardly led to a gaggle of highly attuned palates. Newly educated wine drinkers could buy wines these authors had recommended and impress their peers with their recently acquired knowledge of the best Burgundy vineyards or the finest Bordeaux châteaux, but they were a long way from distinguishing a Pommard from a Pomerol just by sniffing and slurping. They were also unlikely to be able to identify plaster of Paris in their sherry without access to a laboratory. It remained very difficult for wine drinkers to know whether the wine in the glass was pure or defiled. It was up to lawmakers to protect consumers from the adulterers, and while they had been remarkably late to the party, the wheels were starting to turn.

It seemed that time was running out for the wine cheats: wine quality was on the up, reducing the need for adulteration; drinkers were better informed; and the authorities were beginning to step up—after passage of the 1875 Food and Drugs Act, British swindlers could end up with six months of hard labor if they were caught in the act. But new opportunities for wine fraudsters lay just around the corner, as a tiny but mightily destructive aphid landed on French shores. It might have been less than a millimeter in size, but it would have calamitous consequences for the whole of Europe, wiping out entire vineyard regions and turning producers into paupers, a disaster culminating in mass protests in France, with protestors begging the government to protect the nation's favorite drink against imposters.

4

I PREDICT A RIOT

HAVING BEEN ELECTED for a second term in 2012, President Barack Obama served California Champagne with apple pie at his inauguration banquet. While food-and-wine-matching nerds would have sighed disapprovingly, it was not the pairing with dessert that caused the most consternation, but a naming technicality. The menu stated that an "Inaugural Cuvee Champagne, California" would be served. Cue Franco-American fallout. The Champagne wine trade association's American arm declared, "Champagne only comes from Champagne, France" in caps at the top of its website, but a loophole means that a few US wine producers continue to make so-called Champagne 9,000 kilometers from its French home. However, makers of sparkling wines using the Champagne name must state the place their so-called Champagne comes from in a particular way, and there's little flexibility. If the menu makers had used the term "American Champagne" or "Californian Champagne," they wouldn't have incurred the wrath of the Champagne region. The French bristled, but the Americans who had made the error effectively told them it was a storm in a wine glass and amended the semantics in time for Obama's inaugural lunch. However, the affair highlighted a centuries-long issue: what is Champagne, where is Champagne, and who is allowed to use the name?

The issue seems of little concern on a warm September day in the Champagne region. It is the middle of the grape harvest, and the road to the rural town of Aÿ is lined with parked buses; along the dusty lanes that weave between the vines, there are countless white Renault Kangoo vans so quintessentially French that it wouldn't be a surprise to see a man sporting a striped t-shirt and beret and sucking on a Gauloises step out of the driver's door. The buses have offloaded hundreds of pickers brought in from nearby towns, and the fields above Aÿ are speckled with bobbing heads moving along the rows of mint-green vines, collecting this year's grapes. It isn't just the white vans that break up the mass of green on the slopes; portable toilets dot the landscape at this time of year, their blue TARDIS shapes detracting from the beauty of some of the most valuable vineyard land in the world.

Making Champagne is now a rich man's game, with the most prestigious and expensive grand cru vineyards fetching two million euros per hectare (over 809,000 euros per acre). The costs of entry mean young people growing up in Champagne can't hope to own land unless they inherit it from their parents or win the lottery. The wines that Champagne's exorbitantly priced vineyards produce are similarly expensive—and people are prepared to pay for them, for this is the birthplace of the world's finest sparkling wines, symbolizing luxury, love, and celebration. While makers of many other sparkling wines have tried to replicate the style of Champagne using the same grape varieties and winemaking methods, and imitating its branding, Champagne's innate class in the glass is unrivaled. The region's producers sell more than 300 million bottles each year, but the region's current prosperity, illustrated by the grandiose gated mansions along the avenue de Champagne in the town of Épernay, was far from assured at the start of the twentieth century. Facing competition from other wine-growing regions, unscrupulous wine merchants, and globalization, Champagne's growers were forced to fight for their livelihood.

It's difficult to imagine how the quiet town of Aÿ, disturbed only by the whir of tractor engines and the hourly peal of church bells for most of the year, was once the scene of vicious fighting between angry grape growers and the French army. But photographs from the time attest to the carnage wrought on April 12, 1911: the headquarters and warehouses of Champagne firms went up in flames; millions of bottles and casks were broken across Aÿ and beyond, turning cellars and streets into rivers of wine strewn with glass. Protestors from nearby villages—men, women, and children—joined the fray. Undeterred by cordons set up along the roads by the army, growers marched into Aÿ via the rolling patchwork of vineyards they had come to know over a lifetime—a route the army had left unprotected. The government had sent in the cavalry to protect Champagne cellars and maintain order, but it failed miserably, overwhelmed by an estimated five thousand rioters "clinging to their bridles and stirrups" and compelling the dragoons to resort to their sabers, injuring many, as reported by the Press Association.[1]

Despite trying to safeguard the main cellars of Deutz & Geldermann, Gauthier, Ayala, and Gallois, the cavalry was forced back by an angry crowd hurling rocks, bottles, and even a homemade bomb. Later that day, after the crowds had finally been dispersed, the center of the action, the boulevard du Nord and rue Jeanson, were still burning, lighting up the spring night.

The local newspaper, Le réveil de la Marne, described the scene: "By evening, nothing remains of the elegant houses save for charred, blackened walls. The cellars, the shops, all that you can see are their carcasses and twisted iron beams. . . . The boulevard du Nord, along its length, is strewn with all sorts of debris: broken or burnt furniture, accounting books, barrels and harvesting baskets . . . a vault lying in the middle of the rubble."[2]

The same day, the streets of Épernay were the scene of a similar battle. Growers from nearby villages marched in gangs, wives leading their spade- and iron-bar-wielding husbands toward the well-guarded town. Mounted guards brandishing sabers raced down the streets to disperse the masses assembled in the center of the town. *Le réveil de la Marne* reported that there were cries as it seemed that men and women were going to be trampled by the hooves of the cavalry. Residents on one street opened their doors, ushering in panicked grape growers and their families who were fleeing the swords and horses.

News of the events that became known as the Champagne riots quickly traveled to the furthest reaches of the world: the Press Association's reports, which claimed that five million bottles of Champagne had been destroyed in Aÿ in a single day, were published by newspapers as far away as the *Marlborough Express* in New Zealand. And the damage wasn't confined to the cellars: an estimated 35,000–40,000 vines were pulled up and used as weapons, burned, or trampled during the troubles, and it is estimated that the looting, sabotage, and destruction amounted to what would today be millions of dollars of damage.[3]

The roots of the riots can be traced back more than half a century. The golden age of French wine was but a memory; the country's wine industry went from prosperity in the 1850s to desperation in less than a lifetime, and its demise started in the unlikely location of west London's Hammersmith district. In 1863, a local gardener had sent some leaves to Oxford scholar John Obadiah Westwood, who was known as the "Insect Referee" for the popular Victorian journal *Gardener's Chronicle and Agricultural Gazette*. The role of the Insect Referee was to assess and identify any unusual insect life that its readers came across: "If a member of Britain's eager army of amateur gardeners found something unusual scuttling in the conservatory, they might send it in a matchbox care of the journal to the Professor . . . to pronounce in print on just what it might be."[4] The leaves Westwood received in 1863 were covered with tiny galls, a collection of eggs, and a few of the as yet unidentified aphids. The Insect Referee did not know it at the time, but the yellow aphid had already landed on the other side of the English Channel and was about to take French wine producers to the brink. In a small village a few miles north of Avignon in the Rhône Valley, a grower had received a package containing native vines from an American friend. Monsieur Borty planted the well-intentioned gift in 1862; two years later, he noticed that several of his other vines were suffering from an unknown blight. He was unaware that the same thing had started happening in a neighboring village in 1863. The following year, growers further afield noticed their vines were withering, sickened by an unknown killer. A destructive aphid was nibbling at the roots of vines, sucking on their sap. And, as if taking the lifeblood of the vines weren't bad enough, the critters left the wounds open, allowing free entry to any viruses and fungi in the vicinity. The aphid traveled slowly but surely across France. By 1874 it had made its way to Burgundy, some 400 kilometers north of Avignon, and it did not discriminate—it destroyed the vines of humble producers and turreted wine estates alike.

In 1868, the aphid was identified as *Phylloxera vastatrix*. *Vastatrix* means "ravager" or "devastator" and in the next forty years, it would live up to its name, forcing Europe's vineyards to be ripped out and replanted. But in 1868, it was only the rural wine community that seemed to be concerned that the national beverage was in danger of extinction; the French government had not yet realized the implications of this tiny aphid—it was busy hosting the International Exhibition in Paris (1867), opening the Suez Canal (1869), and waging war on Prussia (1870–1871). In 1870, after the culprit of the disease had been identified and it had charted a course not only across southern France but north and to Bordeaux, the government acknowledged there might be a problem that could affect the country's tax revenue and offered a

20,000-franc reward for anyone who found a solution. As village after village succumbed to the plague, the sum was upped to 300,000 francs, generating nearly seven hundred proposed remedies. Weird and wonderful ideas were offered, including burying living toads in vineyards, adding volcanic ash from Pompeii to the soil, or inviting a marching band to play to the vines. Unsurprisingly, the vines continued to die.

A decade later, in 1880, a solution was finally accepted: graft European varieties to the roots of American vines. This remedy had been proposed years earlier at a French farmers' meeting in Beaune, the capital of Burgundy wine. In 1869, Leo Laliman, a viticulturist who championed American vines—and who was likely a bringer of phylloxera, having planted vines from America in the Bordeaux region in southwest France—had suggested that Burgundians should use these varieties as rootstocks. His advice was ignored, and phylloxera arrived in the ancient winegrowing region in 1874. If only they had listened . . . However, grafting their noble French varieties—*Vitis vinifera*—to the roots of these lowly, foxy-tasting American varieties seemed like sacrilege to many growers. It was thought this would affect the purity of their precious French wines. But in 1880, after hundreds of remedies had been proposed and tried and had failed, this was the only effective solution; it meant the vineyards of Europe had to be ripped out and replanted. Between 1868 and 1900, it is estimated that 2.5 million hectares of vines were uprooted, causing French wine production to slump.[5] But the French were still thirsty and their demand had to be met.

In an effort to sate the masses, both wine and raisins were imported. Raisins, which are dried table grapes, could be shipped into France duty free. Resourceful—or disingenuous—makers would rehydrate the raisins in hot water and sugar to induce a fermentation. Splash in a little coloring for good measure, and the result was a makeshift wine known as a *piquette*. Using dried grapes, or grape skins that have already been used to make wine, and adding water to produce a low-grade wine-like alcohol is a practice almost as old as wine itself: ancient

Greeks and Romans gave this beverage to slaves and workers. During the shortages caused by phylloxera, such methods became more widespread, and a how-to guide was published in 1880 entitled *The Art of Making Wine from Raisins*. The book played its part in the production of hundreds of millions of liters of such wine in the 1880s and 1890s, wine that accounted for between 10 and 17 percent of all French wine sold in 1890.[6] Despite a grape shortage, growers faced falling prices for their fruit as raisin wine flooded the market. For honest growers trying to make ends meet after uprooting and replanting their vineyards at great expense, this was yet another kick in the teeth.

Wine continued to be stretched beyond all recognition in southern France into the twentieth century, even though the region was no longer short of wine. The Languedoc region had been hit by phylloxera early on and had been replanted by the time the aphid reared its head in Champagne. By 1900, the Languedoc was producing more grapes than ever before. Local wine associations called on the government to fight fraud, demanding that it outlaw the practice of adding water to wine and penalize those who added sugar to make their crop go further. The government sat on its hands, allowing the undercurrent of disaffection to swell among the impoverished communities of the Midi, which led to the spring and summer of discontent in 1907. Demonstrations grew from hundreds to thousands, then tens of thousands of people, culminating in 500,000 descending on Montpellier on June 9, 1907, which finally prompted the government to act, albeit begrudgingly, on behalf of the local wine trade.

Whereas phylloxera arrived early in the south of France, it came late to Champagne. It finally arrived in the country's most northerly wine region in 1890. It took its time to build its pace: by 1900, just 61 hectares of vine had been infected. But by 1911, the year of the riots, 6,500 hectares in the Marne department alone—more than 40 percent of the region's vineyard area—had been reported as phylloxera ridden.[7] While American rootstocks had been accepted as the solution to the problem, growers reluctant to uproot their vineyards—and lose their income for several years—injected chemicals into the soil, which failed to stem the tide. Sadly, there was meager assistance for affected growers: the vineyard owners had to pay the labor costs of ripping out and replanting vineyards, and there would be no crop to harvest—and therefore no income—for at least three years.

The arrival of phylloxera and the destruction of the region's vineyards coincided with record Champagne sales. From 350,000 bottles in 1780 to 3 million in 1830, the appetite for Champagne continued to rise unabated. In 1861, 11 million bottles were sold, and by 1909, the market had grown an additional 250 percent, to 39 million bottles.[8] But the region couldn't keep up with demand: vines were withering in the fields of Champagne. Honest Champagne houses could draw on reserves in their cellars when the harvest was not bountiful, but unscrupulous *negociants* had no qualms about buying cheap wine, no matter its origin; they would then turn it into sparkling wine, rename it as Champagne, and make a healthy profit.

In a relatively lawless French wine industry, these "Champagne" producers were trucking in wine from cheaper sources, like southern France or the Loire Valley, depressing local grape prices and sullying the region's reputable image. The locals were rightly peeved. Some youths saw no future in the region and decided they were better off taking their skills where there was demand: a newspaper article entitled "Poverty in Champagne" reported "a group of 17 young people from Venteuil left from Damery station . . . for Algeria," hoping to find steady employment in North Africa's rapidly expanding vineyard area.[9] For a village of 800 people, losing its youngest and most able-bodied was a blow, and its population has been in steady decline ever since.

In the Marne Valley, discontent had long been rising like the pearl strings of Champagne bubbles for many years. Twenty years before the town of Aÿ was ransacked by angry grape growers, local man René Lamarre was revving up growers about fraud being committed in the region. In his self-published work *La révolution champenoise,* Lamarre berated those *negociants* who were making Champagne from cheaper grapes.[10] As early as the 1820s, wines that were made far from this small portion of northern France were being called Champagne. Imitation might be flattering for some, but not for the people of Champagne. Madame Clicquot, the *veuve* (widow) whose brand is now in the hands of luxury behemoth LVMH Moët Hennessy Louis Vuitton, took legal action against a wine producer based in Metz who was exporting fake Champagne to Russia. Rulings were made throughout the nineteenth century that only sparkling wines harvested and produced in the Champagne region could use the name, but the abuse continued until the issue came to a head in 1911.

The vat of fermenting discontent was given an extra boost when an anonymously written pamphlet entitled "The Black Book of the Assassins of Champagne" was published in early 1911.[11] It acted as a who's who of wine fraud for local growers, and it was no coincidence that many of the wine producers on the receiving end of grape growers' fury in the weeks that followed were listed in the book. The cellars attacked in Aÿ, Damery, and other villages along the Marne Valley in the winter of 1910 and spring of 1911 were believed to be operating fraudulently.

In the months preceding the main riot in Aÿ, villagers in Hautvillers, the birthplace of Dom Pérignon, had discovered that four 600-liter barrels of bogus wine were going to be transported under cover of darkness to nearby Épernay. The locals weren't having it. The men charged with transporting the wine to Épernay were dealt with roughly; the head of the transport company, a Monsieur Rondeau, tried to reason with 1,500 angry locals but ended up beating a hasty retreat through the vines, losing his hat in the process. His freight went down the drain and his horses trudged back down the hill to Épernay hauling empty barrels.[12] There were similar incidents in Cumières and Damery, with bottles smashed, machines destroyed, and thousands of bottles dumped in the river Marne. The police would eventually arrive, but they were usually too late: the participants had all vanished into their homes, and of course, no one had seen or heard anything. Given the lack of witnesses, the only evidence the police had to go on were the wet, glass-strewn streets.

Nonetheless, arrests were made. In the days following the burning of Aÿ and the cavalry charge in Épernay, there were more than 150 arrests, helped by a rather unexpected source: the local cinema owner had filmed the events in Épernay with the intention of showing the footage at the local movie theater. The police used the footage to identify wrongdoers. The law had no sympathy for those who had stolen bottles of wine or pillaged cellars, and public support for the grape growing community had gone down the drain, just like the millions of liters of wine, after a day's destruction. Children as young as twelve were jailed for stealing and drinking stolen wines, while one cellar worker was handed an eight-month sentence for stealing twenty-seven boxes of matches. The shame that came with imprisonment was too much for some: a father of three from the village of Moussy hanged himself in his cell before the court had ruled on his case.[13]

In the summer of 1911, several months after the riots, forty-six people were put on trial in the mining town of Douai, 150 miles north of Épernay. Those in court weren't just grape growers: records show that a builder, a butcher, a roofer, and a shoemaker were on trial for their supposed part in the events of April. On the last day of the trial, one of the defending lawyers noted, "There were 500 who revolted: you've only got 35 here; they shouldn't be paying the price for everyone."[14] The mining community was sympathetic to the cause of their fellow working men; after deliberating into the small hours of that warm summer night, the jury acquitted twenty-seven of the accused. Six weren't so lucky and were handed sentences ranging from one month for insulting the army to four years for looting and destruction.

Placards reading "Death to fraudsters" and "Down with fraud" were a common sight at protests and meetings leading up to the riots. The practice of importing lower-quality grapes was not only harmful to Champagne's reputation as a quality wine-producing region, but it was depressing the prices that real Champagne grapes fetched. Exactly how much skullduggery was actually occurring in the cellars of the Marne? We'll never know—it's not something producers were keen to document, and if they did, their records were likely destroyed during the riots or lost in the chaos of two world wars.

However, a few historians have dared to share an educated guess. Using an elaborate formula, one economic historian came up with the figure of 17.8 million bottles annually.[15] This would mean that almost one in two bottles of "Champagne" sold in France between 1907 and 1911 wasn't the genuine article. No wonder the growers were peeved. Following the riots, wines from outside Champagne that were made sparkling by adding yeast and sugar to imported still wines had to be declared sparkling wines rather than true Champagne. By sifting through French excise figures in the years after the riots, which is hardly an after-dinner activity, it is estimated that wines from outside Champagne that were made sparkling in the region represented one in every six bottles sold between 1911 and 1914.[16] It's clear that fraud was a very real problem in 1911.

Yet "Down with fraud" wasn't the only demand on protestors' placards. The cry for "Du pain"—bread—reflected the growers' inability to feed their families, and they blamed the Champagne manufacturers for their hunger. The weather had not been kind in the years leading up to the riots. La champagne viticole, a grower-run magazine, reported that 1910 was "a disastrous year" in which the harvest was "completely destroyed following the invasion of mildew." The miniscule harvest produced just 2 percent of the average yield, and it followed a series of difficult seasons: rain at harvest had rotted part of the 1907 crop, 1908 was affected by mildew, and 1909 was a small harvest, although what little there was turned out to be pretty good quality. The abysmal 1910 harvest bore almost no fruit, but growers had tried to save what was on the vine, costing them dearly in labor and anti-rot treatments. "The grower in Champagne has spent his last sou, acquiring debt over several years: what is he going to do to feed his family and how will he maintain his property, which has led him into hardship?" asked the grape-grower's magazine *Le vigneron champenois*.[17]

In 1895, a grower complained that the money he was making from the sale of his wine wasn't enough to cover the costs of tending his vines, buying fertilizer, replacing old vine posts, and feeding his wife and children. This man was no spendthrift—he had saved money during profitable years—but in two bad seasons or so, all the savings he had accumulated, he said, would disappear.[18]

In addition to the angry—and hungry—growers who took the law into their own hands, the authorities also caught up with and officially charged a number of duplicitous wine merchants, thanks to laws put in place after the Midi demonstrations in 1907. An Épernay court heard that one merchant in the village of Damery, Georges Cadel, had received just 860 liters of wine into his cellar, yet 28,095 liters had left his property.[19] He was sentenced to six days in prison and ordered to pay thousands of francs in fines. Unsurprisingly, he fled the village, but he popped up again in the local press three years later, when he was arrested for having failed to pay his fines.

In the same week that Cadel was handed his sentence, Auguste Lemaire, another Damery merchant, was in court for similar offenses. His lawyer almost caused a riot in the Épernay courtroom when he argued that if Lemaire hadn't used wines from outside Champagne to shore up the short supply caused by the poor recent harvests, Champagne's reputation would have suffered further.[20] Lemaire was sentenced to eight days in jail, 3,000 francs in fines, and more than 37,000 francs in damages (the equivalent of more than $160,000 today).

Thirty-two-year-old Romauld Blondel, another local wine merchant, also found himself in the dock for making more "Champagne" than was possible. Blondel had had previous run-ins with the law over illegal alcohol production, but that didn't stop him from protesting his innocence. The prosecuting lawyer didn't much care for his protestations, denouncing Blondel and other slippery merchants in the region: "Five years ago, they weren't wearing shoes, and today they're driving around in cars," he claimed.[21] Blondel was fined 50 francs for falsifying wines from outside the region as "Champagne" and was ordered to pay 7,068 francs to affected growers. He was also charged with "damaging the reputation of Champagne and depreciating the value of Champagne's wines through overproduction."[22] Things would go from bad to worse for Blondel—within days of Aÿ going up in flames, his cellar would be trashed—a hundred barrels of wine were destroyed before government troops could intervene. It was a sour end for a man who had left growers with a bitter taste.

The uprisings of 1907 and 1911 didn't happen in a vacuum; political forces were fermenting in this period, and some historians have pointed the finger at left-leaning movements for agitating the sentiments of impoverished growers across France. It's true that Europe was a seething mass of political turmoil in the late nineteenth and early twentieth centuries. Socialism and trade unionism gained more followers in the last third of the nineteenth century than a Hollywood A-list celebrity on social media. Collective action and strikes were a common occurrence in this period, whether initiated by railway, postal, or factory workers. One celebrated socialist of the time, whose name appears on the street maps of most French towns and cities, was Jean Jaurès. The man behind the national daily newspaper *L'humanité* was one of many politically inspired writers who claimed the Champagne riots of 1911 were driven by socialism.[23]

But the evidence doesn't seem to stack up in Champagne. Admittedly, some individuals involved in the unrest, including a number of the figureheads, such as Émile Moreau, a grower from Aÿ, were ideologically driven, and left-wing symbols and socialist themes appeared during meetings and protests in 1911. The red flag was flown and the

French socialist anthem "L'internationale" was sung, but most historians have struggled to be convinced that socialism played a pivotal role, suggesting that these left-leaning symbols were used "without worrying too much about their deeper meaning." The protestors' political apathy was summed up, according to one French academic in the 1960s, by the actions of Michel Lecacheur, the vice president of the grape growers' federation, who "ripped up the red flag [during a meeting] and not one vigneron attempted to replace it."[24]

OUT OF BOUNDS

The goal of the grape growers of the Marne was to protect the area's winemakers from threats from without and also within. The protests have also been viewed as a cultural reaction to the first wave of globalization—the growers were drawing a boundary around their region in an attempt to consolidate their regional and national identity. This meant making laws that required all Champagne to be made from grapes grown in Champagne. But where was Champagne? It's a question that's still being asked today, but in the minds of the growers of the Marne in 1911, there was no debate: the vineyards that were the true Champagne were in the Marne department. The growers of the Aube, a hundred kilometers to the south, didn't agree, but their exclusion from the region had been on the cards for some time. In 1905, the legal basis for the creation of Champagne produced only in Champagne was set: the *loi de repression des fraudes* made the mislabeling of the origin of any product illegal, providing the foundation for regional appellations. In 1908, Champagne became the first wine region to be delimited. The Aube was granted a temporary stay of execution: the 1908 law required "complementary measures" to become effective, but these were not implemented by the dillydallying French government until February 1911.

It wasn't a Marne-born Champagne grower who managed to push through the February 1911 deal for the Marnais, however. The man of the hour hailed from Marseille and had little in common with the starving growers of Champagne. Paul Bolo was a man of questionable morals: he married a rich widow and enjoyed spending her money on cars, horses, and parties. Before their wedding, he neglected to tell her he was already married, and he is said to have had many extramarital affairs with wealthy women sporting loose purse strings. The pair would entertain France's who's who in their Parisian mansion or Biarritz villa, and Bolo traveled widely, helping set up banks in South American republics. By all accounts he was a ladies' man, but it wasn't just the opposite sex that consumed his waking thoughts: as the president of the Confédération générale agricole pour la défense des produits purs (General Agricultural Confederation for the Defense of Pure Products), he came to Champagne and placed himself at the forefront of the growers' movement. He was celebrated by the growers at the time, but his reputation was soon sullied. In 1918, he was sentenced to death and shot after the French war council found him guilty of collaborating with the Germans, having financed the purchase of a French newspaper with German money to damage morale and spread a pacifist message.

But in the opening months of 1911, Bolo brought welcome change in the Marne. There was dancing in the streets, and bottles of Champagne were opened and enjoyed, rather than being smashed, as they would be two months later in Aÿ. The locals even played a serenade for the locally stationed troops. Newspapers proclaimed "the end of the crisis" as the Marne was declared the only true Champagne region.[25] However, producers in the Aube were not in a similarly celebratory mood: they had been selling their white wines to *negociants* in the Marne to be made into Champagne since the middle of the nineteenth century, and they believed they had a historic right to be part of this exclusive region. In his sweeping history of French wine, the late historian Marcel Lachiver explained, "They clung to the hope of being able to sell wines to the Marne *negociants,* even if they were resigned to the fact they couldn't sell Champagne themselves. But the law of February 6, 1911, which stated that only wines harvested within those delimited areas could produce wines bearing the name of the appellation, destroyed this hope."[26]

Protests and tax strikes revealed simmering discontent in the Aube, with older members of the grape-growing community claiming that, if necessary, they were prepared to go as far as a repeat of the French Revolution of 1830: three days of violent protest that ended in the abdication of Charles X and the Bourbon monarchy. The culmination of the Aube protests was far more tranquil than it would be in Aÿ. In the streets of Troyes, 110 kilometers to the south of Aÿ, 20,000 protestors swarmed the city center, angry that the government had ordered their exclusion from the Champagne region. Bands of men, women, and children, dirty from sleeping on the roadside en route to the protests of April 8 and 9, 1911, included Georges Collot, a grower who walked the fifty-kilometer distance from the village of Urville. Collot was the grandfather of Michel Drappier, who runs Champagne Drappier, now an internationally renowned Champagne house in its own right. The family has lived in Urville since 1808, growing grapes that would be pressed and put into barrels before making their way to a Champagne *negociant* in Épernay or Reims by horse-drawn cart, and later by train from the station in nearby Bar-sur-Aube.

At the time of the riots, few growers in the Aube turned their grapes into wine, other than for local consumption. They left wine and Champagne production to the big companies further north. Today, it takes more than an hour and a half to drive to Épernay from the tiny village where Michel lives and where his son, the eighth generation, will continue the family's wine business in the years to come. "Here in the Aube, where it is so remote, people were more farmers, they were peasants. They weren't revolutionaries. The protests in Troyes were more *bonne enfant*—that means rather happy, convivial. Yes, there were a few speeches but what my grandfather told me was that the army was sent because of years of socialism, communism, trade unionism [rather than a violent uprising by the growers]."[27]

Inspired by their figurehead Gaston Cheq, whose mustachioed bust watches over his birthplace of Bar-sur-Aube today, the Aubois growers, facing an uncertain future, shouted "Champagne or death!" The Troyes protests were peaceful—no swords were drawn and there were no reports of dead horses—but the government nevertheless found them unsettling, and eventually a compromise was offered: the region was given the right to be part of Champagne but only as a "second zone." The possibility of the borders being redrawn to include the Aube upset their Marne counterparts to the north, who just a month earlier had been partying in the streets. This second-zone concession set the stage for the riots of April 1911, which would leave the streets of Aÿ smoldering.

The events of the first two weeks of April 1911 were a turning point for the region. The government had finally been forced to negotiate a deal that would appease both the Marnais and the Aubois temporarily. As the summer months approached, the thirst for violent protest quickly dried up and tensions eased. Further discussions around Champagne's boundaries were left to the official bodies, while the growers returned to long days in the vineyards, hopeful of a decent crop to ease their hunger.

The army retained a presence in the region but as harvest approached, it was time for the remaining cavalry to leave Épernay and for an army of grape pickers to take their place. No longer were there more soldiers than wine growers. There were some fond farewells, according to the local newspaper, between the troops and the young women of these normally sleepy villages where romance had been sparked.[28] Many of those stationed in these communities had been welcomed with open arms, and one soldier did remain: in a story of love conquering all, Brittany native Sergeant Pierre Bosser was stationed in the village of Hautvillers in early 1911 as part of the government's attempts to maintain order in the region. A young local woman, Suzanne Dutarque, the daughter of a grower, caught his eye over a Pinot Noir vine. Bosser and Dutarque's romance quickly developed, and the pair was married within months of the riots. Suzanne didn't come with much of a dowry: her brother would inherit the family business. Within three years, however, the vineyards of Champagne would be stained with the blood of local boys fighting for their country; Suzanne's brother was killed in the trenches of World War I. Pierre survived the war and returned to be with the love of his life, initially working for the Épernay railway. Upon the death of his father-in-law, he and Suzanne took over the family business, and in 1933, the first vintage of Bosser-Dutarque was harvested.[29] Today, their grandson, Jean-Philippe Bosser, can be found running the family wine business in the same village and the same house where love blossomed.

While the enemy had come from within in 1911, the arrival of war in 1914 created a new enemy for the region's grape growers and wine producers: Germany. The vineyards of Champagne became a theater of fighting within months of Franz Ferdinand's assassination, lighting the fuse that would lead to declarations of war. The region's position—en route from Germany to Paris—put it in harm's way. The timing of the start of the war couldn't have been worse for local wine producers—the 1914 harvest was almost ready to be picked when fighting broke out, and the sound of secateurs cutting bunches from the vine was often drowned out the by the crash of shells and patter of gunfire. Some rushed to pick the grapes before the rain of fire showered down on the vines, but this meant some of the wines were made from almost unripe grapes, leaving the drinker pulling a just-sucked-a-lemon face. The bracing acidity in these wines meant that some of the wines of 1914, while eye-watering when young, were endowed with the staying power to mature beyond the events of World War II.

The Germans briefly took the city of Reims in the earliest days of the war but were pushed back. However, relief was short lived. During the course of the war, the people of Reims would endure more than 1,000 days of unrelenting bombardment; the city's majestic thirteenth-century cathedral, site of coronations for 600 years, was heavily shelled, leaving only the walls standing. The once-bustling streets were left in ruins; just forty of the city's 40,000 houses remained. Vineyards in the area were shelled, and craters soon replaced vines. It wasn't just the men who were requisitioned to fight the Germans; horses that once ploughed the soil between the rows of vines were seized. Still, those who weren't called up to fight—the elderly, women, and children—continued tending their vines as best they could, and the wines produced from the 1915 and 1917 seasons were reportedly excellent.

The demand for a border to be drawn around the Champagne region must have seemed relatively inconsequential during those bloody years. Its sons were slayed alongside many others who died far from home, as the roll call of foreign names and regiments on the white grave markers of local cemeteries attest. The orderly rows of headstones standing peacefully in the fields to the north of the city seem to stretch on interminably. While history books state the numbers lost in the muddy trenches of northern France and Belgium, it is difficult to comprehend the sheer waste of young lives without visiting the region's vast cemeteries. More than a century later, speeding along on the twenty-mile-long chemin des Dames, a seemingly benign ridgeline that offers sweeping views of the French countryside, it is difficult to imagine that this was the setting of some of World War I's bloodiest battles. The strategic site pitted Frenchman against German over and over. The cemeteries along the road are the only evidence that thousands of men lost their lives here.

After the 1918 Armistice, it took the region almost another decade to make progress on the rules drawn up in 1911. The region had lost over half of its population, and 40 percent of its vineyards were damaged; entire villages had been razed. "So much land had been chewed up, contaminated by poison gas and irrigated by the ooze of decaying corpses that fifty thousand acres were declared 'zone rouge' or 'red zone' meaning that they were considered forever sterile."[30]

The year 1927 brought relief for those in the Aube—they were reinstated as Champagne proper, no longer a second-class zone within the region. In the Marne, growers continued to grumble that the Aube was closer to Burgundy than Champagne; today, there remains a very real separation between the two: the journey to the rural Aube remains a road rarely traveled by all but the most dedicated Champagne lover; the dense vineyards carpeting the hills, the labyrinth of underground cellars, the stately Champagne houses and fine dining opportunities in Reims and Épernay prove more alluring than the handful of utilitarian wineries that lightly dot the small villages to the east of Troyes.

Yet change is in store for the Champagne appellation. In 2008, a team from France's National Institute for Origin and Quality (INAO) had the unenviable task of reassessing the suitability of villages included in the Champagne boundaries in 1927. It is no coincidence that the decision to reappraise the borders of the region occurred at the same time as demand for Champagne threatened to exceed supply. When the borders were drawn originally, many growers chose to use their land for cereal crops rather than vines and didn't apply to be part of the official wine zone. Given the rise in Champagne's stock, many have regretted that decision. In 1995, a village sandwiched between prestigious grand cru villages in the Pinot-making vineyards of the Montagne de Reims area—Fontaine sur Aÿ—asked that the Champagne laws be revised so that it could be a part of the appellation like its neighbors. The village hadn't been made a part of the appellation in 1927 simply because it hadn't asked. The INAO refused. Undeterred, the village took its case to court and won admission to the Champagne appellation. Fearing there were other Fontaine-sur-Aÿs about to emerge, the local grape growers' union, the Syndicat general des vignerons, asked the INAO to carry out a scientific overhaul of the list of villages allowed to make genuine Champagne and the fields in those villages that could become vineyards.

The reasons for reconsidering the boundaries are no longer associated with fraud: it's about money. Producers want to make more and more Champagne, and there's no more land available to do that. It's almost impossible to buy vineyards. When a good site comes up for sale, there's a bidding war. At around two million euros for a hectare of grand cru vineyard, it has been estimated that it takes at least forty years to see a return on the investment. Pierre Larmandier of Champagne Larmandier-Bernier explains, "There is now no relationship between the cost of land and the return on the vineyard."[31] Australia-based Champagne expert Tyson Stelzer, however, points out that since buying a premier cru vineyard—a site with a slightly less prestigious status than grand cru but still highly desirable—in 2002, Larmandier has seen a decent return on investment: the soil beneath his grapevines doubled in value in a decade. Of course, to meet demand and maximize profits, less quality-conscious producers have found a solution: not by importing wines from elsewhere, as their counterparts did a century ago, but by burdening vines with higher crop loads. Some challenges may have changed for Champagne producers in the past century, but others have stayed the same: the unscrupulous try to maximize short-term profit, while the reputable seek to make the best wines possible and protect the region's honor for the next generation and beyond.

5

APPELLATION NATION

IT HAD STARTED like any other summer morning in the center of Saint-Cecile-les-Vignes: the cicadas were in full voice, the boulangerie had a steady stream of baguette buyers, grape growers were revving up their Renaults and Citroëns for a busy day in the vineyard. But something wasn't quite right. In the heart of the village, between the town hall and the church, the bust of a vinous legend had surveyed the villagers' comings and goings for close to forty years, but as the sun rose higher, it dawned on the locals that one of its longest residents had left his post overnight. It was enough to make them choke on their croissants.

The valuable bronze sculpture of Pierre Baron Le Roy de Boiseaumarié was a tribute to a man who devoted his life to crafting and defending France's wine regions, particularly the Côtes du Rhône and Châteauneuf-du-Pape appellations. But the sculpture was gone. A few weeks earlier, a wine-inspired statue from the fountain in the neighboring village of Cairanne had also disappeared. While there was a rumor circulating that thieves were starting a collection for a wine museum, the investigators paid that far-fetched theory little heed, instead linking it to a spate of thefts from local cemeteries of bronzes decorating graves and tombs. In the village of Sorgues, a town within spitting distance of Châteauneuf-du-Pape, the bronzes adorning around forty tombs had been "patiently unscrewed and taken away" under cover of darkness, according to a local wine grower magazine.[1]

Having gone AWOL for several months, Le Roy's bust was finally recovered and returned to its home just in time for the 1993 harvest. His day-long homecoming was quite the affair, beginning with a ceremonial journey along the river Rhône from Avignon via Châteauneuf-du-Pape and through a few less famous wine villages before reaching Saint-Cecile-les-Vignes late in the day, where he was reinstalled. As part of the celebrations, the *ban des vendanges* was proclaimed, the equivalent of the starting gun for the annual harvest.[2]

The season had been done and dusted when Baron Le Roy's bust was first unveiled in 1955. On a wet autumn day, a 1,500-strong crowd defied the weather to honor the man who put them on the world wine map.[3] Although those gathered were dressed in their Sunday best, their hands seemed remarkably grubby to outsiders: having spent the past weeks transforming black grapes into red wine, the skins on their hands had turned purple. Barrel upon barrel of rich Grenache and succulent Syrah were now safely in the cellars following a superlative harvest that would go down as one of the seasons of the century. But the frenetic pace had slowed by the end of October. The fledgling wines of the summer of 1955 were happily fermenting and could now be left alone in their cellars while their makers stood in the pouring rain at the unveiling of a bronze bust, a tribute to a man who may not have been a winemaker but had been a champion of their corner. It seemed that it was not just the wine community that honored him on that rainy Sunday: for just a moment, "the nascent autumn enjoyed the presence of the sun," reported Robert Joly, a local newspaper editor, who attended the inauguration. "Just once, immediately after the bust had been unveiled, the sky lit up—it wanted to doff its cap to the astonishing personality of Baron Le Roy."[4]

In 1955, Le Roy was the occupant of the highest position in the world of wine, that of president of the International Office of Wine. While the role was meant to rotate across the more than twenty member states, he was clearly so good at it that he was continually reelected for fourteen years before hanging up his hat to focus on his South American stamp collection. He didn't do that by halves either: he became a full member of the Academy of Philately just a few months before his death in 1967, aged seventy-seven. But on this rainy October day in 1955, the wine growers of the southern Rhône journeyed to Saint-Cecile-les-Vignes to pay tribute to him as the architect of their appellations. He had called Châteauneuf-du-Pape home since 1919, after meeting his wife Edmée, whose family owned a wine estate on the outskirts of the village. Without his leadership over the ensuing decades, the now-protected status as quality wine regions, which assured buyers that their wines could be trusted, would have been far from guaranteed.

Le Roy came from an illustrious family; his ancestors had fought on the battlefields of Europe and included several heads of regional governments. His father was a senior officer in the cavalry but after leaving the army, the family headed south to a village close to Montpellier to start a new life as vineyard owners. When they arrived in the village of Vendargues, they found widespread poverty. Overproduction and widespread adulteration of wine had forced grape prices down, and many couldn't cover their costs of production nor repay the loans they had taken out to replant after phylloxera invaded their vineyards. Entire villages relied on wine to stay afloat. If the grape growers weren't making money, they couldn't afford to buy bread at the bakery, meat from the butcher, or pay local tradesman for their services; it wasn't unusual to see baguette makers striking alongside local grape growers in a show of solidarity.

Frustrations that had simmered over the course of the first years of the century came to a head in a wave of protests and mass meetings during the spring of 1907. Politicians were also stoking the rebellious fire: the socialist mayor of Narbonne, Ernest Ferroul, was a key figure in inciting public protest, calling on the "sons and daughters of the Midi" region to join the movement and urging the government to act against fraudulent wine producers.[5] The protests brought communities together in a common cause: entire villages boarded trains to join the action, often assisted by local rail companies offering subsidized fares. They demanded that the government intervene to end their hunger, and their banners threatened "Death to fraudsters." Despite the menacing slogans, most of the protestors were a peaceful bunch. However, there were skirmishes between locals and authorities and, in the village of Coursan, troops opened fire on an angry crowd, killing five and wounding ten. The protests culminated in Montpellier, where more than half a million people, including Le Roy, took to the streets on June 9. Despite the fact that he was studying for a law degree, Le Roy was not one of the law-abiding protestors: inflamed by the hardships he was witnessing on his doorstep, the then seventeen-year-old resorted to violence, dousing the door of the city's courthouse with gasoline and setting it alight. While this act of arson was meant to be a group effort, his partners in crime lost their nerve and scarpered while he stuck to the task. There were troops inside the building, and the aim was to stop them from coming out and shooting at the crowds. Le Roy was apparently not caught, and the incident failed to end his law career before it began, but the plight of the winegrowers had made a lasting impression on Le Roy.[6]

Following the mass demonstration in Montpellier, both sides conceded it was time to make peace: the scale of the protests, the deaths of innocent people, and troops defecting out of sympathy for the impoverished locals forced the government to act. A new law was quickly passed clamping down on the "stretching" of wine. This meant that winemakers couldn't bulk out their harvest with sacks of sugar and gallons of water. It also introduced measures to record the size of their harvests so that any dishonest winemakers could be identified. In 1911, the region's winegrowers' association reported that there were more than 600 fraud prosecutions. The events of 1907 had not only forced the government to intervene, continuing the slow march toward the birth of the appellation system, a process that would take close to thirty years, but marked the start of Le Roy's life-long defense of the wine community.

But first his country needed him. At twenty-four, Le Roy became one of the 8.4 million Frenchmen to be mobilized. He became one of the first one hundred fighter jet pilots to graduate from the Armée de l'Air, the embryonic French air force. He had his share of highs and lows during his time in the cockpit: he shot down several enemy planes, which won him prestigious military awards, including the Legion of Honor, and he too was shot down twice in enemy territory. He spent time recovering in a German hospital and was a prisoner of war but survived to tell the tale, which many of his comrades did not.[7] More than a hundred years later, walking between the vines of Château Fortia with Pierre Pastre, the husband of Le Roy's granddaughter, three fighter jets fly overhead in formation, as if to honor his memory—then Pastre reveals there's an aircraft base in the town of Orange, ten kilometers away.

But you are never far away from Baron Le Roy in Châteauneuf-du-Pape. You can pay your respects to him in the town cemetery opposite the vineyard, where he was buried in 1967. In Châteauneuf, there's an avenue Baron Le Roy and a Baron Le Roy car park. Many southern Rhône towns and villages have a street named in his honor. There's even a rue Baron Le Roy in Paris, in the quartier de Bercy, about twenty minutes by bike or bus along the Seine from the Louvre, and his name is attached to a nearby tram stop.

After the war, Le Roy returned to his widowed mother in Vendargues unsure what to do with the rest of his life. Following the death of her husband in 1912, and with her son away at war, his mother had sold the family vineyard, so that option was off the cards. He pondered returning to law, but his future path was quickly decided when he met Edmée Bernard le Saint, whom he married in 1919. She had inherited her parents' estate, Château Fortia, following the death of her elder brother, Henry, in the first month of the war.

The couple took over the management of one of the most important wine estates in the most important wine-producing village in the southern Rhône valley. Châteauneuf-du-Pape had enjoyed a reputation for fine wine for centuries, its renown no doubt helped by having several popes as clients. From 1309 to 1376, Avignon, rather than Rome, was the seat of the papacy. While Avignon's popes seemed to like a drop of Burgundy, the local wines also enjoyed some divine interest. It was Pope John XXII (1316–1334), the former bishop of Avignon, who put Châteauneuf on the map, setting up a base just far enough away from Avignon to escape the self-serving crowds that buzzed around the papacy. Sitting at the village's highest point, the château of Châteauneuf was built during his reign, and many vineyards appeared—some three million vines were in the ground by 1334.[8] In that period, local wines became known as *vin du pape,* and the name stuck. While the vineyards have since flourished, the actual château is a shadow of its former self, having been burned and pillaged during the Wars of Religion (1562–1598); what was left was partly blown up by retreating German troops in August 1944. It's easy to see why John XXII chose the site: the hilltop provides 360-degree views of the town and its vineyards, which cascade down to the alluvial plains and the wide, watery belt of the Rhône River. By the mid-sixteenth century, the days of the popes in Avignon were just a memory, but the wines of Châteauneuf were still winning fans: the astrologer and physician Nostradamus noted that Châteauneuf made "excellent wines, some of which are shipped to Rome."[9]

In the years leading up to Baron Le Roy's arrival, the village's leading wine estates, including Château La Nerthe and Domaine de la Solitude, were shipping their wines around Europe, but this was the exception rather than the norm. Most vineyard owners would pick their grapes and sell the fruit or the new wine to *négociants*, who would buy wine by the barrel and transport it to their cellars for blending, which left plenty of room for creativity. Even today, there are few domaines in Châteauneuf that don't sell a portion of their wine to a *négociant* to help with cash flow. At the end of a day picking grapes under a cloudless Mediterranean sun, Florent Lançon, the eighth-generation winemaker at Domaine de la Solitude, enters the estate's tasting room carrying several metal suitcases that his grandfather bought from a military supplier. He flicks the catch on one to reveal reams of historical papers documenting the family's ownership of the domaine, which dates to the early seventeenth century. On the winery wall are framed documents, including an 1827 order from Mr Greenwood & Mr Butler of 110 Fenchurch Street, London, requesting five barrels of wine. The journey to London would be long. The barrels would leave the cellar on a cart pulled by horses that would trot the six miles to the port of Roquemaure on the Rhône. From there they'd sail to Marseille or Sète before heading into the Mediterranean for the long journey around Spain, up the coast of Portugal, and along France's west coast before crossing the English Channel. There was also the option of the Canal du Midi, which linked the Mediterranean with Bordeaux and the waters of the Atlantic, cutting out the circuitous route around the Iberian Peninsula. It could take weeks or even months to receive an order, and when it finally arrived, the buyer was lucky if the contents were still intact: dishonest drivers and swindling seafarers were known to siphon off wine by piercing barrels and then sneakily plugging them after they had quenched their thirst.

Despite the challenges of shipping wine in the 1820s, Châteauneuf-du-Pape became one of the most important exporters in the region. A local government report suggested that as many as 200,000 liters of wine were leaving France each year, destined mainly for Europe but also for locales as far away as the East Coast of the US. While the volume may seem small compared with the 12.5 million bottles of Châteauneuf now sold annually, it was significant for a small village that wouldn't be connected to the rest of the country by the Paris-Lyon-Marseille railway for another three decades. When the railway came to the neighboring village of Sorgues (which has since affixed Châteauneuf-du-Pape to the station's name, such is the wine's renown), journey times and shipping costs fell dramatically, opening up new opportunities as well as presenting new challenges.

Estate bottled Châteauneuf-du-Pape remained a rarity even in the early twentieth century. Bucking the trend was Château La Nerthe. The wealthy and titled Tulle de Villefranche family owned the estate from 1560 to 1877, and with their prestigious social networks, La Nerthe built an impressive customer list that included members of the royal family and senior members of the clergy and the military. These customers were prepared to pay high prices for quality wine: a barrel sold for 168 pounds in 1750, equivalent to 200 days' salary for a field hand, according to a history of the estate.[10] While barrels were the order of the day, the domaine's account books show that little by little, bottles were finding favor: the first recorded sale of bottles of La Nerthe, and thus the first recorded sale of bottles of any Châteauneuf wine, was an order for 150 bottles from a Monsieur Bonchot of Avignon in 1782.[11]

Selling wine in barrel, never mind an expensive and fragile bottle, under the name of the estate was still a rarity when Le Roy waved goodbye to his fighter jet and headed for the vineyards of Châteauneuf-du-Pape. He landed in a village suffering an identity crisis. Not only had its sons been slain or maimed during the Great War, Châteauneuf's wines, its pride and joy, had become a mere blending partner for merchants looking to put some flesh on the bones of their weedy red Burgundies. While modern grape growing and winemaking methods, as well as climate change, mean that Burgundy's prized vineyards now make ripe—and often eye-wateringly priced—Pinot Noir wines, in the late nineteenth and early twentieth centuries they were all too often thin, pale, and tart. Those were not qualities anyone was looking for in a glass of wine, but in the almost lawless world of French wine, a splash of something vivid, ripe, and alcoholic from the warmer climes of the south of France or even Algeria could sort out the deficiencies of the latest crop of Volnay.

An important local grower, François Armenier, recalled that before the Great War, a Burgundy *négociant* arrived and stayed in his parents' hotel for a few weeks. He visited the local vineyards, finding out whose vines were healthy and whose weren't, plucking berries from the vines as he walked along the rows to check if they were sweet and tender or chewy and sour. Once the reconnaissance mission was over, the merchant knew which parcels he wanted to buy fruit from. In a village of cash-strapped grape growers, he was well aware that he was in a strong position and, according to Armenier, took up residence in a café and simply waited for producers to come to him. It was a self-assured move, but as he had predicted, a steady stream of producers decided they were in need of a trip to the café. He requested the grapes from the best plots and the growers accepted his offers without negotiation. They needed cash and to free up space quickly: "The cellars weren't large and couldn't accommodate the wine from two harvests, it would have cost too much and you had to make money to live and pay the costs of the next season."[12] The merchant also rented out tanks in the village to turn the grapes to wine before sending the newly fermented barrels off to the nearby town of Sorgues, where they'd board the train destined for Burgundy's wine capital, Beaune. Somewhere between the station platform and the vast cellars of Beaune, the wines of Châteauneuf-du-Pape would likely lose their identity, destined to become a bit part—or a major player—in a bottle of Gevrey-Chambertin or Pommard.

THE ROOT OF EVIL

The source of the great Burgundy deception was the shortage of wine caused by the destructive force of phylloxera. It made its first appearance in France in the vineyards of the Rhône in 1863; Burgundians held out for more than a decade hoping that somehow they would not be touched by the devastation the louse was causing further south, but its journey north was inevitable. In 1874, Burgundy's most southerly outpost, Beaujolais, received its first unwanted visitor, and four years later, a grower in the famed Côte d'Or village of Meursault had his summer ruined by the discovery of phylloxera in his vineyard. The military was called in to cordon off the area and apply toxic chemicals. The solution to phylloxera—grafting their noble grapes to the roots of what were perceived to be plebeian American varieties—was abhorrent to Burgundians, but one of the leading experts in phylloxera at the time, Jules-Émile Planchon, lambasted their baseless prejudices: "Burgundy hopes to defend itself by stifling, even at a very high price, the first outbreaks of evil. It shudders at the thought that American vines, even in a supporting role, would trespass on the vineyards that produce its finest wines."[13] Despite expensive and toxic interventions, the aphid's spread could not be halted. Burgundians, like their counterparts in Champagne, were forced to slowly accept that their vines were sick and the prognosis was terminal. By 1911, Burgundy's most prized wine producing area, the Côte d'Or, had lost more than one-quarter of its vineyard area compared with 1881.

In the years before phylloxera worked its way up to the vineyards of Burgundy, the best wines of the region became a must-pour in the glasses of the middle and upper classes not only in France but across Europe. The Canal de Bourgogne, the Burgundy canal, provided easy access to Paris when it opened in 1832, and the journey was made even quicker when the last railway tie was laid between the two cities in 1851. What's more, when William Gladstone, the Chancellor of the

Exchequer and future British prime minister, cut the duty on French wine in the government budget of 1860 and, a year later, allowed retailers to sell single bottles of wine to customers to take away, sales of French wine flourished in the United Kingdom.

During this so-called Golden Age for wine there was a thirst for knowledge, and a professor at the University of Dijon, the mustard-making city located directly north of the Côte d'Or, aimed to satisfy it. Jean Lavalle compiled one of the first comprehensive guides to the region's vineyards, *Histoire et statistique de la vigne et des grands vins de la côte-d'Or.* Not only did it include intricate maps of this narrow strip of vines from the village of Santenay in the south through Beaune and up to Dijon, it classified them from the top *tête du cuvée* sites, equivalent to today's grand cru vineyards, through to fourth-division generic Burgundy. His work provided the foundations of a quality hierarchy that endures today. It also opens a window to the fame of the area's wines. In his preface, Lavalle explained, "All the world, in France or abroad, speaks about the wines of the Côte d'Or; everyone knows the most popular names; it is both the glory and wealth of our *département* and of the whole country; and yet there is no complete history of these great vineyards."[14] There was now.

Burgundy's winemakers did not want to bid adieu to their prosperity when phylloxera slashed production levels. Instead, they began shipping barrels of wine from the south of France, southern Europe, and North Africa to make up for what nature was failing to provide. This wasn't new: in 1855, almost a decade before the aphid had made landfall on French soil, Lavalle warned of an underground Burgundy scene that had nothing to do with the placement of the vines' roots. He hoped his book would help customers that had never stepped foot in Burgundy by providing the tools they needed to buy genuine Burgundy wine. He claimed his work gave "any foreigner the tools to guard against a certain trade which, under the name of Burgundy, sells wine from anywhere and from anything."[15] In his closing statements he noted that any merchant would reveal the secret to huge profits: "By always selling Burgundy wine without ever harvesting or buying it."[16]

The deceitful trading of "Burgundy" wines that didn't contain anything grown in Burgundy was compounded by shortages caused by phylloxera. Instead of admitting there was a supply shortage and upping their prices accordingly, local *négociants*—even long-standing, reputable ones—started shipping in barrels of wine, whether the source was Châteauneuf-du-Pape, Spain, or Algeria. In the 1880s, some Burgundian wine merchants even bought vineyard land in northern Africa to secure their own grape supplies. The volume of France's wine imports shows the scale of outside sourcing. In the first half of the 1870s, just 42.5 million liters were imported into France; by the end of the 1880s, imports had risen to more than a billion liters.[17] If the locals had few qualms about doctoring their own products, large-scale foreign wine merchants hundreds of miles away were even less concerned about provenance. At the turn of the twentieth century, millions of liters of wine would leave the ports of Hamburg and Rotterdam destined for markets that included the UK, US, and Scandinavia. A study of the Côte d'Or economy in the nineteenth century, written in 1909, revealed that large-scale merchants in Hamburg would blend wines not only to suit the tastes of their customers in northern Europe, but also to suit their wallets. Wines could be watered down or strengthened, and they might have their color deepened with vast quantities of blueberries imported from Norway. These wines would leave Hamburg harbor with labels bearing "Vougeot" or "Chambertin" but had little in common with the real wines.[18]

In the two decades that followed the publication of that report, a series of laws was introduced to stamp out fraudulent activity, but it seemed to have little effect. Maurice Constantin-Weyer, a French writer and winner of France's most prestigious literary award, the Prix Goncourt, explained the seriousness of it in his 1932 ode to wine, *L'âme du vin:* "Of all the wine made in the Côte de Beaune, Pommard is the village that has the most recognition globally. And yet the world drinks more Pommard in a week than it can produce in ten years."[19] While Constantin-Weyer loved the sappy, ageworthy character of genuine Pommard and the aromatic, delicate reds from neighboring village Volnay, the problem was that the masses, and even high-rolling Burgundy drinkers, were no longer keen on these naturally light-in-body Pinot Noirs from the cool and variable climes of northern France. They now wanted buxom Burgundy, and that was a contradiction in terms.

It seemed that drinkers who had formerly paid a premium for genuine Burgundy had moved to the dark side, developing a taste for fake wine in the years of scarcity: "In the 1880s and 1890s, buyers of Burgundy became accustomed to strong, doctored wines. From then on, the natural wines, light in body and with variable quality from one year to the next because of the weather, became difficult to sell. Today, it is these natural wines that are treated as if they are the fakes. We have examples of Parisian families that have become used to drinking the concoctions made in [the wine traders' warehouses in the Paris district of] Bercy, who are unable to enjoy drinking anything other than thick wines that have no sense of place."[20] The members of the wine trade who stuck to the rules were frustrated by these counterfeits, and yet this evidence gives the impression that the final consumer did not feel victimized. Were drinkers being duped by a Beaune from Bercy or a Chambertin containing a dollop of Châteauneuf? There was certainly the intent to deceive customers and to profit by blending wines sourced far from the origin on the bottle, but customers were often none the wiser and frequently more satisfied than they would have been with the real thing. Taste triumphed over integrity.

The Burgundians had shot themselves in the foot, and the news was spreading overseas as fast as phylloxera. In the United States, an Ivy League dropout was spreading the word. Following just a year at Princeton, a teenaged Frank Schoonmaker was disillusioned with college life. He decided he could educate himself just as well as his professors and quit school to travel around Europe on a shoestring budget. The experience provided the basis for his first book, *Through Europe on Two Dollars a Day*. This guide, and his subsequent *Come Travel with Me* series, were published in French, German, and Italian editions and became the 1920s equivalent of Lonely Planet guides, directing Americans to the best places to see, stay, and be merry. The vineyards of Europe had yet to seduce this wandering writer; the nectar that would come to define his life in his roles as author, importer, and expert advisor was still a foreign world to him. But with the repeal of Prohibition on the cards, the scent of European wines was wafting over the Atlantic, creating an inquisitive readership that the editor of *The New Yorker* magazine asked Schoonmaker to address. Learning on the job by asking those in the know, Schoonmaker delivered a series of articles that set him up as the man on the ground who could be relied on for wise wine words, which led to the publication of *The Complete Wine Book* in 1934. It provided the American public with the most up-to-date information on the styles of wines produced in Europe, tips on how to buy, store, and serve wines, and even a few recipes calling for the use of wine.

The Complete Wine Book would be seen as incomplete today. While the bastions of western European winemaking—France, Germany, Italy, and Spain—received plenty of attention, the entire New World received only passing mention. Schoonmaker stated that the likes of "Algeria, Argentina, California, South Africa and Australia" were only good for mass-produced wines that "attempt, but always unsuccessfully, to imitate the great wines of Europe; and which bear, more often than not, world-famous European names [such as port or Chablis]."[21] He did cover his back for future readers who might tut-tut at his narrow view of the wine world: "No one can lay it down as an absolute fact that great wine will never be produced in any of these commercial wine countries. . . . Nor will it be so long as factory methods are followed instead of those of the master-craftsman." These statements hardly endeared him to his countrymen, but within a few years he was buying and selling wines from the Golden State as well as penning another book, *American Wines*, although that too damned US wines with faint praise. That said, he was hardly complimentary about a lot of French wine either, claiming that 50 percent of it was "perfectly terrible."[22]

During Schoonmaker's formative years in France, he befriended Raymond Baudouin, the founder of France's most important wine magazine, *La revue du vin de France*. He had privileged access to wine-makers and their wines, and Schoonmaker was allowed to tag along with him. Baudouin was a relentless campaigner against wine fraud and championed the still-embryonic method of bottling at the estate rather than in a *négociant*'s cellar, where anything could happen to the barrels of wine and frequently did. Bottling at source was expensive and fiddly, due to the need for measures to prevent any tampering en route to the customer, thus ensuring that the wine the customer received was as the winemaker, rather than the overseas merchant, intended. In *The Complete Wine Book*, Schoonmaker raised a glass to Baudouin, who was "not only one of the outstanding oenological authorities of Europe, but who has, for more than a decade, waged unrelenting warfare upon fraudulent practices in the wine business."[23] He also gives a shout-out to Le Roy, to "whose vigilance and energy the present standing of the Rhône wines is in no smaller measure due,"[24] as well as to a Beaujolais producer who had introduced estate bottling rather than allow merchants to take his barrels and blend away their contents.

Schoonmaker was also influenced by a Burgundian whose wines he would later introduce to the American market: Marquis d'Angerville. After studying at the illustrious École des Beaux-Arts in Paris, Sem d'Angerville turned his back on engraving in 1906 when he inherited his childless uncle's vineyard in the Burgundian village of Volnay. Over the course of the next four decades, he became a "vigilant protector"[25] of Burgundy's reputation, leading one of the local wine producers' unions in the interwar years. In collaboration with several other growers, d'Angerville vehemently opposed the creative blending that was an everyday occurrence in the warehouses of *négociants* and doggedly pursued anyone misrepresenting Burgundy's most famous wine villages. He was involved in scores of court cases, taking on merchants, restaurateurs, and anyone else misusing Burgundian names. It won't come as a shock that *négociants* stopped buying wine from d'Angerville and other anti-fraud champions, including Henri Gouges and Armand Rousseau. These little guys were forced to bottle their own wines, which they had never done before. However, it guaranteed their customers that the wines were the genuine article, setting a precedent for others.

Surrounded by these steadfast, straight-shooting wine personalities, it was only natural that Schoonmaker railed against those who were dragging down the name of Burgundy with their imitations. His French friends were some of the country's most ardent supporters of the appellation system as a legal solution to the issue of fraud. He claimed that his book's greatest merit was that it "stands up boldly for the strictest application of that elementary principle of commercial honesty the French call 'appellation of origin' (which over here, unfortunately, is still quite as often honoured in the breach as in the observance), preaching and exemplifying it throughout."[26] His advice to buyers? "One should buy Burgundy only from the most trustworthy dealers and should regard every brand as suspect until it proves its worth." Many of the village wines, whether Beaune or Pommard, he declared "are, in the vast majority of cases, cheap ordinary wines in fancy dress and . . . should be shunned like the plague."[27]

HOLDING BACK THE TIDE

In a tide of doctored wine, it was up to the little guys to act. Despite barrel loads of red wine leaving on the swift train ride north to be blended and relabeled in the cellars of Burgundy, the endorsements of popes and the likes of Nostradamus and the high bar set by leading estates like La Nerthe, Fortia, and Solitude meant that this village in the southern Rhône was already on the fine-wine map for those in the know. Châteauneuf-du-Pape was mentioned in the same breath as the famed sweet wines of Sauternes or the finest sparkling wines of Champagne, but there were plenty of producers and merchants endangering its hard-earned reputation. The village needed a leader to unite the growers and champion their cause. There had been two previous attempts to create a winegrowers' association, but they had failed due to a combination of apathy and infighting. In 1923, however, the local growers had their sights set on a man who was not only a part of the wine-producing community but an eloquent law graduate and a war hero: Baron Le Roy.

"A group of growers . . . came to me to ask me to defend Châteauneuf, ruined by the arrival of grapes from many other places while the authentic wines remained unsold in the cellars," recalled Le Roy in a local magazine in 1954.[28] He turned out to be a strict leader who demanded discipline from members, which included remaining united in the face of a strong but fragmented opposition. As his exploits in Montpellier and the cockpit had demonstrated, he was a man who could be counted on: within a year of accepting the role as president of the local growers' union, he was leading his wine troops to the nearby town of Orange, appealing to the courts to enforce strict rules on those wanting to use the Châteauneuf-du-Pape name. The growers' demands included restricting the area of production, which would exclude those on the inferior plains close to the river; limiting the varieties used to the thirteen "noble" and "traditional" grapes that form the base of all Châteauneuf today; and banning irrigation. They also called for wines to have a minimum 12.5 percent alcohol, which seems laughably low by modern Châteauneuf-du-Pape standards, but in the 1920s, this required growers to keep yields low so the grapes would ripen fully, producing concentrated and balanced wines. However, there was no prescriptive ruling on what a wine ought to taste like, or that it should conform to a certain typicity. This is a more modern construct that has since been created.

France had been inching toward stricter appellations, but Châteauneuf leapfrogged them. Parliamentarians were thrashing out the terms of a new law in the first half of 1914, but it had been put on the back burner following the outbreak of war; when it made it onto the statute books in 1919, it proved to be rather ineffective in preventing fraudulent activity. The new law compelled growers to declare the size of their harvest and how much wine they had made if they wanted to use an appellation name—whether Chablis, Champagne, or Châteauneuf—but the practice was widely abused, and trying to prove that a declaration was erroneous required a lot of time and effort. The opportunity to jump on the Châteauneuf bandwagon after 1919 was too good to miss, even if it meant having to pay a small tax for the privilege. As a result, as many as 30,000 barrels of wine were given the official Châteauneuf-du-Pape stamp of approval in 1924, of which just 5,000 were true Châteauneuf, claimed an article in the local daily newspaper, *Le petit orangeois*.[29] The wines pretending to be Châteauneuf were often of inferior quality and cheaper, dragging down not only the prices of genuine wines but also the reputation of the village.

As Baron Le Roy and representatives from the growers' union made the short journey to the court in Orange, they were outnumbered by their opposition. As many as 150 vineyard owners were hostile to their proposals, often for their own financial reasons: they did not want to pay the levy to use their village's name, and they had vineyards or varieties that might be excluded, which would lead to a loss of business. There was no need for immediate concern—the union's requests were initially refused. But their cause was far from lost: a panel of experts was appointed by the court to get to the root of the matter and five years later, the panel returned to court in Avignon, recommending in its report almost the same set of rules that Le Roy had previously demanded. The regulations imposed on wine growers in Châteauneuf-du-Pape in the courtroom in 1929 were more stringent than anywhere else in France—and the world. The self-imposed rules laid the foundation for the rest of the country to follow as it moved toward a fully fledged appellation system, adopted in 1935, that not only put boundaries around vineyards but also introduced guarantees of quality and authenticity. Châteauneuf can lay claim to being the first wine appellation in the world, even though its official date of birth was 1935, a date shared with other entrants to the national appellation register.

If Le Roy was the horse that pulled the Châteauneuf-du-Pape plough toward the destination of a meaningful appellation, the rest of the country was reined in by two politicians: Joseph Capus and Edouard Barthe. Provence-born Capus worked at a Bordeaux plant research station before climbing the career ladder to regional and then national politics, including a brief stint as minister for agriculture. Long before Le Roy set foot in Châteauneuf-du-Pape, Capus had the ear of high-flying politicians and was fighting at the national level for appellations that not only drew a perimeter around an area, but also provided consumers with quality assurances. What was the point of drawing a line around a vineyard area if there were no rules on where to plant, what to plant, and how those plants were cared for?

As early as 1911, Capus had met the future war minister, André Lefèvre, who shared his views on the then nascent system. In his account of the evolution of appellation laws, written shortly before his death in 1947, Capus quoted Lefèvre: "The law is dangerous, because in giving a fictional value to anything that's harvested in its boundaries, it rewards those who plant questionable varieties on poor land, creating mediocre wines, which, by virtue of their administrative boundaries, would be perfectly within their rights to be sold using the name of a prestigious appellation."[30] This was exactly what was happening in the world's foremost sweet white wine producing area, Sauternes. Govern-

ment officials with no wine expertise had created the Sauternes boundary but, surprise surprise, they had made a mess of it. Vineyards on the
inferior plains, which had previously made bog-standard red wines,
had sneaked into the area and soon enough, the local growers were
grafting over their red vines with white varieties to profit from their
association with the Sauternes name. Unsurprisingly, the quality was
not up to scratch, endangering the reputation of those who had worked
hard to build it. For the next twenty years, Capus railed against what
he saw as ineffective regulations, and in the early 1930s, a global economic depression and national wine crisis pushed the industry to the
breaking point.

Following the war, the world no longer had an appetite for French
wines. Russia, previously an important market for French wine, particularly Champagne, closed its doors after the Revolution. Meanwhile,
Germany, burdened by onerous reparations drawn up in the 1919 Versailles treaty, was no longer in a position to buy. Across the Atlantic,
the United States government ratified the 18th Amendment, ushering
in Prohibition. The country remained dry until late 1933, but when the
borders did reopen for imports, it was hardly to the sound of popping
corks: the Great Depression left Americans in no position to buy cases
of fine wine. Meanwhile, the French were having a good crack at home
winemaking: having returned to their villages after the war, many
Frenchmen planted easy-to-grow varieties to quench their thirst, rather
than buy wine. Throw in the 1929 stock market crash, which plunged
the world into a global economic depression, and there were few reasons to raise a glass in the early 1930s.

Had there been reason for celebration, there was plenty of French
wine going spare: in 1934 and 1935, nature provided two abundant
crops. France's national harvest exceeded more than 7.5 billion liters in
both years, which outstripped the country's consumption by around
500 million liters.[31] Exports were certainly not going to mop up the surplus. And that's not all: the overflow of wine became a flood of biblical

proportions when Algeria enjoyed a similarly bountiful crop. Algeria, a mainly Muslim, teetotaling country, had been invaded and annexed by the French a century earlier. The North African country became an increasingly important source of grapes when phylloxera ravaged France's wine supply, and buoyed by their success, and spurred on by the arrival of famed French wine families, growers in Algeria had continued to plant in the postwar years, more than doubling the area under vine between 1920 and 1935. In 1934 and 1935, Algerian production hit a record high; the combined French and Algerian crop hit a whopping 10 billion liters in 1934. It came close to the 10 billion mark again the following year.[32] Some French wine producers pointed their fingers at fraudsters, and they were still at large—the Châteauneuf-du-Pape union had managed to bring about sixty-seven convictions since its inception, including one for a particularly delicious instance of stretching nine barrels of genuine Châteauneuf with two barrels of Algerian red, 24 liters of blackcurrant juice, 250 grams of metabisulfite, and 250 grams of beef blood.[33] Others, including Capus, blamed the Algerians for France's wine woes, but the French were their own worst enemies. While the producers of Châteauneuf-du-Pape had imposed a cap on how much each hectare of vines was allowed to produce in a bid to ensure the fruit was of high quality and ripened fully, other French growers weren't as exacting. Capus claimed some wine producers were managing to reap massive yields from their fertile lands, providing 200 hectoliters per hectare of undoubtedly dilute and underripe grapes, which certainly wasn't helping the overproduction crisis the country faced.[34] What's more, there was certainly an element of creative license in their declarations, in which they purported to have harvested more than they had, thereby giving their customer—the wine merchant— the ability to flesh out genuine wines or simply sell lesser wines under a more famous appellation.

It was no surprise that producers and merchants were taking advantage of the loose laws. In 1923, 500 million liters of wine had claimed appellation status; by 1934, it had risen more than threefold, to close to 1.6 billion liters, or 20 percent of national production. The increase was labeled an "appellation scandal,"[35] although that statistic seems rather inconsequential today, when over 50 percent of France's wine bears the name of an appellation, and a lot of that can be of pretty basic quality. Stricter rules that were rigorously enforced couldn't come soon enough, and on July 30, 1935, almost thirty years to the day after the first tentative steps were taken toward regular state intervention in wine, Capus and his supporters won over the doubters. It was a victory that Le Roy had won in his corner of the country several years earlier, setting a precedent for the nation. Key to its success was the creation of a ruling body and a team of fraud detectives, working under the auspices of the ministry of agriculture, who would chase the fraudsters both at home and overseas. The anti-fraud effort included employing an inspector in the United States. (The makers of Roquefort, which had beaten Châteauneuf to the title of first appellation with its smelly, cave-aged, blue sheep's cheese, had their own dedicated special agent on American soil to stamp out fraud.) The fraud police had their work cut out for them: Capus revealed that in 1942, the force had prosecuted 56 producers in Champagne for violating the rules on the size of the harvest; in 1945, they had uncovered 113 cases of fraud in Paris alone; and in 1947, they were dealing with 15 cases overseas, as far afield as Venezuela.[36]

In the elegant offices of the Châteauneuf-du-Pape wine association, now-retired vineyard manager Catherine Armenier tells me how her grandfather Emile had been one of the original cohort to ask Le Roy to lead them. A century after Baron Le Roy took up his post at the helm of the growers' union, Armenier played her own role in the defense of the appellation, leading its advocacy body for six years. While the Burgundians no longer need the wines of Châteauneuf to flesh out their Pinot Noir, there's still much work to be done. During her presidency, Armenier had to deal with plenty of pretenders who sought to profit from the appellation's renown. The most memorable was a brand created in the UK in

2006: Chat-en-Oeuf. The wine label featured an illustration of a cat (*chat* in French) sitting on an egg (*oeuf*). Its maker claimed it was the "perfect gifting wine for cat and wine lovers alike" (although it failed to mention that it would also have appealed to egg lovers). Produced in the nearby Côtes du Ventoux area with a Châteauneuf-like blend of Grenache and Syrah, it also had the audacity to say, right on the back label, that it was a lot less expensive than Châteauneuf. While some thought it was all a bit of fun in an era of silly wine names—including "Cat's Pee on a Gooseberry Bush" Sauvignon Blanc, or the South African winery Fairview's "Goats Do Roam" and "Bored Doe" cuvées—the producers of Châteauneuf-du-Pape hadn't become France's first appellation just to let a rip-off like this slide. Following legal proceedings that culminated in 2013, Chat-en-Oeuf was renamed Le Petit Chat, although the cat's still sitting on the egg. "It's thanks to those who did the work [in the 1920s and 30s] that we now have something we can defend and [can] act against those who misuse our name and our bottle design. Their mission was successful."

The creation of the *appellation controlée* system had been a long time coming. It was the culmination of more than thirty years of work that began on August 1, 1905, with the passage of the wordily titled "Law on the prevention of fraud in the sale of goods and falsification of foodstuffs and agricultural products." That marked the beginning of regular state intervention in many other products in addition to wine, but wine had taken on a symbolic role as the country's treasured national drink. It was imperative to protect French pride by protecting French wine as well as its cheeses, lentils, chickens, ham, garlic, sausages, and more. Wine producers stumbled toward the creation of the appellation through crises in the vineyard, a world war, and an economic depression. The appellation system would survive German occupation and become the model that other European wine-producing countries would follow to encourage quality over quantity and deter those who deliberately intended to mislead customers at the expense of conscientious producers.

The French appellation system, as well as its Italian and Spanish equivalents, continues to be the cornerstone of wine law, but it is far from perfect. There have always been those disgruntled by the strait-jacket it imposes on them, from the grape varieties that growers must plant to the permitted vinification techniques. High-profile desertions have ensued; in Italy, one of most famous defectors was a wine called Sassicaia. In the early 1970s, it was one of a handful of nonconformist wines nicknamed Super Tuscans, which shunned the traditional grape of Tuscany—Sangiovese—in favor of Bordeaux-style red blends. Because the Super Tuscan wineries were operating outside of the local rules, their wines were classified as lowly table wines, but it soon became clear that they were superior to 99 percent of traditionally made Tuscan reds. Little by little, the original laws had to evolve to embrace these superstars.

Despite their flaws, appellation systems have provided a framework that wine lovers can trust. The contents of a bottle, whether it's a Saint-Émilion or a Saint-Amour, can be assumed to come from the place stated on the label, although it is no guarantor of excellent quality. But the authorities have the power to punish those who fail to abide by the law, as one Bordeaux family found out in the notorious Winegate scandal.

6

WINEGATE

ON AUGUST 8, 1974, Richard Nixon, the thirty-seventh president of the United States, became the first president ever to resign. Suffering the ignominy of impeachment following a slew of scandalous revelations relating to a botched break-in of the opposition's election offices and the ensuing cover-up, he finally fell on his sword. Over a period of two years, American investigators discovered the country's president, the political elite, and its most senior law enforcers had flouted the constitution, lied to protect their own interests, considered themselves above the law, and threatened the freedom of the press. Meanwhile, a very different scandal had been unfolding in the wine cellars of Bordeaux. In August 1973, the French press broke the story that the Cruse wine merchant business was under investigation for fraudulent activity. In a regrettable comparison, Cruse declared that he would be "the Nixon of Bordeaux," believing that the president was the victim of a witch hunt and would be proven innocent. But Watergate was not a "pseudo-scandal" orchestrated by a left-leaning press that would disappear in a "cloud of gossip," as the wine merchant suggested to the media.[1] Instead, the US president was impeached, and on the morning of October 28, 1974, a dark cloud hung above the city of Bordeaux as the world's attention shifted from the White House across the Atlantic. Forty years after the birth of the appellation system, the world discovered that its laws were flouted on a daily basis by those who were perceived to be upstanding members of its community. The turreted towers of the Bordeaux wine trade—and the nation's vinous integrity—crumbled in court.

When the international media landed to cover what became known as the Winegate case in late 1974, Bordeaux was a melancholy, unwelcoming city that had earned the nickname *la belle endormie*—sleeping beauty. At the time, once-beautiful buildings blackened by pollution and neglect sat alongside abandoned warehouses, which stretched the length of the city's riverbank, blocking the view and access to the Garonne. In the nineteenth century, these storage units had welcomed sugar and spices from far-flung lands and dispatched local timber and barrels full of wine. It was a working waterfront. While the commercial port moved away from the city center in the 1970s, the unsightly warehouses remained, as did the businesses that had long catered to the all-male dock crews. Charles Sichel of Maison Sichel, a wine merchant company based in the Chartrons district since 1883, explains: "There were a few seedy bars [on the *quais*] and where the new bridge is [Pont Chaban-Delmas] there were working girls. It was interesting taking customers out to lunch when there were girls standing in the doorways waiting for business—it was quite something—but I can't remember them ever saying anything!"[2]

Throughout its history, Bordeaux's sons have portrayed the city in a none too flattering light: the novels of Nobel prize–winning writer François Mauriac (1885–1970), whose bust now stands in the leafy public gardens, depicted Bordeaux and the surrounding areas as a bleak and uptight place to live in the early twentieth century. Similarly, one of Alfred Smith's (1854–1932) best-known paintings, *Le Tramway devant les Quinconces par temps de pluie*, depicts a gray, wet day on the banks of the Garonne, umbrellas up, and those without hurrying along with heads bowed. It was not an aspirational place to live until very recently.

On a tour of the city a local guide recalls her rented ramshackle apartment in the 1980s: "The building's bathroom was in the attic, so I had to leave my apartment to use it. At that time the city was trying to push residents to improve the inside of their buildings. It wasn't until the late 1990s that they started to focus on cleaning up the outside of the buildings and the public places." Today the buildings are impeccable—a mass sandblasting effort has unveiled the natural caramel and blonde tones of the local limestone, which were long hidden. Here and there, a few reminders of the past can be seen along its narrow streets—a façade or two that's blackened, as if smeared with charcoal—but overall the city is now as elegant as its wines.

The waterfront is now the people's playground, filled with joggers, cyclists, and pram-pushers promenading along its length, a place for concerts, festivals, and open-air markets. The magnificent squares—once used as car parks—have regained their former splendor. On a sunny summer's day, a cruise liner has dropped anchor at the edge of the city center overlooking the water mirror, a slick of water that, as its name implies, reflects the classical architecture of the Place de la Bourse (Stock Exchange Square). It has become Bordeaux's iconic postcard picture, an unwitting urban water park, and represents the new face of the city—clean, bright, and optimistic.

The reawakening of Bordeaux has been noticed far beyond its traffic-choked ring road; it has become the most desirable place to live in France, according to a survey commissioned by the *Observatoire du bonheur* in 2015. Asked in which French city they would most like to live, nearly one in five respondents answered Bordeaux. It came in ahead of Montpellier and Toulouse, and far ahead of Paris. Just an hour's drive from the beaches of the Atlantic and three hours to the ski slopes of the Pyrenees, Bordeaux is now only a two-hour commute to Paris thanks to the opening of the high-speed rail link (TGV) in 2017.

The spruce-up has continued beyond the city center. Gliding north along the dock past the Chartrons district, the tram has started to deposit an unprecedented number of tourists in the Bacalan district. It's certainly not the prettiest of suburbs, home to run-down docks, abandoned factories, and a huge concrete mass that was once a submarine base, but the magic dust has been sprinkled here too, and the opening of the Cité du Vin in June 2016, a towering gold and silver Frank-Gehry-meets-Zaha-Hadid construction, has been a pivotal part of its transformation, as has the futuristic Chaban-Delmas bridge.

Amid the hustle and bustle of the Quai des Chartrons, the aristocracy of the Bordeaux wine scene made their fortunes buying, blending, and bottling wine that would be shipped along the Garonne toward the gray expanse of the Gironde estuary and into the waters of the Atlantic. From the 1700s on, merchants from Britain, Ireland, Germany, and, in the case of the Cruse family, Denmark made their way to the docks to buy and sell wine to their home nations. Settling on the outskirts of the city center, these mainly Protestant newcomers in a Catholic community were outsiders from the beginning. Several families came to dominate the region's wine trade, and the term *Chartronnais* became a byword for the closed world of Bordeaux wine's high society. These families would go to church together, socialize—often in German or English rather than French—intermarry, and, while the French monarchy was just a memory, were coined "the aristocracy of the cork" by author François Mauriac in *Préseances,* a novel that fails to hide his distaste for this closed yet coveted social circle.

Mauriac published his stinging novel in 1921, earning him plenty of enemies among the Bordeaux wine glitterati, but remarkably little in this privileged world had changed by June 28, 1973, when a team of government inspectors knocked on the door of 124 quai des Chartrons.

The beautiful blonde building with its grandiose racing-green door is now home to a company specializing in unblocking toilets, but in 1974, a discreet plaque on this four-story townhouse revealed that it was then the headquarters of the noted Cruse family. The head of the family, Lionel, was not pleased to receive a surprise visit from the tax department. The family had been part of the Chartrons community for five generations, and he was not having them poking around his offices unannounced. But why not let them in? Surely, this reputable member of the wine trade had nothing to hide. His reason for turning them away, he claimed, was that orders were stacking up and he simply didn't have time to welcome them when the company was so busy. An audit would force him to close the office of one of the region's major wine exporters for eight days, a claim the inspectors flatly denied—they would only need a couple of days to go over the paperwork, they said. It was also the eve of the summer holidays, couldn't the inspectors just come back in August? They turned away, but Cruse's obstruction went on the record, and off the record, the visit set tongues wagging across the city. To quash the rumor mill, Lionel publicly declared that nothing untoward had occurred in the family's cellars; fellow Bordeaux wine merchants closed ranks and rallied behind one of their own, condemning the authorities' tactics as "similar to the Gestapo."[3]

But the evidence was starting to pile up: a paper trail would lead the law back to the Cruse family and the case would end up in the city's courts. It was fueled by incriminating evidence that had been found by another team of inspectors. A raid on a wine trader in the little-known village of Saint-Germain-de-Grave, an hour's drive southwest of Bordeaux's center, led to the discovery that wines trucked in from the Languedoc region were leaving the cellar and being sold to larger merchants, including the Cruse family, as more valuable Bordeaux appellation wines, thanks to some creative paperwork. A truck driver would later admit to the courts he had fiddled the documents en route to the Cruse cellars to throw investigators off the fetid scent. The offenses were first laid out by the weekly magazine *Le nouvel observateur* at the end of August 1973[4]—less than two months after the Cruse office had received its unwanted visitors. All roads seem to be pointing to a wine dealer named Pierre Bert.

Born in the sweet-wine-making village of Barsac, which neighbors the more famous Sauternes appellation, Bert had twice been caught by the fraud squad for illegal blending, forcing him to sell the family wine business to pay his fines, but that didn't stop him from repeating history: "He has a taste for scandal," sighed the trial judge in 1974. Bert would end up behind bars for the role he played in the Bordeaux affair, and while serving his sentence, Bert penned *In vino veritas,* a book that dished the dirt on the closed world of Bordeaux wine. If the convicted fraudster's words were to be believed, it was rife with blending, stretching, and false paperwork. The book also laid bare events leading up to and during the court case and his conviction. Despite his two previous convictions, he had been able to set up a new business using an unsuspecting front man, who didn't seem to be the sharpest tool in the box, considering the substantial amount Bert was paying him for doing very little. Bert revealed he was able to buy barrels of cheap and cheerful wine from the south of France, fiddle the paperwork, and sell them for a healthy profit. He sold wines on to larger merchants, including the Cruse family—who, based on his previous indiscretions, should have known better. In his far from impartial book, Bert suggests their eyes were wide open: "Did the Cruses really believe that I was pulling appellations out of the hat, like a magician, at a time when I didn't have a single glass in my possession?? Did they really think me crazy enough to sell them [appellation wines] way below the market value?"[5]

As the initial drops of the scandal filtered through global newsrooms, it became clear that this would be damaging not just for the Cruse family; it threatened the respectability of the wine world's most regal red region. This backroom blending was not harming drinkers' health, but the possibility that profiteering Bordeaux winemakers would flagrantly flout laws designed to protect ordinary customers from fraud jeopardized the reputation of this historic wine area. The timing could not have been worse.

UNWANTED ORPHANS

Bordeaux was on the brink of a precipice in 1973. Wine prices, fueled by speculation, had soared to new heights, and "the big claret fraud" or the "vintage vinegar scandal," as it was variously dubbed by journalists, pushed the region over the edge.

In the years leading up to the Cruse case, loyal claret drinkers saw their favorite wines priced beyond their means. As the story broke on the other side of the Atlantic, the *New York Times* reported that the price of a single bottle of Château Latour 1953, which had sold for around $12 five years earlier, had risen to $125.[6] While the prices of wine from all the major wine regions of France had steadily increased over the course of the previous decade, Bordeaux had made the biggest gains, leaving the rest of France confounded by the prices the region's winemakers were able to charge. The first signs of the upward trend appeared with the release of the 1969 wines. In the same year that a man walked on the moon and The Beatles performed for the last time in public, there were hopes of another great vintage in Bordeaux. The first growths— the top-ranking estates in the Bordeaux classification—upped their prices as much as threefold compared to 1967. In his legendary annual vintage reports, which spanned five decades, the late *négociant* and château owner Peter Sichel revealed, "There were mutterings of 'another 1961' [a superlative year for wine] and even if there were some six weeks to go before the vintage was over, there did not seem to be much that could go wrong." How wrong they were: the settled, sunny weather of the summer was ruined by a soggy run-in to the harvest. Sichel explained, "Appalling rainfall in September 1969 put paid to any possibility of it producing great wines."[7] As much as the trade tried to build it up to find willing buyers, the final vintage of the 1960s was, in truth, a pitiful way to end the decade. Thankfully, the weather was more forgiving at the opening of the 1970s. A sunny season paved the way for the largest crop the region had gathered since the end of the war. While there's a theory that a small crop often leads to better quality wines— the vine putting all its effort into making the best of a few bunches, rather than spreading itself thinly across a heavily laden plant—there are plenty of years where quality and quantity go hand in hand, and 1970 was one of them. The wines were big on color, concentration, and character.

The wines had plenty of thirsty customers beyond the traditional markets. The region's wines were no longer the preserve of British gentlemen. The ex–private school boy crowd that attends London's private members' clubs and wears red trousers without a hint of irony continues to be a staunch supporter of the claret tradition today, but Americans developed a taste for Bordeaux's red blends in the 1960s. Stetson-wearing, cigar-sucking Chicago wine man Max Zimmermann embodied the new breed of Bordeaux wine buyer. Having opened a liquor store the day after Prohibition ended, he came to be known for his hat, first a fedora and later a Stetson. Known as The Hat in Chicago, Chapeau Max in France, and Capello in Italy, Zimmerman would take up residence at Château Loudenne, where several British Masters of Wine, including Philip Goodband, had been installed in the late 1960s. Their brief included reviving the run-down seventeenth-century estate and putting on a warm welcome for American buyers like Zimmerman. As Goodband remembers, "Max would come and stay with us— Stetson on, pockets filled with cigars—to buy as much wine from Bordeaux as he could get hold of."[8] And following a couple of sorry seasons, Zimmerman and his compatriots were thirsty.

Luckily an abundant crop in 1970 meant that there was plenty to go around, or so its makers thought. Due to the high volume of wine produced, prices were initially lower than for the wines eked out from the rain-diluted 1969 harvest. One of the leading authorities on Bordeaux wines at the time was Edmund Penning-Rowsell, an "engaging bundle of contradictions" who had a decent claim to being the only journalist to have been a regular contributor to both *Marxism Today* and the *Financial Times*. According to one obituary, Eddie was "a Communist who worked for the *Financial Times* and liked his lunches with Baron Philippe de Rothschild," the owner of Château Mouton Rothschild, which gained promotion to Bordeaux's most prestigious club—the premier cru—in 1973.[9] His connections endowed him with the inside track on the wines of the Gironde department, which culminated in his claret bible, *The Wines of Bordeaux*. The book revealed the chess-board-like moves of the Bordeaux wine trade in the early 1970s and the idiosyncrasies of selling fine wine. In 1970, for example, Mouton Rothschild launched its wines at less than half the price of the 1969, which he explained was an attempt by the baron to curb the "upward spiral of leading-growth prices." However, Mouton Rothschild's rival, Château Lafite Rothschild, ignored the sledgehammer-like hint. But the baron hadn't yet played his hand. Bordeaux's finest don't release all their wine at once, instead releasing a little at a time in tranches. "When it became apparent that there was a tremendous demand for the '70 clarets from investors as well as normal trade buyers, prices shot up."[10] Not wanting to be outdone by Lafite, the baron increased the price of his second tranche of Mouton Rothschild by a whopping 85 percent. Where the top estates went, the lesser châteaux followed, and prices crept up. Still, the demand for Bordeaux continued to rise.

Mother Nature clearly didn't receive the instruction that the Bordelais needed another bumper harvest the following season. In the spring, grape growers pray for settled weather to help the vines flower and set their berries, which form the year's crop. But in 1971, it was cold and rainy. As a result, the harvest was small, and what was picked was hardly going to set the world on fire. Master of Wine and Bordeaux expert Clive Coates questioned whether quantity rather than quality was on the minds of the Bordelais when they went out into the vineyards and were overly enthusiastic with the secateurs that autumn: "One is inclined to wonder if some growers, seduced by the short crop, high prices and unprecedented demand, might not have been quite as ruthless as they should have been in excluding from the final blend vats made from young wines or parts of the vineyard badly hit by the weather."[11] Unsurprisingly, a mixed bag of wines flowed out of the cellars, but that didn't stop the producers from doubling or even tripling prices over the year before. For many smaller producers, this was a long overdue opportunity to make some money after years of struggling to make ends meet. Others saw it as profiteering. Sichel was not only a wine merchant by now but owner of several estates, including Château Palmer, with its fairytale turrets. While he admitted that people were shocked that the 1971 wines had doubled in price despite being inferior in quality, Sichel didn't think it altogether unreasonable. There was demand for their product and the market was willing to pay, he reasoned: "As soon as any classed growth or equivalent of a good vintage has been put on the market it has immediately sold—the protests from buyers that the price is suicidal mingling unharmoniously with their pleas for a larger proportion of the crop." It was also high time that those who toiled in the vineyard—not just the merchants, retailers, and speculators who traded the wines as if they were stocks and shares—enjoyed the fruits of their labor, he added. "It is not perhaps surprising that when he reads of his wine fetching many times his original selling price, he is tempted to feel that he was a sucker to have sold so cheaply. . . . Why should others make so much more profit from his wine than he himself?"[12]

In just a couple of years, the wines of Bordeaux had seemingly become a luxury good. Prices remained red hot in 1972 despite the wash-out summer. The city's annual exodus to the beach resorts of Arcachon and the exclusive Cap Ferret peninsula was dogged by drizzle and cool temperatures. The vines, lacking their injection of summer sun, were well behind schedule, causing growers to wonder if they would even be able to ripen their grapes. The markets started to panic that there would be no wine to buy. But late summer and early autumn finally brought fine weather, and the grapes staggered their way toward being just ripe enough for the armies of itinerant pickers to reap in October, making 1972 the latest harvest on record since the end of World War II. However, even the best producers couldn't hide the fact that the cool season and lack of sunshine meant the resulting wines were frequently sour.

But what did it matter if the wines were unpleasant to drink? Everyone wanted to buy Bordeaux wine and customers were prepared to pay whatever it cost, so when the wines were launched in the spring of 1973, the asking prices were as eyewatering as the wine's acidity. Even Sichel, who had publicly justified the hikes only a year earlier, was now denouncing the greed of the locals: "By no stretch of the imagination can it be claimed that in relation to recent price levels the wines of 1972 can by their quality justify the prices being asked. . . . They are grossly overpriced."[13] And just as the rapacity of Bordeaux's wine producers was starting to leave a bitter taste, eight tax inspectors knocked on the door of 124 quai des Chartrons. The boom ended as sharply as it started, and by 1974, as the region's leading wine merchants were led to the dock, the wines of Bordeaux had become "unwanted orphans of a shattered marketplace."[14]

FROM THE QUAY TO THE DOCK

Following their unannounced visit to the Cruse family offices at the end of June 1973, investigators paid Lionel and his cousin Yvan several more visits to pore over the company's records. They weren't happy with what they found, and their report noted that some documents that had given them cause for suspicion had been amended or even mysteriously gone missing. For example, the investigators noted that one lot of wine was initially labeled as *V.R [vin rouge] type Nuits-Saint-Georges*, suggesting that it was not from the village of Nuits-Saint-Georges in Burgundy but emulated that style. On their next visit, the official form had been crudely changed to the less specific *V.R cuvée Royale,* but the investigators weren't idiots—they'd noted the lot number, and the hastily changed wine names weren't enough to cover the Cruse family's tracks.

Over the course of the next year, the inspectors compiled a fifty-five-page document detailing the case against not only the bosses of the Cruse operation but smaller merchants, brokers, and the director of a wine laboratory, all of them mixed up in doctored documents and bogus blends. On October 28, 1974, a flock of international journalists flew into Bordeaux to witness the very public humiliation of eighteen defendants, including one of its most prestigious players. During the trial, Americans found out they'd not been drinking the delightful wines of Burgundy's Puligny-Montrachet, as the label had stated, while Germans were angry to hear the contents of bottles bearing the illustrious name of Graves, a Bordeaux appellation home to some of the region's most famous estates, was just ordinary *vin blanc.* What's more, unsuspecting American drinkers had also been set to receive a tank of rough red that was marked "Sell as Beaujolais in the US." Even so-called experts had been deceived and humiliated. Surely they should have been able to notice the difference between these contrasting wine styles?

The report also revealed that there had been an assortment of illegal adjustments to faulty wines, wines that should never had made it to the bottling line, let alone people's glasses. Thanks to the director of a local laboratory, faulty wines that were more like vinegar were revived, while foul-smelling wines had their unpleasant aromas removed using activated charcoal (which is now a legal processing aid for filtering and improving color). Following the trial, Pierre Bert defended the merchant, saying the attempts of Cruse and his winemakers to save spoiled wine reflected their love for a drink to which they had dedicated their lives, rather than a grab at financial gain. You may find that difficult to reconcile, as did the trial judge.

Other modifications included adding generous amounts of powdered acid to make wines seem fresher than they were naturally: nearly half a million liters of wine were perked up with more than ten times the legal dosage of citric acid. Conversely, wines that were too tart were softened with sack-loads of calcium carbonate, which is often found in toothpaste to brighten smiles. Investigators unearthed a large delivery of the deacidifier-cum-dental-aid during their inquiries. While a little bit of adjustment here and there is deemed legal to make up for what nature has failed to provide—depending on what region you're in and the nature of the season—the Cruses and their colleagues had overstepped the mark by some distance. In total, the report calculated that more than 28 million liters of wine, equivalent to almost 37.5 million bottles, were not made and sold according to the letter of the law. In summary, the officials concluded, "The Cruse company respects neither the concept of appellation, since it labeled table wines as appellation wines; nor the notion of place, since the same wine bears several different châteaux names; nor the vintages, which were wrongly given."[15]

The evidence was damning, but a court case isn't a court case without a defense, and for that the Cruse family brought in loyal customers from across Europe and as far away as Puerto Rico to vouch for their professional integrity. UK wine merchant David Rutherford claimed there had never been an issue with any of the wines he received from Cruse apart from the occasional corked bottle, but that was hardly unusual in a world before screwcaps. Similarly, the Cruses' Dutch importer took his opportunity on the stand to praise the family for promoting not only their own wines in Holland, but those of the entire Bordeaux region.[16] The trial risked undoing all that work.

THE FERRARI CRASH

As the Cruse trial approached its grand finale in October 1974, memories of a high-profile case from just a few years earlier were fresh in the minds of the Bordelais, and there were fears that Winegate would do to the French wine industry what the Ferrari family had done to Italian wine. Ferrari was one of the first modern wine brands in Italy, making everything from Frascati to Chianti and heavily promoting its wares. In the days before advertising standards existed, television commercials made all sorts of unsubstantiated claims about the power of their products. A Ferrari wine ad featured "an exhausted businessman returning home from work. His wife ran to embrace him, and, noting his fatigue, offered him a glass of Ferrari wine," reported a *Life* magazine exposé on Italian food and drink in 1968.[17] The man started "jumping, somersaulting on the rug, laughing and shouting 'Wow, I'm a new man.'" Whatever went into the wine had to be good, and the thirsty nation glugged it: on the eve of a scandal that was about to unfold, as many as one in ten Italian households enjoyed a bottle of Ferrari with their evening meal. Unfortunately, a police investigation found that Ferrari's wines were not as wholesome as claimed. In a case involving hundreds of lawyers and witnesses and thousands of pages of documents, the Ferraris were put on trial on charges of conspiracy and fraud dating back more than a decade. Newspaper reports covering the case revealed that wines had been doctored with ox blood and figs to give reds a deeper color, while other additives included banana skins, ammonia, Cuban sugar, and grape juice from Tunisia. Additionally, evidence in the case had clearly been tampered with: when the judge turned up to examine the wine cellar that had been seized by the Italian fraud squad, many of the tanks were empty, while others contained only water dyed red with food coloring. Where had the incriminating evidence—more than three million liters of it—gone? No one knew. Despite the extent of the fraud and the number on trial—close to three hundred individuals—international coverage of the case was muted compared with Winegate, but then again, the image of Italian wine was nothing compared with the grandiose grands crus of Bordeaux. At the time, the few bottles of Italian wine shipped overseas were mostly basic Chianti, presented in traditional straw flasks and typically served up at homely Italian trattorias complete with the stereotypical red-and-white-checked tablecloths. The case simply did not have the same star appeal.

Back in France, the Cruse cousins attempted to explain away the inclusion of lowly Riviera red in their Bordeaux blends. They were very strict about what they bought from brokers and had faith in their suppliers—even Pierre Bert, whose reputation was hardly spotless—and they were the ones who had been wronged, they claimed. But as one of the most eminent merchants on the quai des Chartrons, surely they could taste the difference between a Merlot from Margaux and a Grenache from the Mediterranean? The Cruses and their network of international distributors claimed they could not, which for some of the most qualified in the business was difficult to believe. Lionel told the court, "I don't want to be the gravedigger of Bordeaux wine, but yes, I dare say that confusion is possible if the wines are young, fermenting, and arriving in tank."[18]

His cousin Yvan backed him up, claiming that the character of Bordeaux wine didn't truly develop until it had been aged. Like human bobbleheads, the witnesses for the defense all nodded and agreed that it would be difficult to distinguish the difference. The Dutch importer declared he wouldn't want to oversee a tasting panel that would try, while Raymond Le Sauvage, the president of the local wine brokers' union, gave a real-life example of the pitfalls of blind tasting. Wines had to pass a tasting panel to win the right to use the local appellation name, and in the village of Saint-Estèphe, he had sneaked an imposter in the line-up: a wine from Buzet, a small wine-growing area more than a hundred miles southwest of Saint-Estèphe. No one clocked that it did not belong in the tasting.[19] This was hardly a ringing endorsement for the appellation system, which was based on the authenticity and typicity of a product. The system was flawed, and the defense aimed to prove that simple human error rather than intentional lawbreaking was the cause of this debacle. There were calls in court for a tasting to take place as if to prove the point, but no corks were popped inside the courtroom.

It was difficult to ignore the testimony of wine broker Pierre Bert, who suggested that this case was just a drop in an ocean of wine trading that was not above board. Bert seemed to have little to lose and appeared happy to take down the rest of Bordeaux with him. In one of the first articles to break the story, he had claimed that "90 percent of *négociants* and 50 percent of property owners" were guilty of such frauds. He went as far to claim that "200,000–300,000 hectoliters of wine arrives in Bordeaux from the Languedoc each year. It has to go somewhere."[20] He was probably stretching the numbers a little, but he was happy to go on record in the court of law stating that rule-breaking was a daily occurrence. On the stand he admitted that he was guilty but denied that he was the cause of fraud; he was merely facilitating it, and he claimed that his customers knew exactly what he was doing—a claim that the Cruses denied—and that he had received no complaints from them. "If a business doesn't satisfy its clients, it goes out of business. I haven't stayed in this profession for thirty years by ignoring what the customer wants."[21] Intriguingly, the Cruse's British importer, David Rutherford, whose company had been selling wine since 1714, also seemed to imply that if the quality of the wine was up to the expected standard, then some liberal blending didn't matter: "If the wines are good, the customer will continue to buy," he told the court, supporting the theory that the victims only feel victimized if they find out they have been misled.[22] At this point the appellation laws had been in place for close to forty years, and these arguments seemed to make a mockery of all that Le Roy and Capus had fought for: protecting the customer and producers from fellow producers.

Unsurprisingly, in a bid to save the reputation of the national drink, the country's wine associations scrabbled to show how diligent they were. The national appellation institute, INAO, declared that its task force, set up by Le Roy and Capus four decades earlier, had conducted 10,000 checks in France in the previous year alone, resulting in 2,786 convictions. These infractions had failed to attract the attention of the wine trade press, let alone make the international broadsheets.

Crisis management was in full swing during the case. Not wanting to miss an opportunity to influence the opinion formers of the day, Bordeaux's top brass wined and dined the visiting international media after the long days in the courtroom. While it seemed in poor taste to some, the press lapped up the free hospitality but still printed stories predicting the end of an era for Bordeaux wine. "Never has there been such a gastronomic display around a trial; lunches, cold buffets, cocktails, dinners at Dubern [restaurant]," reported *Le Monde* during the trial. "The regional wine association has even pushed it to the point of providing a bus service between the courthouse and its receptions. Of course, good Bordeaux wines are served."[23]

MIXING POLITICS WITH PLONK

Blending and mending wine was an everyday occurrence along the quai des Chartrons, according to Pierre Bert. But it was fraud, and it was illegal in the eyes of the law. Why, then, did the authorities clamp down solely on the Cruse family and not go after the rest of the merchants Bert supplied? Could it have been a case of dirty politics?

There was plenty of speculation that the case went further than the wine world and had its roots not in the vineyard but the Élysée Palace. The theory was that the targeting of the Cruse family and Bordeaux was part of a power play for the French presidency by candidate Valéry Giscard d'Estaing. One of his main rivals was the Bordeaux mayor and former prime minister Jacques Chaban-Delmas (the man whose name is now attached to the city's new lift bridge). Although Chaban-Delmas was not Bordelais by birth, he became a friend of the Chartronnais, particularly the Cruses, Lawtons, and Calvets, following his arrival after the war, and they had been generous supporters of his bid to become the city's leader. It was a role he held for eight terms over forty-eight years, and on election nights, they would be part of the inner circle that joined him in his offices, according to reports at the time. Conspiracy theorists thought the timing of the tax inspectors' visit to the Cruse family and the resulting investigation of Chaban-Delmas's associates was no coincidence. Giscard d'Estaing, who went on to win the presidency by the smallest of margins, happened to be the country's finance minister at the time the tax men started sniffing around the Cruse cellars. The investigation put Chaban-Delmas in a compromising situation, but he didn't come running to the aid of his allies, instead calling for tough action in an affair that he claimed threatened "the world reputation of all the wines of France." *Libération*, a left-leaning daily newspaper based in Paris, later claimed that Chaban-Delmas hadn't wanted to "find himself involved with a godfather who had suddenly become cumbersome."[24] Despite the fact that he distanced himself from the affair, it acted as another setback in his thwarted presidential campaign.

On the other side of the Atlantic, the sitting president of the United States was having more trouble than Chaban-Delmas. Despite winning the race for the presidency with an overwhelming majority in 1972, the sweet victory had quickly turned sour, a little like the wines in Pierre Bert's cellar. A failed attempt to bug the Democrats' campaign offices located in the Watergate building in Washington, DC, was dismissed by the president's press secretary as a "third-rate burglary," but it would end in the impeachment and resignation of Nixon less than two years after his inauguration. In June 1973, the televised Senate committee hearings called the major players from the White House and reelection campaign office to give evidence, and the nation tuned in to the courtroom drama that unfolded. The ratings of the year's hit shows—*All in the Family*, *The Waltons*, and *Hawaii Five-O*—were dwarfed by the viewing figures for this real-life tale of bungled break-ins, political lies, cover-ups, and hush money. There has always been an appetite for a scandal.

There were damning testimonies but no physical evidence of wrong-doing by the president until a relatively lowly White House assistant was asked whether conversations in the White House were recorded. Tapes were eventually handed over confirming that Nixon was directly involved in the Watergate cover-up, proof that he had lied repeatedly to the nation. Within days of the tapes being released, Nixon announced that he would resign, but there was no apology.

Just two months after Nixon stepped down in disgrace, the man who had defiantly announced a year earlier that he would be "the Nixon of Bordeaux" was also due in court, to face charges of wine fraud. Lionel Cruse had claimed that Watergate, and Winegate, would disappear in a "cloud of gossip." How he must have wished they had. Both Nixon and Cruse seemed to feel they could fool the authorities through manipulation of evidence: paperwork went missing at the Cruse cellars and potentially damning documents were edited, while Nixon's transcripts were shown to be a censored version of the White House tapes. Both cases played a part in the country's leadership: Nixon resigned, and Chaban-Delmas failed to win election. And both men ended up getting away relatively lightly: Gerald Ford pardoned Nixon, while his henchmen, many of whom had testified at the Senate hearing, were given prison sentences. Both Lionel and Yvan Cruse received suspended sentences. Pierre Bert was jailed but made use of his time there to write his tell-all book, which was published in 1975.

The Winegate scandal "led to a fantastic slump in sales,"[25] according to journalists at the time, but hindsight suggests the case and the much-publicized trial were merely part of a bust in a boom-bust cycle that has plagued the region throughout its history. The market was flooded: greed and speculation had led to swollen price tags that seemed disconnected from reality, but it all came crashing down. Clive Coates explained that the "bubble finally burst and with such savagery that there was hardly a merchant in Britain or France who was not wounded and several who found themselves in acute financial difficulties because they had continued to pay high prices—and, moreover, for the indifferent vintage of 1972—in anticipation of a further increase in demand which never materialised and were then forced by their accountants and bank managers to destock in a great rush."[26] As one rain-soaked harvest followed another, Bordeaux had a lot of dilute wine filling the cellars that no one wanted.

It didn't help that Bordeaux's most promising market, the United States, was in a state of disarray after the presidential crisis. In Vietnam, the US had suffered defeat at the hands of the Viet Cong, losing 58,000 American soldiers and suffering more than 300,000 wounded in a war that the public had gradually come to loathe. Rampant inflation meant that the average American family was poorer than the year before. Rising oil prices hit the country hard in 1974, and owners of the year's most popular cars, the Chevrolet Monte Carlo and the VW Beetle, couldn't go very far in their vehicles. "Sorry, No Gas" signs were a common sight at gas stations, and even if there was gas available, the lines were long and the prices high. In a bid to conserve fuel, the national speed limit was reduced to fifty-five miles per hour. The nation was on a go-slow, and drinking overpriced wine was out of fashion.

America had lost its way. So had Bordeaux. But they'd both be back.

7

YOU SAY "PROST," I SAY "FROST"!

IT STARTS WITH A PRANK in the boys' bathroom at Springfield Elementary School. Eternal fourth-grader Bart Simpson drops an innocuous cherry-shaped explosive into the bowl and flushes the toilet, but the watery explosion is badly timed: Principal Skinner's visiting mother just happens to be paying a visit to the school's loos and is launched off the seat by the eruption. A rather unusual punishment awaits: instead of detention or having to write more lines, Bart is sent on a foreign exchange to France. His hosts are not a French family but a rather unsavory pair of *hommes:* Cesar and Ugolin, the owners of the ramshackle wine estate Château Maison. Bart's exchange is not filled with freshly baked croissants, a cruise down the Seine, or the sounds of the accordion; he is treated as slave labor during the grape harvest. In this episode, the bright colors and comforts of Springfield seem far, far away as Bart sleeps on the hard floor of a barn while Maurice the donkey snuggles down on a cozy bed of straw.

Bart refuses to taste Château Maison's newly fermented wine, which has been doctored with antifreeze. He's only ten years old and has no desire to drink alcohol, nor to be poisoned, but his hosts don't take no for an answer, and he is forced to sample the beverage. Of his antifreeze additions, Cesar admits, "If you put in too much, it can be lethal, but the right amount gives the wine more body." Judging that it is a success—Bart does not die or lose his sight—Cesar and Ugolin send him out on a push bike in the pouring rain to buy more antifreeze in Paris. Once in the capital, Bart flags down a policeman. "You gotta help me," he cries. "These two guys work me night and day. They don't feed me. They make me sleep on the floor. They put antifreeze in the wine, and they gave my red hat to the donkey." The officer's reply? "Antifreeze in the wine? This is a very serious crime!" Cesar and Ugolin are arrested and told that they'll be doing their winemaking in prison from now on. Bart leaves France a hero.[1]

Cesar and Ugolin weren't the only winemakers in prison for adding so-called antifreeze when the episode aired in 1990. That the first season of *The Simpsons,* which has gone on to become one of the longest-running American television shows, as well as *Time* magazine's best show of the twentieth century, featured unscrupulous vintners making illegal additions to their wine shows just how widespread the awareness of this fraud had become. But the scriptwriters sent Bart to France, not Austria, where the antifreeze-which-wasn't-antifreeze wine scandal had dealt an icy blow to the fortunes of the country's grape growers. Viewers of *The Crepes of Wrath* episode may have thought it funny, but to the Austrians, the events of 1985 were no joke.

"Toxic," "highly tainted," and "lethal" were just a few of the descriptors used in attention-grabbing headlines across the globe as news trickled out during the summer of 1985 that a few Austrian winemakers and merchants had been illegally adding a little-known substance called diethylene glycol to plump out their thin, sour wines. For centuries, creative winemakers have been trying to supply what nature failed to provide in a bid to make more pleasurable wines, but the Austrian case seemed far more serious: this substance might harm the health of the drinker. As with most wine fraud, it was done in the name of greed. A University of Vienna dissertation on the scandal revealed that adding diethylene glycol to lowly table wines could result in an almost sixfold increase in the price of wine, raising it from 3.50 to 20 schillings per liter.[2]

Fear spread from rural vineyards to the skyscrapers of New York City. Would this wine cause blindness, as the two French winemakers in *The Crepes of Wrath* had feared? Could drinking a glass of Riesling kill you? As bottle after bottle was pulled from the shelves and national governments recommended avoiding Austrian wines or even placed a ban on them, uncertainty and fear gripped wine lovers around the world.

WUNDER STUFF

Today, Michelin-star restaurants proudly list Austrian Grüner Veltliners and Rieslings on their wine menus, but in the years before 1985, the country's wines tended to be destined for the bottom shelves of the supermarket rather than for white-tablecloth fine dining rooms. Despite attempts to clean up the Austrian wine scene through strict regulations—including defining what could be called wine as early as 1896, tightening controls on winery practices and the contents of wine vats in the 1920s, and setting minimum quality requirements in 1961—wineries could continue to milk the vines for all they were worth and blend their wines with those from other countries and still call them Austrian. In 1971, however, annual inspections, which had been carried out since the 1920s, were abolished, and Austrian wine drinkers were left to rely on the honesty of producers.[3] As it turned out, not all members of the wine community had their moral compass accurately set.

The country's rules did not demand high standards of its makers, nor was there an insatiable desire for fine Austrian wines at home or abroad. After 1945, Austrians and Germans wanted to drink cheap, and having endured rationing and hunger at home under the Nazis, sweetness was highly desirable; producers were happy to oblige. Consumers had money to spend: Austrians joined in the postwar economic boom, the *Wirtschaftswunder,* which spread prosperity from Boston to Berlin. The Austrian government also gave the local grape growers a hand up by keeping taxes on wine low, and Austrians responded by doubling their drinking in the decades after 1955. It soon became a race to keep up with demand, and the old ways of growing vines couldn't handle the pace. Growing individual vines up stakes in the ground was labor intensive and time consuming. And wine wasn't necessarily the growers' focus: many of them were farmers who also grew other crops and kept livestock. But they needed to find a more efficient way of slaking the nation's thirst, and the solution came in the form of Lenz Moser. The Beetle-driving vintner was born in 1905 in a small village on the banks of the river Danube. In between fathering five children, indulging his love of opera, and building a house—complete with Roman atrium—he embarked on a mission to modernize the country's traditional and inefficient grape growing. Since the 1920s, Moser had been experimenting with a system of growing vines along wires, with enough space between rows of vines to allow tractors to trundle up and down the vineyard, reducing the workload and improving profits. He shared his ideas in his book *Viticulture with a Difference: The Progressive Farmer's Book of Viticulture,* and visitors to Austria's wine-growing region are likely to see vines trained along Lenz Moser lines today.[4]

Moser's idea of training vines high and wide started to gain traction in the middle of the century; the move from nurturing individual vines to wire-trained vines in rows was hastened when freezing temperatures descended on Europe in February 1956. From Burgenland to Bordeaux, the continent shivered; average daily temperatures in Austria registered a record low of -9°Celsius, with Salzburg dipping as low as -31°Celsius. Nearly a thousand people are estimated to have died across the continent because of the cold, according to Lee Allyn Davis, author of *Natural Disasters*.[5] Crops were destroyed before spring had begun and vines were wiped out, never to produce again, requiring mass replanting. The wine harvest of 1956 was 39 million liters, less than a quarter of the 1954 crop.[6]

By the late 1960s, the country's vineyards had adopted Moser's method, or a variation of it. The now-wide rows and straight lines of vines allowed for growing mechanization, and fertilizers were embraced by both farmers and grape growers. Larger crops could be produced with less manual labor, which was a win-win if no one had high expectations for their glass of Austrian wine. Luckily, most of the customers weren't fussy. Despite the quantity over quality approach, the nation's thirst could still not be satisfied; imports had to make up for the shortfall. The law allowed local wines to be mixed with a very generous splash of wine from other countries (as much as two-thirds of the blend, at one time) and still be labeled as Austrian. In addition, restrictions on planting more vines were lifted in the country's largest state, Niederösterreich (Lower Austria), home to more than half of the country's vineyards today, including some of the most historic and prestigious sites. However, in the 1970s, growers picked sites that were easy to farm rather than suitable for making fine wine. As a result, a stream of cheap, low-quality wine had turned to a raging torrent by the early 1980s. Austrian wine production hit a record high in 1982, almost topping the 500-million-liter mark. Austrians were doing their best to drink local but could only manage to imbibe 300 million liters. The export markets—primarily Germany—had never mopped up a surplus of this magnitude, managing to consume just 45 million liters in the years leading up to 1985.[7] There was simply too much wine and nowhere to put it, with some vintners going as far as storing it in their swimming pools before it eventually flowed to the closest distillery.

A surplus of wine and depressed prices had not been anticipated a decade earlier. A study had been commissioned in 1973 to predict how much wine Austrians would drink in the future. The List Study, named after its author, engineer Karl List, predicted that the country's thirst would be even greater by the mid-1980s. Consumption had risen steadily in the late 1950s and 1960s and would continue to rise, according to List. But it turned out that Austrians had already hit peak wine; they were not going to drink an extra nine liters of wine per person by 1985, as List had anticipated. The wine community went about planting vineyards to meet a need that never materialized. In fact, Austrians began to drink *less* wine, a decline that would continue into the 1990s and 2000s, while beer boomed. Planting more vines was a "poor decision," according to Austrian wine expert Klaus Postmann.[8] Things seemed to be going badly for Austrian wine in the early 1980s, but they were about to get a lot worse.

On July 23, 1985, the English-speaking world first got wind of the grubby underbelly of Austrian wine. It was not deemed big news initially and was given just five sentences in the "In Brief" section on page seven of the *New York Times*. Reuters reported that Austrian authorities "had impounded nearly five million bottles of Austrian wine laced with a poisonous chemical used in antifreeze and urged consumers to stop drinking Austrian vintages pending further tests."[9] The report followed an announcement made by the Austrian health minister the previous day. But the government had known for months that there was a problem and had allowed Austrian wines to continue to be sold and consumed, despite not knowing if they were fit for consumption. Following the discovery of a wine containing a hefty 16 grams per liter of diethylene glycol on June 19, the authorities judged it time to come clean. Just a few days after this announcement, a very sweet wine, known as a *Beerenauslese*, made by a Burgenland-based wine company, Sautner, was discovered to contain a record amount of 48 grams per liter.[10] At the time, the ministry of health claimed that 14 grams could be lethal to someone in poor health. Understandably, there was fear in the wine aisles.

The country's minister for agriculture during this debacle was Günther Haiden, and he'd picked up the scent of the unfolding scandal in late 1984. The authorities had received an anonymous tip accompanied by several bottles of wine that were claimed to have been adulterated and that were sent for analysis. There wasn't a test for the compound diethylene glycol at the time, as it wasn't meant to be in wine. Scientists scrabbled to come up with a technique to detect it, which took several months. At about the same time, a wine producer attempted to claim back the sales tax on an unusual amount of diethylene glycol he'd bought. What on earth would he do with such a quantity? While the evidence was starting to stack up, Austrian wine still flowed freely in local wine taverns and across the German border. However, a lengthy exposé in the German national weekly *Die Zeit* in early August revealed that the Austrians had informed the West German authorities of the adulterated wine in April, shortly after the first tanks, mostly destined for West Germany, were seized. But the buying and selling had continued. Tankers of Austrian wine kept rolling into the Federal Republic in May and June thanks to the German ministry of health's decision that "there was no need to fear an acute health hazard."[11] It wasn't until July 9 that the German public were warned off Austrian wines and they were pulled from store shelves.

The media was soon filled with scaremongering articles. Josef Schuller, a Burgenland boy who would later become Austria's first-ever Master of Wine, was in Hamburg touring with his folk band in the summer of 1985 when he picked up a copy of the German tabloid *Bild*. A front-page headline read, "11 Poisoned by Antifreeze Wine at Grandma's Birthday Party,"[12] while a Viennese daily claimed "German Died of Poisoned Wine."[13] The latter story recalled the case of a retiree from Munich who vacationed in Vienna four years earlier and, after drinking plenty of sweet wine there, developed severe pain on way home. It was reported that he went to the hospital, his kidneys failed, and the doctors said he'd suffered glycol poisoning from consuming large amounts of wine. The problem was, the man hadn't died. He turned up alive and well in a rival newspaper article, claiming, "I'm fine now." That this lethal, illegal ingredient had not yet killed anyone was a relief for wine drinkers, but the fact that the man had developed glycol poisoning from drinking wine several years earlier set alarm bells ringing. How long had this been going on? The answer was years.

A so-called blacklist of adulterated wines was published by the Austrian authorities. The list grew daily and eventually included wines dating back to 1978, forcing wine lovers to cross-check the contents of their dusty cellars. Friedrich Hümer, a representative of a winemakers' association in Vienna, told a *New York Times* reporter that the problem could stretch back at least a decade: "Wine traders signed lucrative contracts over the last 10 years with major supermarket chains and other outlets in West Germany and elsewhere to supply large amounts of sweet Austrian wines, the kind the Germans like to drink, at constant levels of quality." He added: "What nature didn't supply they added themselves."[14] By the time all of the glycol-laced wine was rounded up, the equivalent of 33 million bottles had been seized and destroyed, representing around 10 percent of the annual harvest.[15]

Nature had failed to provide grapes ripe enough to make the sweet wines that customers coveted. While summer temperatures have risen steadily since the 1980s due to global warming, allowing even late-ripening red varieties to fully mature, in the 1970s, Austria was still a cool-climate white-wine-making region. The lack of warmth made it difficult for the vines laden with bunches to ripen their fruit. If there had been fewer bunches, the vines might have stood a chance, their ripening energy spread less thin. What's more, many seasons were wet, causing further dilution and rot. But there were contracts to be fulfilled and pockets to line, and there was a cheap substance that would turn the sour grapes to succulent wine and couldn't be traced. Until the scientists caught up.

Diethylene glycol is a sweet-tasting, viscous liquid that turns a thin, sour wine into a full, rich cuvée. Vintners had previously used glycerin to conjure up that oily feeling in the mouth, but after a ban was implemented, they were on the lookout for a replacement, and it came in the form of glycol, which was both soluble and cheap. Theo Müller, a teacher at a wine-growing institute in Trier, Germany, said: "It was cleverly thought out. . . . You'd need a certain prior knowledge of chemistry and audacity to figure that out."[16] However, diethylene glycol was not antifreeze. It never has been and never will be. The media claimed it was an ingredient in the automotive de-icer, but that was either a mistake or a sensational way to sell newspapers, or both. It is ethylene glycol, not diethylene glycol, that can be poured into car radiators to stop the freeze. Both are colorless, sweet liquids, but ethylene glycol is far more toxic than diethylene glycol. The body breaks down ethylene glycol into oxalic acid, which in a worst-case scenario can cause kidney failure and death. That's not to say that diethylene glycol is harmless—it isn't. But the international media whipped up an antifreeze frenzy; *Der Spiegel* distastefully—and incorrectly—suggested that drinking two of the most potent wines, which added up to a total of 61.5 grams of diethylene glycol over two liters, was "enough for two people to commit suicide."[17] However, the news broke at the height of the summer, which meant it was the media's silly season—known as *Sauregurkenzeit,* which literally translates as "sour cucumber time," and the scandal came along just at the right time. Instead of stories about cats getting stuck in trees, the world came to learn about Austrian wine for all the wrong reasons.

Diethylene glycol was, however, responsible for at least 600 deaths in the twentieth century. The first, and perhaps most infamous, mass poisoning occurred almost fifty years before the Austrian scandal. If Austrian vintners had picked up a copy of *FDA Consumer Magazine,* the US Food & Drug Administration's now defunct monthly publication, in the summer of 1981, and read the article "Taste of Raspberries, Taste of Death," they might have thought twice about the liberal addition of diethylene glycol to their wines. The 1937 Massengill Elixir Sulfanilamide incident killed 105 people across 15 states that year, including 34 children. At that time, Sulfanilamide was commonly prescribed to patients in powder or tablet form for its antibacterial properties, before modern antibiotics replaced it—it is now used mainly to treat itchy vaginas. But there was a request for a liquid form of the drug. The Tennessee-based Massengill pharmaceutical company fulfilled the request, but instead of dissolving the drug in glycerol, as with many of today's children's medications, the company used diethylene glycol infused with a raspberry flavor. At the time, no safety tests needed to be carried out before the medicine hit the market, and doctors prescribed it innocently. One doctor was left distraught after it killed six of his patients, including his best friend. As suspicions mounted, the FDA sprang into action to seize all the medicine in circulation: "The entire field force of 239 FDA inspectors and chemists were assigned to the task. . . . Newspapers and radio stations continued to issue warnings. . . . One doctor postponed his wedding to help an FDA chemist search for a 3-year-old boy whose family had moved into mountain country after obtaining a prescription."[18]

You would think that lessons would have been learned from this tragedy, but it seems that memories are short and fatal mistakes are still made when it comes to manufacturing and administering pain relief. In a 2008 report investigating the safety of diethylene glycol in toothpaste, the European Commission's Scientific Committee on Consumer Products referred to several other more recent mass poisonings: in 1990, 236 Bangladeshi children died from kidney failure after receiving acetaminophen (paracetamol) that had been dissolved in diethylene glycol, and in the same year, 47 Nigerian toddlers suffered the same fate. A few years later, another 90 children died of renal failure after taking acetaminophen syrup that was discovered to contain a fatal dose of diethylene glycol. The most recent mass poisoning was in Panama in 2006, where 51 patients died after taking a glycol-laced antihistamine.[19] Based on the evidence presented in the European Commission report, it was hardly surprising that it banned its use in toothpastes.

But in 1985, the world of science only had the Massengill case to go on, as well as a fifty-year-old study looking at lethal doses in rats, mice, and guinea pigs. The European experts used the poisonings in the 1990s to gauge how much diethylene glycol would kill humans. They came up with an approximate figure of around 1.6 grams per kilogram of body weight. The average man in the United States weighs around 90 kilograms (199 pounds), and based on the calculations, it would take nearly three liters of the most heavily laced Austrian dessert wine to prove fatal. Alcohol poisoning might also come into play at that stage. For those mistakenly ingesting any of the glycols, however, help is at hand thanks to a drug called fomepizole, which prevents the body from breaking down the molecule into its toxic byproducts. In the US, there's also a 1–800 hotline to the Poison Control Center, if required.

"WE ARE THE VICTIMS, NOT THE PERPETRATORS"

Rust, the self-proclaimed "prettiest wine-growing town in Austria," turned from beauty to beast during the summer of 1985. The historic village, with its cheerfully painted houses and cobbled streets, sits on the shores of Lake Neusiedl. In the summer, sailboats bob on its waters while children splash in the shallows. Tourists have long flocked to Rust to see pairs of regal storks sitting in their nests on top of its chimneys, before touring the historic town's wine cellars and taverns. But even the storks couldn't lure the crowds once Rust's name became tarnished in the unfolding wine adulteration scandal. In the summer of 1985, the village's wine-producer-run taverns—known as *Buschenschank* or *Heurige*—should have been packed with wiener-schnitzel-eating, wine-drinking visitors from the continent. Instead, *Der Spiegel*'s roving journalist Inge Cyrus was one of the few tourists walking its cobbled streets: "The evenings have become quiet despite the high season. In the otherwise cheerful Buschenschank on Haydngasse and Hauptstrasse, cats roam around sparsely occupied tables. The 110 winegrowing families aren't comforted by the fact that the innkeepers' beer sales have tripled."[20]

The name of the village kept appearing in the government's blacklist of wines, published in both national and international newspapers, and it was nothing short of a public relations disaster for Rust's quiet corner of the world. Its reputation was built on its naturally sweet, botrytized wines, a result of Rust's misty lakeside mornings and dry, sunny autumn days, which allow noble rot to develop. Noble rot—a fungus known as *Edelfaüle* in Austria—attacks the berries, leading the grapes to shrivel and concentrating their sugar and flavor, creating luscious, golden elixirs. The good name of Rust had already been abused before the scandal hit. Wines made as far as seventy miles from the village were allowed to use its name on the bottle; they might be labeled Rust, Rust-Neusiedlersee, or Ruster, but it was only the last that truly hailed from the village, with its gently sloping vineyards, long-held traditions, and superlative sweet whites. It was no surprise that wine producers in the wider district of Burgenland wanted to piggyback off the town's reputation, but it backfired spectacularly.

"We are the victims, not the perpetrators of a criminal act," the local mayor, Heribert Artinger, declared, and the town's producers put up banners and posters protesting their innocence.[21] At the annual wine festival, a banner was erected over the main road telling passing motorists that this was "the prettiest wine-growing town in Austria—with unadulterated wine," while the trickle of visitors to the wine cellars was met with homemade posters that demonstrated the divide between small growers in the traditional areas and the bulk-wine traders. One read: "Wines from the Rust-Neusiedlersee area? No thanks! Genuine quality wine from Rust? Yes, please."

The start of the decade had already been tough due to the wider region's new vine plantings, which had started to produce baskets full of grapes and a flood of wine, forcing prices down and spelling financial trouble for many. "It is the worst disaster to hit this region since World War II," Artinger continued, comparing its effects on the growers with that of phylloxera.[22] The following year, the nation's wine exports fell by 90 percent, and they would not reach pre-1985 levels until the new millennium—a sixteen-year-long recovery period.

It wasn't just innocent Austrian growers who became embroiled in the diethylene fiasco. Despite Germany's claim that it had the best wine laws in the world, the biggest importer of Austrian wine became enmeshed in a web of wine lies. The Germans initially pinned all the responsibility on the Austrians when any German wines were found to contain glycol: it must have been stored in a tank that had contained a tainted Austrian vintage, they claimed, or bottled on the same line as an adulterated wine. The argument was hard to believe coming from a country that prided itself on its meticulous cellar hygiene. Bulk bottlers in huge wine factories had been buying cheap, sweet wines by the tanker load from Austria to blend and stretch their German wines for the bargain-basement prices that German supermarket customers had come to expect. One of Germany's oldest wine families was at the heart of the scandal. Based in the village of Burg Layen in the Nahe wine region, a short drive west of Mainz, the Pieroths have records of their ancestors producing grapes and wine in the area as early as 1675. By 1984 they had become one of Germany's biggest wine businesses, employing more than 3,500 people in Germany and overseas.[23] The family was also involved in state and national politics: Elmar Pieroth was a member of Germany's parliament, the Bundestag, from 1969 to 1981, and when his family's company become embroiled in the scandal in 1985, he was working as an economics senator in Berlin. He claimed ignorance of any wrongdoing when it emerged that Pieroth wines contained diethylene glycol. A spokesman for the company initially claimed that none of the tainted wines had been put on the market, having been produced for the company's own employees (which suggests they didn't highly value their work force). However, government testing on both sides of the Atlantic showed the spokesman wasn't telling the truth—the wines were in circulation. On a single day in August 1985, nine different wines bottled and sold by Pieroth were found to contain a decent dollop of diethylene glycol. The US Food & Drug Administration later announced that several Austrian wines sold under the Pieroth name dating back to the late 1970s were laced with the substance. It took more than a decade for the case to be decided in court, and in April 1996, six former senior employees, including two family members, were finally handed a one-million-mark fine.[24] Of course, the history section of the Pieroths' website does not mention this unwholesome episode.

When it came to blending Austrian with German wines, the complicit parties had been careful to cover their tracks. Austria had adopted a maturity-based quality control system based on the one used in Germany. Producers had to have paperwork stating their wine was from grapes that had reached the desired ripeness and that the wine was of superior quality, a *Prädikatswein*. Without the certificate, it couldn't leave Austria. However, many producers didn't export their wines, instead selling directly to private customers and restaurants within Austria, leaving them with a certificate that they didn't need and that could be sold illegally for a few schillings. This loophole was exploited by two Austrian brothers, Josef and Richard Grill, who bought certificates for 308,347 liters of wine, according to court records.[25] Many clients must have turned a blind eye, as the rough wines arriving in the tankers hardly matched the official papers.

The reputation of German wine was already at a low ebb, bouncing from one public embarrassment to another. Excessive amounts of water and sugar, often delivered as liquid sugar in easy-to-carry and easy-to-pour tins, were a blight on the German winescape. In a climate that struggled to ripen its grapes, a liberal dose of sugar before the fermentation began would increase the wine's body and alcohol, while the addition of some sweet grape juice just before bottling to even out the sour taste, as well as water to increase volume, was commonplace. In the mid-1970s, some regions were making far more wine than they'd harvested. It wasn't just the cash-strapped producer desperate to make ends meet; high-profile individuals were also flouting the law, including the former president of the German Winegrowers' Association. Werner Tyrell was a respected member of the German wine trade, having spent sixteen years in the presidential role, and his wines were much admired for their purity. While thousands of wine producers faced prosecution in the early 1980s for selling adulterated wine, Tyrell was supposedly fighting the good fight during the day, but it seemed he was sneaking about after dark. Tyrell almost evaded the law, thanks to his powerful position; the chief chemist at the wine control board found signs of adulteration in one of his wines dating from 1979, but her superiors stopped her from informing the public prosecutor. After Tyrell finally confessed the truth in court, he was given a mere one-year suspended sentence, while the poor chemist received anonymous death threats for her law-abiding efforts.[26]

The diethylene glycol scandal became one of the biggest news stories of 1985, not only in Austria but around the world. A government-sponsored language society, Gesellschaft für deutsche Sprache, chooses an annual word or phrase of the year; in 1985, it was *Glykol*. (In 1989, after the Berlin Wall crumbled, *Reisefreiheit*—"freedom of travel"—was deemed worthy of the title; in 1999, "millennium" got the nod.) Meanwhile, in England, an auto mechanic shop with a sense of humor posted an ad in the local newspaper promoting its services for the coming winter: "IMPORTANT NOTICE: NONE OF OUR ANTIFREEZE HAS BEEN CONTAMINATED WITH FOREIGN WINE!!!"[27]

Distant countries were also drawn into the scandal. The Australian wine industry suffered when both Japan and China mistakenly banned wines from Down Under, having confused the Antipodean nation's name with that of Austria. It wasn't the first or last time the mistake would be made. In 2007, President George W. Bush thanked Australia's prime minister for visiting Austrian troops in Iraq[28] and in 2008, Reuters reported that Austria "narrowly" won its seat on the UN Security Council after one country confused it with Australia.[29] In February 2016, US news network CNN reported that Australia would be building a fence on its Slovenian border, despite the two countries being separated by nearly 9,000 miles of land and ocean.[30] It's a constant source of frustration for well-traveled Austrians, many of whom have given up correcting various taxi drivers and hotel receptionists. A slew of t-shirt designs has been created around this case of mistaken identity bearing the slogan *Keine Kängarus in Österreich*—"there are no kangaroos in Austria."

Ultimately, the kangaroo-free Austrian courts charged more than three hundred wine producers, traders, and merchants for their involvement in the diethylene scandal, and fifteen people were sent to jail, including the mayor of Fels am Wagram, a quiet wine village sixty kilometers northwest of Vienna. Josef Grill and his brother had not only been buying up unused export certificates to ship their wines off to Germany, they were also charged with creating fraudulent wines from 1978 to 1985, according to Austrian court records.[31] There was even evidence they'd been tinkering with their wines as early as 1965. Their winemaker, Otto Nadrarsky, was a linchpin of the operation, preparing the concoctions, making the additions, and passing on his knowledge to winemakers at other companies—for a consultancy fee. The Grill team cooked up more than 23 million liters of rule-breaking table wine and close to 6 million liters of Prädikat wine with grape juice, excessive amounts of sugar (5.2 million kilograms), glycerin (15,000 kilograms), diethylene glycol (27,000 kilograms), and a host of other additives—some illegal and some permitted. Damages were estimated to be at least 295 million Austrian schillings (equivalent to 21.4 million euros), and millions of liters of wine had to be confiscated. The Grills had bribed inspectors to overlook their illicit behavior, and they weren't the only ones handing over envelopes stuffed with cash.

Herbert Wolf, the head of the wine department at an official testing institute, should have been leading by example. Instead, he was receiving under-the-counter payments totaling tens of thousands of schillings, free (unadulterated) wine, and hunting invitations, from not only the Grills but from other Burgenland wineries, including Tschida, Steiner, and Klosterkellerei Siegendorf. He was convicted of aiding and abetting fraud, having allowed at least 300,000 liters of adulterated wine to be given the official seal of approval.[32]

One upstanding and innocent inspector, Josef Mitterer, was so overcome by the events of the summer of 1985 that he took his own life that September.[33] He was the man behind the tennis ball trick: underhanded grape growers would try to claim they'd harvested more high-quality grapes than they had by getting the same receival bin inspected and certified multiple times—one load of grapes looks pretty similar to the next. Mitterer started throwing a tennis ball into each load when no one was watching. If he found the tennis ball in the next batch, he would have proof that the harvester was not playing by the rules. A stickler for the rules, he had had the windows of his car shattered when news of the scandal broke, possibly by a disgruntled winemaker or a less scrupulous member of his own department. It was rumored that he knew what was going on but had been forced to keep it quiet and could no longer bear the pressure.

The Grills appealed their convictions; Richard's lawyer asked for leniency after a ten-year sentence was doled out. He noted that the courts had given a drug dealer just eight years for importing 52 kilograms of heroin. The court was rather unsympathetic, concluding that the Grill brothers were aware "that under no circumstances could they have sold the wine produced using prohibited chemical additives, in particular diethylene glycol." The court continued: "Consumers would not have bought the drink if they had known about its true consistency and its inherent worthlessness, especially as they expected to buy a product made according to the norms and principles of the Wine Act, free from additives."[34] The Grills didn't have blood on their hands but in the eyes of the law, they had put profit over probity; the scent of money was as sweet and intoxicating as the glycol they added, and they could not resist its heady allure.

A VINTAGE DEMISE

Within months of the Austrian wine industry's fall from grace, news broke that Italian wine drinkers were dying after sipping wine blended with methanol, a wood-based alcohol. The methanol could increase a wine's finished alcohol level by a percentage point or so, and it would sell for a few more *centisimi* than weaker equivalents. Today it would seem almost laughable that growers would have trouble reaching 12 percent alcohol, given the heat of the Italian sun, but with heavy crop loads burdening the vines, there was too much fruit to attain full ripeness. Since it was illegal to add sugar to boost final alcohol levels in the southern reaches of Europe, a group of unethical wine companies took to this cheap but harmful alternative. The blenders were heavy handed, and over the course of two months, more than twenty-five people died and many more were hospitalized after a glass of rough *vino rosso*. Parallels were drawn with their northerly neighbors. "The whole Italian wine industry shivers and prays it will be spared an Austrian-style hammering over the black sheep in its flocks," reported the *Irish Independent*, but it was not to be. The Danes were the first to ban the sale of Italian wine, while the Swiss, French, West German, and Belgian authorities issued warnings not to drink Italian wines; France and Germany seized any shipments attempting to enter the country. The United States' official response was rather confused, as Frank J. Prial, longtime wine columnist for the *New York Times* explained in his front-page story on April 12: "The Bureau of Alcohol, Tobacco and Firearms, the Federal agency responsible for wine imports, initially directed importers to tell their retailers to remove all Italian wines from the shelves. Later the same day that statement was withdrawn, and a spokesman said only that the bureau felt Americans should not drink Italian wines for the time being 'simply as a precautionary measure.'"[35]

Italian wine associations and officials were at pains to point out to anyone with a Dictaphone and a potential byline that the offenders were a small group of dealers making cheap wines who were quickly rounded up and punished. However, the fraudsters managed to shatter the hard-earned reputation of an entire country's wine industry in just a few weeks. The coverage might have been more extensive, but world events meant that the methanol scandal quickly became a low priority for international news agencies. On April 26, 1986, the fourth reactor at the Chernobyl nuclear power plant exploded, immediately killing thirty-one people and sending a cloud of radiation across Europe. The methanol scandal paled in comparison. A few weeks later, the world was given a much-needed dose of escapism with the release of *Top Gun*. Our breath was taken away by Maverick and Iceman in their flying suits and aviators, rather than methanol-laced wine.

The Italians and the Austrians were both were left licking their wounds in the late 1980s. In Austria, many walked away from their vineyards; others limped on. On the bright side, the scandal proved to be a catalyst for long overdue change: within months, the Austrian government passed a strict new wine law to prevent history from repeating itself and to restore faith in the country's wines. The act clamped down on the use of sugar and other chemicals. Loopholes were closed and inspections were reintroduced, while precise record keeping became as important to winemakers as washing out tanks and filling barrels. It was also the first time that maximum yields were included in Austrian law, to prevent overproduction and maximize the concentration of the grapes. And Austrian wine had to be 100 percent Austrian, rather than mostly Austrian with a bit of ripeness or color added from a splash of Italian or Spanish wine. It was fair to say the rules were far more onerous than they needed to be, and some producers felt they were oppressive, expressing their displeasure by driving their tractors into the Austrian capital, holding up traffic and making a nuisance of themselves. The government wasn't about to make a U-turn, however, with the whole country's vinous reputation in tatters thanks to the actions of a minority of offenders.

The next time you open a bottle of Austrian wine, pause for a second and take a closer look at the circular stamp on the top of the cap. Sporting the colors of the national flag and a unique code, it's known as a banderole and signifies that it's a quality wine that has conformed to the rules that have been in place despite 4,000 tractor-driving vintners kicking up a fuss in central Vienna. In addition to the vineyard and winery rules, every wine undergoes chemical analysis and must be tasted by a government-appointed panel to get the seal of approval before it leaves the winery. The number on the banderole is the inspection number and means that it has ticked all the boxes and is considered worthy of representing Austria on the international stage. It's been called the strictest wine law in the world, and it probably is, but then the Germans said that about their rules in the early 1970s and that failed to stop those who claimed to be its most important representatives.

That said, the image of Austrian wine has been overhauled since a minority of corrupt cellar masters and dodgy dealers placed it at the top of the wine world's naughty list. Instead of "Prost," people joked, Austrians now said "Frost" when they clinked glasses. Although overseas sales fell through the floor, local consumption only suffered a minor and temporary dip, with the nation's breweries benefiting from the downturn. While Austrians have, like many of their European counterparts, steadily reduced their wine intake since the 1980s due to lifestyle changes, health concerns, and stricter drink-drive laws, among other things, the rest of the world has more than made up for what the small population of this landlocked Alpine nation no longer consumes. You'll find Austrian wines in the best restaurants and the fanciest wine shops in London, New York, and Tokyo. And that's because the wines are a million times better than they were before the scandal. The attitude in the pre-scandal years to sell it sweet, cheap, and not particularly cheerful (mainly to German supermarkets) was thrown out. Improvements were not instantaneous: in the vintages immediately following the scandal, Austrian producers were keen to disassociate themselves from sweetness but seemed to confuse dryness with austerity, and consequently there were plenty of eye-wateringly sour styles that emerged in the wake of the glycol scandal. Antacids were hardly an accompaniment that Austrians wanted to recommend with a glass of their Riesling, and there was a swift realization that ripe grapes were needed to make balanced dry wines.

On the shores of the Neusiedlersee today, fine sweet wines continue to be made in the historic cellars of Rust. Known as Ruster Ausbruch, they astonish even the fussiest of drinkers: luscious and concentrated Austrian sweet wines, intensified by the effects of noble rot, have taken the title of best sweet in the world at major international wine competitions, and the route was paved by a tireless young chemistry graduate born on the eastern shores of Lake Neusiedl. Alois Kracher joined the family firm in 1986, an inauspicious time to enter the market. Undeterred by the implosions going on around him, he shaped his own style of sweet wine and carried other quality-conscious growers along with him. Not only did he win countless awards for world's best sweet wine in the 1990s and 2000s, but the International Wine Challenge renamed its sweet wine trophy the Alois Kracher Trophy in his honor—after his untimely death from cancer, aged just forty-eight.

Despite not being involved in the scandal, it was a major financial blow for many companies, including that of Lenz Moser, which ran into financial difficulties and ended up in the hands of a consortium. Lenz's grandson, Lenz Moser V, continued to run the business for more than a decade under the new owners. He remembers getting the company's first computer to input all the data required under the new wine act.[36] Despite the help of computers, vintners were drowning in paperwork and exhausted by constantly having to jump bureaucratic hurdles. The 1985 wine law needed to evolve in the years that followed to consider those that it governed.

Bulk-wine grape growers and producers reliant on German supermarket sales found themselves out of business, while many small producers no longer had the energy to continue after the events of 1985. The nation's vineyard area ebbed like an outgoing tide. In 1987, there were close to 60,000 hectares planted. By 2019, with plantings shy of 45,000 hectares and just a quarter of the wine producers that there had been in 1987, Austria found itself several rungs lower in the world's grape-growing league. It sat at number twenty-seven, between Georgia and Morocco and far below Algeria and Moldova.[37] And when it comes to wine production, it accounts for less than one percent of the entire world's output, making it a bijou wine nation on a similar scale to New Zealand. However, Austria remains far less famous than its Kiwi counterpart, since most bottles of Austrian wine don't stray too far from the cellar: they are mainly sold in Austria, Germany, and Switzerland.

It is wonderfully evocative to compare the Austrian wine community to a phoenix rising from the post-1985 ashes, but that might be taking things a bit far. Change was already happening within Austria prior to the scandal. A new generation of well-trained winemakers was taking over the reins from their parents. They had attended the wine schools that were sprouting up around the country and were the first generation to travel beyond Austria, working harvests in France, Italy, and the New World. They brought their training, outward-looking attitude, and youthful determination back to their villages.

In a bid to show the world that Austria's best were worthy of a place on the world's finest tables, in 2002 a Swedish dentist-turned-wine-merchant organized a blind tasting with Austria's finest Grüner Veltliners up against Burgundy's best Chardonnays.[38] The thirty-nine participants were trained professionals and the results suggested that Austrian Grüner Veltliner had the goods to take it to the big Burgundy boys. Intrigued by the results of this tasting, the world's most successful female wine writer, Master of Wine Jancis Robinson, decided that Londoners should have a piece of the action and instigated another sparring match later that year.[39] The results were yet another blow for the Chardonnay grape and gaiety for Grüner. Out of thirty-five wines tasted by a group of Britain's finest palates, seven of the ten highest-scoring wines were Austrian, including an Austrian Chardonnay. And they were all white, dry, and significantly cheaper than the lesser performing wines.

Despite Robinson's claims that these results would "seem to point to a glorious future," Grüner Veltliner, Grüner, Gru-Vee, or GV, as it is variously known, is still one of those great white hopes that never quite achieves its international potential. But in Grüner, Austria has a signature variety that is distinctly Austrian and increasingly respected, with producers across the globe trying to emulate the heights of the wines produced from the very finest terraced vineyards on the banks of the Danube. Many have tried but none has yet succeeded in capturing the satisfyingly spicy singularity of Austrian Grüner.

WHAT'S IN YOUR WINE?

Following the revelation that diethylene glycol was lurking in their wine undisclosed, people began to question what was in their glass. The list of permitted additives was laid out in the mainstream media, and those without a wine degree were shocked: what were tartaric acid, sulfur dioxide, and egg whites doing in their glass of wine? There was a call for listing ingredients on wine labels; decades later the debate rages on, but that hasn't stopped at least one Hollywood actress from entering the fray. Cameron Diaz, who got her break as the female lead in *The Mask* in 1994 and went on to star in such box-office hits as *There's Something about Mary* and *Charlie's Angels*, launched her own "clean, delicious wine" brand, Avaline, after finding out wine didn't make itself. "I just thought it was fermented grapes," said Diaz.[40] And when

Diaz and her co-founder Katherine Power found out that the grapes weren't washed before they went into the tank, and that egg whites might be used to clarify their wines? "We were mad for a while," says Diaz. So the two launched an organic wine brand that claimed to offer "total nutritional transparency." They don't state if they give their bunches a wash, however.

If they'd bothered to look back to Roman times, the horrified pair would have realized that prior to the invention of modern winemaking techniques, wine was often undrinkable and would quickly turn to vinegar. Sulfur dioxide is commonly used in winemaking to prevent oxygen from having its wicked way with wine. It's a natural byproduct of fermentation, and the levels are often topped up to ensure nasty microbes don't ruin the wine. And if the grapes haven't gotten enough of the nutrients needed to ensure all of the grape sugars are turned to alcohol to make a dry wine, diammonium phosphate—or as Diaz labels it on her wine, yeast nutrient—can be added to the tanks. Vegans might object to the use of egg whites, milk, or isinglass (a fish extract) to improve clarity, but these processing aids are settled out or filtered from the wine.

Wine is a natural product made from grapes grown in a particular year, and no two years are the same: the summer could be hot or cold, dry or wet, and the grapes reflect the season. In cool regions where grapes struggle to ripen, sugar can be added to boost the final alcohol level of the wine, while the deacidifying agent potassium bicarbonate is also permitted, to make the wine less sour (certainly an improvement on the toxic lead salts used in the seventeenth century). Grapes grown in the heat of the Mediterranean might have ripened to such levels that they need a little added acidity in the form of tartaric acid—which is found naturally in grape juice—to give them a sense of freshness. These are not toxic products but naturally occurring additives. What's more, unlike the ingredients in a chocolate cookie or a bag of chips, the products used in the winemaking process are not necessarily found in the finished bottle. They may have been converted to something else, such as sugar to alcohol, or they may have been filtered out before bottling.

There's no denying that most modern wines are ameliorated in some way, from adding yeasts to sulfur dioxide. But is that adulteration? For purists, additions are the devil incarnate and reflective of the dominance of large-scale commercial winemaking. They insist that at the very least, grapes should be grown organically, and wine should be naturally fermented using only the yeasts found on the grapes' skins and in the atmosphere. No sulfur should be added, and certainly no nutrients or additions that have been bought in a packet. This is what is known as natural wine, and it has created a divide in the wine-loving community. The naturalists believe it's their way or the highway, but for more mainstream types, the funkier—and frequently faulty—wines that emerge from such methods can be undrinkable. What's more, lower levels of the antibacterial and antioxidant sulfur dioxide also mean that natural wines are more likely to travel badly, particularly if they are shipped halfway around the world. Wine has always needed a helping hand to get it from grape to glass; without human intervention, there would be no wine. What is deemed acceptable intervention, however, is a matter of taste.

8

INDIANA JONES AND THE
GLASS CRUSADE

IT WAS ALL OVER in ninety-nine seconds.

Kip Forbes, the son of US magazine magnate Malcolm Forbes, had dropped a record-breaking £105,000 ($155,295) on a single bottle of wine. And it had taken less than two minutes. Sent to do his millionaire father's bidding, the younger Forbes wasn't leaving the packed Christie's auction room without his prize—a bottle of Lafitte 1787 bearing the initials Th.J., a bottle the vendor claimed was once the property of Thomas Jefferson, the third president of the United States. Within hours of the gavel slamming down on December 5, 1985, the bottle engraved with Jefferson's initials was comfortably installed in its own seat on a private jet, leaving behind the gray skies of London for a new home on New York's glitzy Fifth Avenue.

Despite the breakneck pace of the sale, the whiffs of skepticism concerning the authenticity of the bottle sold on that December day caused a life-long hangover for its vendor, former pop-band manager Hardy Rodenstock, and the Christie's auctioneer, Lancashire-born J. Michael Broadbent. The pair were ensnared in years of speculation and numerous court cases and became the leading characters in Benjamin Wallace's book *The Billionaire's Vinegar*, whose long-awaited screen adaptation has been linked to various Hollywood A-listers, including Matthew McConaughey.

It was the wine discovery of the century: a stash of bottles in a cellar in the Marais district of Paris. While the French capital's finest wine cellars, including 80,000 bottles from the historic restaurant La Tour d'Argent, had been pillaged by German soldiers during World War II, these pre-Revolution bottles had remained untouched by friend and foe alike until an elderly gentleman stumbled across the bricked-up cellar. Covered in the thick dust of centuries of repose, a quick wipe revealed the dozen or so bottles belonged to the who's who of Bordeaux: Lafitte, now known as Lafite Rothschild or simply Lafite; Yquem; Margaux; and Mouton Rothschild, then known as Brane Mouton. Not only that, they dated from the 1780s. And the bottles were engraved with the initials Th.J. It was an unbelievable find. Who did the Frenchman call? How about "the most envied wine tracker in the world," Hardy Rodenstock?[1] The former band manager turned rare-wine collector and dealer, whose real name was Meinhard Görke, raced to Paris from Munich to inspect this cache. He took possession of the bottles on the spot and drove away with a piece of history. Or at least that was Rodenstock's story. It was an account decidedly scant on detail, including the all-important location of the stash, information that went with him to his grave.

But Rodenstock was to be trusted, wasn't he? He was part of an elite circle of wine collectors in Germany. He hosted finely orchestrated wine-tasting events that equated to expensive binge drinking sessions daubed with an intellectual façade. Dozens of incredibly rare bottles dating back decades or even centuries would have their crumbling corks carefully prized from their fragile necks; the wine would be poured carefully into a decanter to separate the delicate liquid from the gritty sediment formed over years of captivity. Rodenstock had also ingratiated himself with the fine-wine world, inviting prominent wine writers, château owners, and auctioneers to his exclusive events, which started as long lunches and later extended to wine weekends, culminating in a week-long wining and dining extravaganza dedicated to the most famous Sauternes estate, Château d'Yquem, in 1998. His extensive collection of old wine and his obsession with finding the rarest bottles drew drooling guests from Europe, the US, and Asia.

His events required more stamina than the Médoc marathon, and a forgiving waistband. The late Michael Broadbent remembered flying to Düsseldorf in the mid-1970s, in the early days of Rodenstock's regattas, for a black-tie lunch. He arrived at 11:00 a.m., sat down for lunch at midday, and got up at midnight—seven courses, seventy-five wines, and twelve hours later. "I had the most fearful headache halfway through and I was sick in the middle of the night and had to fly back on an early-morning flight for a sale at Christie's at 11 o'clock."[2] He learned to take it more slowly the next time, avoiding the rich food and drinking large amounts of water to counteract the alcohol. In the year following the sale of the first Jefferson bottle, Broadbent and fellow Master of Wine and author Jancis Robinson were two of the fine-wine glitterati attending the annual Rodenstock tasting. The venue was Château d'Yquem; the host was then owner Count Alexandre de Lur-Saluces. It was another endurance event. In *Confessions of a Wine Lover*, Robinson recalls, "We sat down at about noon on a crisp autumn day and rose from the table at one or two the following morning. Sixty-six wines were served, with a dozen courses, by chefs specially shipped in from Germany and Bordeaux. . . . There was not a spittoon in sight."[3] She admits that she and Broadbent had a sneaky doze under a tree during the late afternoon, in a bid to revive their flagging energy levels, and had to wash down several aspirin with the nearest drink to hand: a glass of twenty-two-year-old Champagne Lanson.

It was at these carefully choreographed tastings that Broadbent came to know Rodenstock and some of the world's wealthiest wine collectors. He was not one of them. He was born into a manufacturing family in a mill town in Lancashire in 1927.[4] While he was privately educated and well-spoken, with not a hint of a northern accent, he did not consider himself part of the establishment; he rubbed shoulders with them, but his life in wine had started in the lowly cellars of a London wine merchant, sweeping floors and delivering orders. His mother, a whisky drinker and chocaholic, had seen the job advert and urged him to apply. He needed a job—he was twenty-five and had dropped out of his architecture studies and was dithering, he later admitted. Broadbent applied and was unexpectedly offered the job—his employer later revealed his decision was based on Broadbent's elegant handwriting. The Lancastrian moved to London, where the "mad as a hatter" merchant Tommy Layton set him to work, paying him such a meager wage that Broadbent was forced to pawn his stamp collection, despite living on a diet of carrot, onion, and potato stew.[5] He stuck it out for a year, which was a lifetime for a Layton trainee, but the merchant gave him one piece of advice that would prove to be invaluable in his life's work: write a note on every wine you taste. Starting that day in Layton's cellar in September 1952, Broadbent compiled more than 85,000 wine tasting notes in more than 130 identical red notebooks that became the basis for his series of wine books.[6]

Just fourteen years after starting life in the wine trade as the delivery boy and cellar rat, Broadbent enjoyed a heady ascent up the wine ladder. He heard a rumor that auction house Christie's was looking to set up a wine department and decided to take the initiative, writing to the chairman to ask if it was true—as well as asking for the job. While he was worried that he might have jumped the gun, he was successful, no doubt due to some excellent references from some of the wine trade's top brass. "It was one of those rare things like proposing marriage," he remembers. "I just felt in my bones that it would work."[7] On

October 11, 1966, the first season of wine sales began at Christie's, with Broadbent acting on tip-offs in order to secure fine wine to sell. He had no competition from other auction houses, and there were plenty of aristocratic cellars whose vinous treasures had lain untouched for decades and not yet been mined.

His most important sale that first season was the cellar of Lord Rosebery, which he discovered while doing a recce of another wine collection. A few miles west of Edinburgh city center lies the seat of the marquess of Linlithgow, Hopetoun House. Then marquess Charles Hope had a cash flow problem and needed to raise some funds. Years later, the family would open the house and grounds to visitors to stay afloat, but at that time the marquess had a lot of mature wine in the cellar that was unlikely to be opened. That's how Broadbent ended up in Edinburgh one evening. He turned up at Hopetoun House at just the right moment—the marquess and his butler had been watching the Miss World contest, and Miss India had just been crowned champion. The television was duly switched off and Broadbent sipped on a whisky with the aristocrat before retiring.[8] The next morning, Broadbent set about the job of making an inventory of the Linlithgow cellar, looking for auction-worthy bottles. There were some decent old wines, a couple of interesting old ports from 1911, but this cellar was to prove a doorway into a world of wine fantasy.

Breaking Broadbent's concentration on the dusty bottles, the marquess appeared with a small roll of paper that turned out to be a list of his neighbor's wines. His neighbor was none other than Lord Rosebery, the son of a former prime minister and Hannah de Rothschild, at one time Britain's richest woman. Harry was now in his eighties. In his heyday he'd been a first-class cricketer, a celebrated racehorse owner, and a politician. Now he had a cellar full of wine that he would not have time to drink before he passed away (in 1974, aged ninety-two). Broadbent couldn't believe what he was reading: pre-phylloxera bottles, double and even triple magnums of Château Lafite Rothschild, bottles of Hungary's jewel of a sweet wine—Tokaji—dating from 1830. He hurried over to see Rosebery; he was met by the butler and led into the cellar, with its magnificent stone arches and gravel floor. Over lunch, which included a carafe of 1920 Taylor's port, Rosebery explained that his entertaining days were largely over, and the incredibly rare triple magnums of 1865 Lafite would require him to invite more than twenty people, and most of them would not appreciate the elixir in their glass. Broadbent duly listed all the wines and then had the dirty job of packing up all the bottles in the cellar, ready for their journey to new owners.

The tip-offs and calls kept coming, and Broadbent, typically accompanied by his wife Daphne, would be found over the coming years in the damp cellars of the aristocracy uncovering a stream of vinous delights: fine wines that were made a century earlier were emerging from the dark confines of these country manors and castles. It was dirty work, scrabbling around in cold, dusty cellars, so the Broadbents would swap their city clothes for fishermen's boots and trousers. They would then quickly change to enjoy lunch or dinner with the owner of the cellar, who was often an earl or prince. Within a year of his joining the auction house, Christie's had run thirty-two sales and Broadbent had been made a director (although it would take five years to get a raise from his employer, he recalled).

Broadbent's star was rising. Not only was he transforming the fine-wine market, but he also passed the Master of Wine exams, the trade's most rigorous qualifications, cementing his position as a respected figure in industry circles. He was also becoming a personality, penning articles for magazines and attracting attention as he whizzed around the London wine scene on his Dutch bicycle, set off perfectly with a large basket.

The burgeoning American market beckoned, and Broadbent was invited to be a guest auctioneer at some of the country's first wine sales. Compared with the rather conservative British wine trade auctions, the American affairs were far more glamorous, with hundreds packing ornate ballrooms to bid on rare bottles in front of TV crews. Flying around the world to inspect cellars, host auctions, and join collectors at special dinners meant a packed schedule. Clients became dinner companions and invitations to special tastings regularly came Broadbent's way. That's how he was able to fill his red notebooks with reviews that would be published many times over and become a reference for anyone looking to understand wines and vintages they could only dream of tasting. (His notes often entertained as well as informed: like many forty-year-olds, the 1942 Château Lascombes from the Margaux appellation of Bordeaux had a "body sagging like the belly of superannuated footballer," while a red burgundy from the Chambertin Clos de Bèze vineyard offered "sweaty tannins like old socks.")[9]

Broadbent's books also became a wine diary of sorts, noting not only the wine and its taste but also where he had tasted it and when. In *Vintage Wine*, published in 2002 to mark his fiftieth anniversary in the wine trade, he explained, "If some names crop up more frequently than others, Hardy Rodenstock for example, it merely serves to emphasise the number of his events which are of a scale, comprehensiveness and eye for detail without equal."[10] For some time, there had been questions asked about Rodenstock's wines, in particular the authenticity of that Jefferson bottle sold by Broadbent to Forbes on that record-breaking night in December 1985.

The murmurings of suspicion were first cast in an article by the *New York Times* before the first bid had been placed. Broadbent told the *Times* reporter that the Christie's glass experts had "vouched for the authenticity of the bottle and engraving date, that the cork was original and covered with an original wax seal. 'We've taken every precaution short of pulling the cork. . . . But knowing Rodenstock, having the 1784 Yquem—it must be right. He's a wealthy man and not after money. It took a lot of persuading to get him to sell it. Of course, who can actually prove it is authentic?'"[11] In the same article, Broadbent said that he had drunk a bottle of 1784 Yquem from the cache with both Rodenstock and the then proprietor of Yquem, Count de Lur-Saluces, who had declared it "remarkable, unbelievable—soft and sweet, beautiful balance." In an effort to prove the veracity of the stash, Rodenstock claimed he had sent samples off to a laboratory for analysis and that he could prove that the bottle dated from somewhere between 1780 and 1800. He also claimed he had correspondence that validated the ownership, which raised eyebrows among Jefferson scholars. One of those experts was Lucia "Cinder" Stanton (née Goodwin), who worked at Jefferson's Monticello home between 1979 and 2011, becoming the world's foremost expert on Jefferson's personal life and slavery at Monticello. If there was anyone who could trace how the bottles had come to be in an undisclosed Parisian cellar, it was she.

Based on her daily dealings with Jefferson's comprehensive diaries and correspondence, Stanton too cast doubt on the authenticity of the bottles. Unbeknownst to the public, she was scouring the vast archives of Monticello for evidence and finding plenty of holes. Her research formed what came to be known as the Monticello Report, and more than twenty years later, it would be used by a billionaire wine collector as the basis of a legal action against Christie's. However, in the lead-up to the auction, the historian made it clear that she, unlike Rodenstock and Broadbent, was doubtful of the wines' authenticity: "I am unable to make the same leap of faith they have, by connecting the bottles to Jefferson because they bear his initials."[12] Indeed, Jefferson never ordered or received any 1787 wines while he was in Paris, according to the records. By the time he left Paris for the US, the wines wouldn't even have been bottled, Stanton noted. Admittedly, he had purchased 1784 Yquem, which was one of the wines discovered in the secret cellar, but there were no records of the Lafitte 1787, the wine that fetched a six-figure sum, while Brane Mouton didn't get a single mention in Jefferson's notes or accounts. Despite the lack of evidence and hazy backstory, the well-respected Rodenstock, Broadbent, and Christie's experts became the rubber stamp that many wine lovers relied on.

Harvard alumna Stanton had plenty of documentation at her disposal to conduct her research into Jefferson's wine cellar: the president was an almost obsessive note taker and record keeper. Before his arrival in the French capital, he was already developing an interest in wine. He had a taste for the wines from the volcanic island of Madeira and was convinced that his native Virginia could be a great place to make wine, but his attempts at growing grapes were thwarted not only by nature but also grape thieves. His inner wine nerd was naturally nurtured in France; he spent three years in Paris (1784 to 1787) as a representative of the fledgling United States of America, and a sabbatical around the country's regions cemented his love of all things vinous.

It took an accident to make the sabbatical happen; while in Paris, the Virginian fell and broke his wrist. The break was slow to heal, and he was advised to bathe it in the mineral waters of Aix-en-Provence, nearly 500 miles to the south. In February 1787, he told his eldest daughter that he'd be taking the doctor's advice. She was less sure of its medical benefits: "I am inclined to think that your voyage is rather for your pleasure than for your health."[13] Jefferson almost admitted as much: "Other consideration also concurred. Instruction, amusement and abstraction from business, of which I had too much at Paris."[14] His three-month tour de France began on February 28, but it was not all play; his travel diary was a meticulous study of the country, documenting everything from the cost of bread (3 sous—there were 20 sous in a franc) or manure (10 sous for 100 pounds) or even a donkey (1–3 Louis d'or, equivalent to 20–60 francs), to where to stay or how vines were planted in 1787. From Champagne, through Burgundy, and south toward the Rhône Valley and the Mediterranean coast, Jefferson describes rural scenes, crops grown, and agricultural practices. Vines and wines inevitably make regular appearances. The reader finds that remarkably little has changed since then in the parcellated nature of Burgundy's vineyards, while the best whites of the northern Rhône continue to come from the same amphitheater-like vineyard that Jefferson singled out—Château Grillet (Grillé in Jefferson's notes) in Condrieu.[15]

Having journeyed south to his intended destination, he immersed himself in the healing waters of Aix-en-Provence. Many dips of the wrist later, he saw little improvement from its soothing minerals, so he decided to do what we would all do when we are in pain: cross the Alps on the back of a mule. His brief foray into Italy introduced him to the Nebiule (Nebbiolo) grape of Piedmont, the one responsible for producing the regal reds of the region: Barolo and Barbaresco. He also went on a reconnaissance mission to discover how parmesan was made. Around two weeks after he'd made the uncomfortable three-day journey across the Alps from France to Italy, Jefferson was on the return leg, ready for a visit to Sète, home to some of France's most ingenious wine blenders-cum-adulterers, before making his way via canal from the Mediterranean coast to the Atlantic fringe of Bordeaux for a class in claret. It was here that he would take a crash course in the great and the good of the Gironde. From the reams since written about Thomas Jefferson and Bordeaux, and the prices paid for bottles he supposedly owned, it might seem like he spent a lifetime there. He visited for just four days.

His trip to this port city was not his first encounter with its wines. His accounts show he had ordered wines from what remain Bordeaux's most prestigious estates today: Château Haut-Brion, Margaux, and Lafite ("de la Fite"), along with white wine from the area named Graves. In a letter to the owner of Lafite, Jefferson implies that there are doubts in the late eighteenth century about the authenticity of wines bearing such famous names, and that only estate-bottled wines would assure him of the provenance: "If it would be possible to have them bottled and packed at your estate it would doubtless be a guarantee that the wine was genuine, and the drawing off and so forth well done."[16] It's an oft-quoted line, used as evidence that buying direct from the château was the only way to assure authenticity, and yet the only time he managed to buy wine bottled at source was from Château d'Yquem. What's more, most of his wine orders were fulfilled by acquaintances, colleagues, or merchants, so he was hardly practicing what he preached. Jefferson wine expert John Hailman has also noted that the former president may have written a lot about Bordeaux but his orders were negligible and even those weren't particularly successful: correspondence took so long that purchases were missed, wines that weren't available were swapped for others, and orders went astray. He "only placed three orders: one for Haut-Brion, one for Yquem, and one for Lafite. Only in the case of Yquem did he receive what he ordered [in 1788]."[17] The Haut-Brion didn't turn up—he was sent Château Margaux as a replacement, while there was no Lafite available and, after what can only be called a cock-up, Jefferson canceled the order and set sail for America.

The evidence seems to suggest that when he left Paris, the contents of his cellar included some bottles of white Graves, which he didn't seem to like, a little Château Haut-Brion, and Château Margaux. And yet Rodenstock uncovered bottles of Lafite and Château Brane Mouton, which Jefferson never ordered, in the mysterious Parisian cellar, alongside Yquem and Margaux. Despite the lack of documentation for these wines—which was out of character for Jefferson—it wasn't beyond the realm of possibility that these bottles were genuine. A generous admirer might have sent him several personalized bottles of his favorite wines as a gift, although he would likely have recorded it. The wines he didn't order or receive, according to his records, simply may have been another example of his Bordeaux contacts swapping one wine for another, which wasn't unusual. Did someone else order the bottles for him in anticipation of his planned return to Paris? After all, it was only when he landed on American soil that George Washington sprang the unrefusable secretary of state job on him, upending his plans for a return to a country that had captured his heart as well as his palate. It wasn't impossible—Jefferson artifacts had previously turned up out of the blue without any paperwork to verify them, but Stanton was quick to point out they generally "have passed to us from Jefferson's descendants, cases in which provenance is so strong that authenticity is unquestioned."[18] The case of the wine stash was rather more questionable.

The timing of the discovery of the cache was opportune, however: America was gearing up for the 200th anniversary of the Constitution. Patriotic parades, dove releases, gun salutes, and reenactments of its signing became ubiquitous; commemorative mugs and coins couldn't be made fast enough, and memorabilia relating to any of the founding fathers, including Jefferson, attracted a premium. What's more, the vineyard at Monticello had just been replanted according to Jefferson's plans and was set to produce its first harvest in 1988. If there was a time to discover Jefferson's wines, it was the mid-1980s.

There was an unprecedented appetite for fine and rare wines and prices soared accordingly. Finance writers and mainstream media were suddenly talking about wine as an alternative investment to stocks and shares. In the summer of 1987, US money magazine *Changing Times* claimed, "If you're only now getting serious about collecting fine wines, the missed opportunities are so numerous you may find yourself awash in self-pity."[19] It quoted a survey of Bordeaux wine prices at auction from 1970 to 1982 that revealed an impressive year-on-year increase of 23 percent. What's more, the finest Bordeaux wines from superlative years, like Château Lafite 1961, were selling for close to $5,000 a case, when they had cost in the neighborhood of $80 upon release. The cost of a case of 1961 from the small Pomerol producer-turned-cult-wine Petrus was a hundred times what it had been two decades earlier. The *Changing Times* article coincided with the publication of *Liquid Assets*, a book dedicated to wines that would not only quench your thirst but could also boost your bank balance, according to its wine-merchant author.[20] For true wine lovers, the birth of the phrase "investment-grade wine" had a whiff of decay and would cause a stain darker than a red wine spill.

If anyone could turn up a stash like the Jefferson bottles, it was Hardy Rodenstock. He had already turned up the scarcest of Bordeaux beauties and Sauternes sweeties in places as unlikely as Scotland, St. Petersburg, and even South America. Germany's weekly current affairs magazine *Stern* dubbed him "the Indiana Jones of bottles" and served up the story with a large splash of satire.[21] He "claims to have tracked down ancient wines in mysterious places, in the humid latitudes of the Venezuelan tropics as well as in the icy lengths of the glorious Soviet Union when it still existed."[22] His ability to sniff out such rarities was uncanny, and although he was turning a profit, he was also considered extremely generous with his finds.

It is that sense of achievement in going undetected that has long spurred wine fraudsters to perpetuate their criminality, explains Ezra Stotland in "White Collar Criminals": "Sometimes individuals' motivation for crime may have originally been relative deprivation, greed, threat to continued goal attainment and so forth. However, as they found themselves successful at this crime, they began to gain some secondary delight in the knowledge that they are fooling the world, that they are showing their superiority to others."[23]

Indeed, Rodenstock was happy to share his bottles from this Parisian treasure trove, as well as sell them. His first deal was with a fellow wine lover in Munich. Hans-Peter Frericks was a wealthy businessman whose love for one Pomerol wine had earned him the nickname "King Petrus" in elite wine circles. He purchased a bottle of 1784 Lafitte and a 1787 Lafitte from Rodenstock before the record-breaking Christie's auction took place and reportedly paid less than $10,000 for the pair. Following the jaw-dropping December auction, Frericks thought he'd hit the jackpot. Not only did he have a bottle of Thomas Jefferson's wine, he had two, and he was ready to sell. Despite having bought most of his fine wines from Christie's, he made the decision to approach rival auction house Sotheby's, which had established its own wine department. It was a bolt from the blue. One of the founders of Sotheby's wine department, David Molyneux-Berry, received Frericks's letter and recalls, "I've been chasing this man for some time. He's called King Petrus because he had one of the finest collections of Petrus in the world, but he'd never bought from Sotheby's—he was a Christie's client. I'd always tried to get hold of him, but he didn't want to, never played ball. Suddenly he writes to me and says he's thinking of selling his cellar. . . . I thought 'Strange,' but I was on the next plane."[24] But things didn't go the way he hoped.

Molyneux-Berry traveled to Munich with a German-speaking colleague who could act as a translator. They arrived at the gates to Frericks's swanky house in an upmarket part of the city and headed straight for the cellar, a magnificent shrine to the fermented grape. Frericks had plucked several jewels from his collection for Molyneux-Berry to inspect, and first up was the 1787 Lafitte that he'd bought from Rodenstock. "I felt the bottle, held the bottle . . . I knew it wasn't right," said Molyneux-Berry.[25] He then picked up an imperial of Mouton Rothschild 1924, of which only three were ever made. It had an imperial-sized label on it, but Mouton Rothschild only had one label size for all its bottles at that time; in addition, the colors seemed off. Molyneux-Berry now had a theory. To test it, he asked his colleague, Heinrich, who was not a wine expert, to lend a hand.

> Frericks had a brilliant cellar book—everything was there: who he'd bought it from, the price, when, everything, and I just gave him [Heinrich] the book and said "I'm going to call out certain bottles [that I think are fakes] to you, and if a certain name appears as the supplier—and you know the name [Rodenstock]—just say yes." So, I said:
> "Mouton '24?"
> [Heinrich said] "Yes."
> "Mouton '46."
> "Yes."

"Mouton '51."

"Yes."

"Mouton '54."

"Yes."

"Mouton '56."

"Yes."[26]

Things did not look good for Frericks—nor Rodenstock. Frericks may have had a wonderful cellar with many genuine wines, but the Sotheby's expert realized the cellar was also "stuffed full of fakes." As a result, Sotheby's refused to sell the collection. Frericks was understandably unhappy and wanted justice. The man he had called a friend seemed to have sold him duds. He wanted proof, and it just so happened that local scientists might be able to help him. The German Research Center for Environment and Health, based in Munich, could carbon date wine, and in 1991, Frericks sent the bottle of 1787 Lafitte engraved with Thomas Jefferson's initials to the lab in a bid to get a birth certificate for his wine. The lab would test for the unstable isotope carbon 14, which decays over thousands of years and is commonly used to date fossils. However, when the world started using and testing nuclear weapons, the amount of carbon 14 in the atmosphere dramatically increased, particularly in the 1950s and 1960s. Frericks's wine had far more carbon 14 than it would have had if it had been produced in 1787. According to the report from the lab, "Either all the wine is from 1962 or there is a mixture of old and young wine, with more than about 40 percent of the bottle contents being younger than 1962."[27] Frericks sued Rodenstock, but Rodenstock claimed Frericks had doctored the contents of the bottle after he bought it. As The New Yorker explained, "In December 1992, a German court found in his [Frericks's] favor, holding that Rodenstock 'adulterated the wine or knowingly offered adulterated wine.' Rodenstock appealed and sued Frericks for defamation. (The matter was ultimately settled out of court.)"[28]

Rodenstock was at pains to offer scientific evidence for the genuineness of the wines he had found in the secret Parisian cellar, citing testing he'd had done to disprove the doubters. In his note on the 1787 Lafitte, Broadbent recalls the testing of a bottle in a Munich laboratory in 1987 that reported what Frericks had found: there was at least some wine in the bottle that was made after 1960. But in 1992, a half bottle was analyzed by the same pair of scientists who had helped carbon date and upend the myth of the Turin shroud, and Broadbent reported the wine in the half bottle was deemed "absolutely correct."[29] However, a closer inspection of the findings revealed that the pair of scientists had actually found that the contents of the bottle, although containing no post-nuclear-era wine, dated from between 1795 and 1865, but the bottles unearthed by Rodenstock were all dated before 1795. Rodenstock spun the story as if he had been vindicated. Meanwhile, an investigative journalist sought out the chemist Heinz Eschenauer, who Rodenstock claimed had confirmed that the cork from one of the Jefferson bottles of 1787 Yquem did hail from the pre-1800 period. But a little digging revealed that wasn't the conclusion at all. According to Eschenauer, "From all the results that Rodenstock got from me," it was impossible "to draw any conclusions about the age of the wine."[30]

It wasn't just Frericks and Forbes who became owners of some of these dubious bottles in the late 1980s. *Wine Spectator* owner Marvin Shanken, who was outbid by Forbes at the original Jefferson auction, secured his own half bottle of Château Margaux, while a Jordanian bought a bottle of 1784 Yquem. Unfortunately for Rodenstock and Christie's, US billionaire Bill Koch had also bought four of the bottles, and while many cases of fraud go unreported—the victim is generally a white middle-aged man who does not want to publicly admit he has been scammed— Koch was prepared to admit he'd been duped and go after the perpetrators.

The billionaire industrialist was a wine connoisseur as well as collector of samurai swords and old Greek coins, and had bought a quartet of Jefferson bottles in 1988, the year that Rodenstock appeared on the cover of *Wine Spectator* magazine. Based on the fact that Broadbent and Christie's had given the Jefferson wines the seal of approval, Koch was delighted to have these rare editions in his cellar. Later, while reading up on his favorite drink, he came across several articles casting doubt on the wines he had spent more than $300,000 on, and he also discovered the Frericks case. According to legal documents, Koch hired lawyers to investigate in 1993, but the evidence was inconclusive: "Some [tests] confirmed the wine as authentic and some . . . indicated that it was counterfeit."[31] Koch would not return to the Jefferson bottles until the turn of the century. In the meantime, Rodenstock continued to host fine dinners and lavish events, but he was growing increasingly irate, lashing out at anyone who dared to question the integrity of the wines he had served or sold. He called one skeptic, a writer for the leading French wine magazine *La revue du vin de France*, "an outspoken hater of Germans," while a Swiss critic was lambasted for the "steaming shit you left everywhere."[32] Despite the nagging doubts and the continued lack of clarity over the provenance of those Jefferson bottles and more, Rodenstock could still draw a crowd. In 1998, a week-long Yquem extravaganza attracted some of the globe's leading wine writers, winemakers, collectors, and even German soccer legend Franz Beckenbauer. Jancis Robinson attended the event and dared to mention, in the *Financial Times*, the doubts that were circulating about the authenticity of the wines. She too was on the receiving end of Rodenstock's wrath: "The result was a red-hot fax machine for the next few days as he fired off copies of pages from auction catalogues explaining various provenances."[33]

It was about this time that the chatter about fraud began making fine-wine merchants and auctioneers nervous. Serena Sutcliffe, who had joined Sotheby's wine department in the early 1990s, had become increasingly aware of a rise in the number of fakes a decade earlier. "The motivation of course was money—surprise, surprise—and that happens when wines go up phenomenally in price, and that's what they did in the second half of the '80s," she said. "It never used to be a trade that had a problem. Because the people who bought fine wines were a small group, they knew what they were doing and there were no ridiculous price hikes." But the trade did have a problem, and the top brass in London's wine scene met to discuss the issue and attempt to tackle it. Over the course of three meetings in a London hotel, however, no agreement could be reached. "It was absolutely clear that we were not going to get a common policy or consensus," Sutcliffe recalled. "They were frightened of losing their competitive edge."[34]

BILLIONAIRE'S "MOOSE PISS"

In 2000, Koch turned his attention back to the Thomas Jefferson wines. He had two bottles of 1787 Brane Mouton, as well as a bottle each of 1784 and 1787 Lafitte, and he was ready to pay for the best technology to determine if he had bought wines made before the Bastille was stormed. He sent samples of the wines to the Massachusetts-based Woods Hole Oceanographic Institution, which set about determining their age through yet more carbon dating. The results didn't provide conclusive proof: according to legal files documenting his case against Christie's, the report "showed that there was a 26.5% probability that the wine was from the period between the year 1680 and 1740 and a 68.9% probability that the wine was from between 1800 and 1960. The report indicated only a 4.6% probability that the wine was from the period between 1740 and 1800."[35] The judge also pointed out that there was a wide margin for error. Koch decided not to take any action. He had another 40,000 bottles in not one but two cellars that he could uncork instead.

Koch could also enjoy the magnificent art hanging on the walls of his homes in Cape Cod and Palm Beach. Such was his collection that in 2005, the Boston Museum of Fine Arts ran a two-month exhibition sourced from Koch's personal collection of paintings and sculptures, as well as some of his more eclectic acquisitions: firearms, including the gun that killed Jesse James and General Custer's hunting rifle, were on display. The plan was also to include the Jefferson bottles. But when the museum requested proof of provenance for the exhibit, it became apparent that the backstory of the Jefferson bottles was as shaky as a maraca. Koch unearthed the unpublished report written by Monticello historian Stanton, who had queried the authenticity of the stash before the first Jefferson bottle went under the hammer. When Koch read that this Jefferson expert could find "no solid connecting evidence"[36] between Jefferson and the engraved bottles, it would be an understatement to say he was not amused. He also learned that among the wine bottles found during archaeological digs at Monticello, there were "none bearing any sort of engraving, and no references to Jefferson's asking for engraved bottles has been found."[37] There were occasions when Jefferson requested that cases be marked so he could distinguish his wines from those he had ordered on behalf of friends and colleagues, but he did not use "Th.J.," which was the marking on the Rodenstock bottles, explained Stanton; he used a colon to separate his initials, "Th:J."

Stanton found herself on the receiving end of a torrent of abuse from Rodenstock after she dared to question the authenticity of the bottles. Never mind that she was an impartial academic who had devoted her career to Jefferson's life; according to Rodenstock, one "should courteously keep back one's dubious and unfounded remarks and one shouldn't make oneself important in front of the press." Stanton's colleagues backed her unreservedly, but that didn't appease the German. "Can you study 'Jefferson' at university?" Rodenstock asked. "She doesn't know anything about wine in connection with Jefferson, doesn't know what bottles from the time frame 1780–1800 look like, doesn't know how they taste."[38]

The fact that so few genuinely know the authentic taste of a wine dating from more than a century ago has been an issue since Roman times. Broadbent was the world's authority on old, rare wines, but could he guarantee that the 1784 Yquem or 1787 Lafitte was genuine from taste alone? Even if someone had tasted a genuine old wine many times—a 1945 Mouton or 1811 Yquem—wine changes over time. What's more, two bottles of the same wine that have never left the estate's cellar, open and tasted on the same day, can taste different because of bottle variation: the way a wine has been stored over time, the health of its cork stopper, and a multitude of other factors make picking out fake wines an inexact science. It can be an expensive, lengthy process to prove the truth behind a well-made fake bottle, and results have often proven inconclusive. Rodenstock was perceived to be a true wine collector who had an aura of authenticity bestowed upon him by the illustrious guests he invited to his tastings. He harnessed that trust to enhance both his bank account and his standing in elite wine circles.

But with Stanton's findings now in his possession, and surrounded by a crack team of experts, Koch ramped up the pressure. Money was no object: he hired the best investigators, including former FBI agent Jim Elroy and ex-Sotheby's man Molyneux-Berry, who had refused Frericks's cellar. Now Koch's cellar was inspected bottle by bottle. Meanwhile, Elroy called in a master engraver and another ex-FBI colleague to inspect the markings on the bottle. In 1985, the relevant Christie's specialist had vouched that the Th.J. inscriptions on the bottles were consistent with an eighteenth-century wheel engraver. It was time to put that endorsement to the test. In an attempt to re-create the markings on a bottle, Koch's men used an authentic wheel engraver and quickly realized this machine could not engrave neatly, nor could it make the perfectly round periods found on the bottles. The likely tool? A dentist's drill, they concluded.

In the summer of 2006, Koch finally sued Hardy Rodenstock, which revived the media's interest in the case and led to an exposé by German magazine *Stern*. Its investigative reporters knocked on the door of his house in Bad Marienberg, the small spa town that was one of Rodenstock's less glitzy addresses—he also owned pads in Munich, Monte

Carlo, and Marbella. It was here that a family printing business admitted to printing old wine labels for him over a period of seven years. Rodenstock denied the claims: he had commissioned flyers and concert posters from this company but never wine labels, he said. A member of the family, Rudiger Kluth, recalled reproducing fine wine labels for Rodenstock some thirty years ago earlier: "If my memory doesn't deceive me, Rothschild was there, Petrus, many well-known names." The vintages? "Late nineteenth, early twentieth century, really really ancient! I thought to myself, my goodness! The labels look really old."[39] The journalist then tracked down a former attendee at one of Rodenstock's tastings who had received a gift of a framed label from an imperial of 1945 Mouton Rothschild. The 1945 vintage was particularly special for the estate, marking a return to peace and the homecoming of its Jewish owner, Baron Philippe de Rothschild. Following a hard frost that cut the potential size of the crop and led to intensely concentrated fruit, the weather was then kind to the vines and the people, both of which had suffered greatly under German occupation. To mark the end of the conflict, Rothschild commissioned an artist to create a special "V for Victory" label for the 1945 wine. It marked the beginning of a new tradition: every year since, an acclaimed artist has designed a unique label for the Mouton Rothschild bottle, from Kandinsky to Kapoor, Haring to Hockney. A label of this special bottle was something to cherish, but the recipient of Rodenstock's framed label agreed the journalists could send it to France for inspection by the team at the château, as well as to a Bordeaux laboratory for specialist testing. The wine estate's manager confirmed the label's paper, coloring, and misplaced letters meant it was "clearly wrong to the naked eye."[40] The laboratory also found a glue on the back of several labels that was not produced until decades after the wine was supposedly made.

The evidence was stacked against Rodenstock, who failed to show up in the New York court and told the judge he had no intention of taking part in the case. Rodenstock's default meant the court automatically ruled in favor of Koch, but he wouldn't get his money back from Roden-stock or have the satisfaction of seeing him serve a prison sentence on the other side of the Atlantic. He was also thwarted in his suit against Christie's. Koch made the case that the auction house "promoted as authentic the Jefferson bottles," which he trusted and relied on in mak-ing his purchases, when in fact, "Christie's knew or was reckless in not knowing of the wines' dubious authority." However, he filed the suit more than twenty years after he had bought the wines and far too long after he started having doubts about their authenticity. The district judge delivered a pithy summary: "For wine, timing is critical. The same is true for causes of action."[41]

Nevertheless, Koch's cases spelled the demise of the world's "most extravagant wine collector"[42] and also left a blemish on the otherwise stellar career of auctioneer Broadbent. But this was just the beginning for Koch, who would spend the next decade taking on the vendors of 421 fraudulent bottles in his cellar, on which he had spent $4.5 million. The cost of the cases would far exceed the money he had lost on those dodgy bottles, but for the billionaire, it was small change. "I want to shine a bright light on this whole fraud to show how bad it is," he said in 2013. "I'm tired of the aggravation of being violated by these con artists and crooks."[43]

What was in these fake bottles if it wasn't Yquem or Lafite? "Moose piss?"[44] ventured Koch. Or the world's most expensive red-wine vine-gar? That was effectively what became of the £105,000 bottle of 1787 Lafitte. While on display in its immaculate glass case in Manhattan, the heat and the bright gallery lights shining on the precious exhibit had shriveled the cork, which dropped into the wine. It was a sour end for all concerned. "I wish Jefferson had drunk the damn bottle himself and saved me the expense," rued Forbes.[45] His anger should not have been directed at the third president of the United States but the wine dealers trying to profit from his name 200 years later.

9

A MESSAGE TO
YOU, RUDY

SPRING MEANS ONE THING in the fine-wine calendar: *en primeur* week. Thousands of wine merchants, bedecked in their uniform of red trousers and dark blazer, descend on Bordeaux for the annual launch of the latest vintage. It is an elaborate mating ritual: the region's producers fan their plumage, courting the world's wine media and merchants, seeking their approval and custom. Processions of rental cars crisscross the Dordogne and Garonne rivers, carrying the good and great of the fine wine trade. Thereafter, verdicts are published, prices set, and orders made.

The wines on offer are not ready to drink, however. They have been drawn from the barrels in which they are still maturing and are blended to reflect the final cuvée that will be bottled more than a year later. These unfinished wines can taste rather raw, particularly in what the wine trade likes to call "challenging" seasons, which typically means "it was pretty bad so we're going to roll it in glitter and try and sell it to you." It's in these lesser years that the Bordeaux winemakers really lay it on thick: the winemaker or owner of the estate will shake hands, kiss cheeks, and deliver a glowing introduction to the vintage. There is lavish indoctrination: a fancy lunch or sumptuous dinner with rare wines pulled from the cellar are all part of the sales strategy.

Within weeks of returning from Bordeaux, the fine-wine merchants, whose financial year can rely on a successful Bordeaux en primeur campaign, are on tenterhooks. When will the first estate hit the go button on the sales campaign, and will they ask too much for the wines (yet again)? The tension is both palpable and slightly absurd: no one can get their hands on a bottle of the stuff for at least another year despite having to pay for it up front, and then most of the red wines won't be ready to drink for another decade. In the wine equivalent of the hundred-meter sprint, no château wants to come out of the blocks too early, particularly if they've misjudged the market and priced their wines too high or too low. Likewise, once the starter's gun goes off, everyone's quick to join the race. After securing a few cases of the finest wines, merchants will offer their most loyal claret drinkers a case or two. Those who bought Château Lafite or Latour consistently over the past five or ten years have first right of refusal. There's also some vinous bundling going on to shift less popular wines: a number of the region's finest producers own vineyards in lesser areas of Bordeaux or make the delicious yet difficult-to-shift sweet wines of Sauternes and will only sell an allocation of the best wine if you agree to buy the less desirable wines as part of a package deal.

The idea of buying an item that you won't receive for at least a year and consume a decade later is a peculiarity of this futures system, but in the early 2000s, it made sense for wine lovers to buy *en primeur*. The wines would never be cheaper. Having purchased Château Calon-Ségur 2003, primarily because it had a heart on the label, and Lynch-Bages 2000, because a former boss called it Lunch Bags, I had every intention of drinking these wines five or ten years later. But over the course of the next decade, the value of many of Bordeaux's top estates increased massively. The £350 twelve-bottle case of Lunch Bags soared in value to £2000, which made drinking it over lunch difficult to stomach.

The rising prices of Bordeaux's finest wines were once again hard to ignore. It had happened in the early 1970s, followed by a crash; in the 1980s, followed by a slump; and then the noughties came along and repeated history: dozens of articles appeared in the mainstream press extolling the benefits of fine wine as an alternative investment—even teetotalers couldn't fail to realize there was plenty of cash to be made. The numbers were impressive: in the ten years leading up to August 2011, wine offered an annual return of nearly 15 percent to the savvy investor, while the Financial Times Stock Exchange offered an unimpressive return of close to zero in the same period. Prices of the world's finest wines, known as blue chip investment-grade wine, were experiencing a trajectory similar to that of gold as the super-rich in emerging markets like China sought out cases of the very best Bordeaux reds and rarest Burgundies.

The International Monetary Fund also took an interest in wine as an alternative asset class, publishing a paper comparing the returns made on a barrel of oil versus a barrel of wine. Using data from the London-based fine-wine trading platform Liv-ex, its authors calculated that fine wine prices had risen a whopping 269 percent in dollar terms between January 2000 and July 2008.[1] When the world's finances went into meltdown in late 2008, wine prices likewise tumbled, but they recovered within eighteen months—if only the rest of the global economy had followed suit. The market was thrown a lifeline by the Hong Kong government, which abolished duty on wine in 2008, and the Chinese wine market lapped up Bordeaux first growths as if they were luxury fashion brands. Châteaux upped their wine prices to record highs on the back of two excellent harvests, 2009 and 2010, and it seemed like fine wine had entered a new pricing era.

It couldn't, and wouldn't, last.

Many investors were attracted by the Bordeaux wines of 2009 and 2010, as well as the wines of previous harvests, which now seemed a good value compared with the release of these two expensive vintages. Fellow collectors had purchased Lynch-Bages 2000 for £350 (roughly $500) on release, but it released its 2009 vintage at £845 (approximately $1,300), an increase of 125 percent compared with the previous year. Lynch-Bages wasn't the only château to hike prices. Suddenly, loyal collectors couldn't afford to buy the new wines *en primeur*. What's more, it didn't make financial sense to buy these wines and cover the cost of cellaring them for the next decade when it was possible to buy older wines that were ready to drink at prices far cheaper than those just released. The 2010 wines may have been—and remain—excellent, but the eye-watering prices had left drinkers with a sour taste.

While the Bordelais were getting greedy, one of their biggest customers was becoming increasingly abstemious. The arrival of Xi Jinping as Chinese president in late 2012 ushered in a new era of austerity. Gone were the extravagant state dinners, lavish banquets, and flashy wine bottles to lubricate wheeling and dealing in the corridors of power. The phones of wine dealers in Hong Kong stopped ringing. Just a few months earlier, reputable wine merchants had recommended spending thousands of dollars on cases of Lafite, Latour, and Mouton Rothschild as a worthwhile investment. Those unlucky enough to believe them found themselves with a rapidly depreciating asset, or, at best, a case of claret that was stagnating like a dirty pond.

On the eve of the arrest of wine fraudster Rudy Kurniawan in 2012, the fine-wine market was nursing a hangover, and worse was to come as the world woke up to its unsavory side. The bull market had been intoxicating in the first decade of the 2000s, and many wine buffs with legitimate collections built up over decades cashed in, selling off many bottles they would never get around to drinking in their lifetime at record prices. There was money to be made, and Kurniawan was not the only one who wanted a piece of the pie.

WOULD YOU LIKE A CAR WITH YOUR WINE?

The state of Texas is a world away from the wine trade's epicenter. The rarest wines on earth are traded like works of fine art in the cosmopolitan cities of New York, London, and Hong Kong. But in the weeks leading up to Christmas 2015, the eyes of the wine world were laser-focused on an auction house in Pflugerville, an unremarkable town eighteen miles north of the state capital, Austin. Auctioneer Gaston and Sheehan was selling off 5,000 bottles of wine—both rare and ordinary—alongside an impounded 1993 Honda Accord, fridges from a liquidated restaurant, and a two-seater swing set.

This was no high-brow wine auction. Champagne and canapés were certainly not served to wealthy bidders as they raised their paddles in a gilt-edged ballroom. The auctioneer's stock-in-trade was selling off seized goods for clients like the US Marshals Service, the Internal Revenue Service, various unnamed law enforcement agencies, and bankruptcy companies. So why on earth was Gaston and Sheehan selling off some of the finest and rarest wines in the world, several of them worth thousands of dollars a bottle?

The previous owner of these wines was Rudy Kurniawan, a man who traded fine dining for prison food after having conned many respected wine collectors to buy fine and rare bottles that turned out to be fakes. Kurniawan was handed a ten-year sentence for selling counterfeits and committing wire fraud. But not all of his wines were bogus; among the bottles seized from his house by the FBI on a cool morning in March 2012, nearly 5,000 were deemed by experts to be genuine. For those willing to take a punt, they could pick up rare vintages of the most prestigious estates in Bordeaux, coveted domaines in Burgundy, and luxury Champagne brands.

Given Kurniawan's indiscretions, these auction lots were a case of buyer beware. Yet for many years, wealthy collectors and connoisseurs were part of an exclusive drinking group that included a Hollywood director and a high-flying New York realtor. They would spend evenings sipping Rudy's wines and declare them complex and profound. No questions were asked about their provenance. Kurniawan mixed with the glitterati, wining and dining in some of the America's most exclusive restaurants, driving fast cars, and flashing cash. He was attracting media attention for his lavish wine sprees, dropping $500,000 in a single afternoon on wine and shelling out $75,000 on a case of half bottles of Bordeaux's Château Cheval Blanc 1947.

The rather geeky looking, bespectacled Indonesian was also generous with his wines. A *Los Angeles Times* reporter met Rudy at one of his favorite restaurants in late 2006, where he opened what was supposedly a rare bottle of red Burgundy: Domaine Roumier's Bonnes-Mares 1962. Over lunch, he cradled a two-month-old chihuahua inside his white leather jacket and the staff didn't blink when it lapped at the water glass. He boasted about his social circles, the historic wines he had tasted, and his lavish dinners, which included flying chefs to Los Angeles to cook for his friends.[2] At his trial, his American Express account showed he spent big: in 2007, he racked up $6 million on his credit card, with more than $200,000 spent at luxury goods store Hermès. He returned to the store the following year, engaging in a $350,000 shopping spree.

Despite his magnanimity, Kurniawan clammed up when it came to his roots. He was reluctant to discuss his family. His father, he told the *LA Times* reporter, gave him an Indonesian surname that was "different from the family's Chinese name to allow him to maintain his autonomy." The real Rudy Kurniawan is a brilliant Indonesian badminton player. Even those who guzzled thousands of dollars of wine with the grape pretender didn't really know who he was or where he came from, but Kurniawan, whose real name is Zhen Wang Huang, charmed his way into a small circle of wealthy wine-loving collectors. He was young, likeable, and had a knowledge of wine that impressed many—the Great Gatsby of the wine world. Where his money came from, no one was quite sure, and Kurniawan was politely evasive. However, the 2016 documentary *Sour Grapes* revealed that his uncles included Eddy Tansil, a fraudster on the run, and Hendra Raharja, a Chinese-born Indonesian banker who committed fraud on an epic scale before fleeing to Australia.[3] No wonder Kurniawan wasn't forthcoming with his family tree.

He was, however, happy to discuss the issue of counterfeits before he was rumbled: "Only after he'd tasted hundreds of bottles did Kurniawan learn how to spot the fakes," it was revealed. "He studies the corks for signs of tampering, knows the telling details of the labels for all of the top wines, and can spot bottle markings that don't match that bottle's label."[4] In an email to Jancis Robinson, wine columnist for the *Financial Times,* later used as evidence at his trial, he wrote, "I'm very careful to ensure empty bottles are trashed or the labels are marked so they can't be reused [by counterfeiters]."[5] But the FBI discovered that his Hotmail account showed otherwise: he asked Robert Bohr, then wine director at downtown New York restaurant CRU, to send him empty bottles that still contained the sediment left behind after an old wine had been decanted, "to look original" for what he claimed was a photo shoot.

Michael Egan, the expert witness at Kurniawan's trial in New York, is based in the city of Bordeaux. He's actually a Londoner who uprooted his Irish wife and two young daughters for a new life in this part of southwest France in 2005. We arrange to meet in Bordeaux's city center one evening during *en primeur* week. En route, the manager of a renowned wine estate, who would later be handed a three-month suspended sentence for adding too much sugar to his wine, whizzed past on a Segway in a tuxedo, on his way to a fancy dinner. At our rather more informal meal, Egan and I shared a plate of cold meat, as well as a strange albeit delicious concoction involving bacon and *frites,* and a bottle of wonderfully ordinary white wine.

Egan's days in the wine world also started out with a very ordinary white wine. "My first job was in Oddbins in London when Liebfraumilch was the most popular white wine," he says. He then landed an entry level job at auction house Sotheby's, where he spent twenty-three years rooting through dusty cellars across Europe, cataloguing and selling fine and rare wines. He is a man who knows what an old bottle should look and feel like.

That's how he ended up in a New York courtroom in December 2013, testifying against one of history's most prolific wine fraudsters. He had a cold at the time, and between throat lozenges and snotty tissues, he walked the courtroom through the fakes and mistakes that led to Kurniawan's downfall. The evidence was stacked against Kurniawan: early one morning, the FBI raided his lavish four-bedroom home in Arcadia, California, which he shared with his elderly mother. They found rooms full of damning evidence. In the spare bedrooms, there were boxes of unlabeled wines and bags of corks; downstairs there were silver cups containing wax to seal the tops of bottles, hundreds of corks and a machine to insert them, drawers containing reams of fine wine labels and glue, as well as rubber stamps bearing the names of famous wine estates and rare vintages. "He tried to claim he wanted to wallpaper his house in the labels, but we could prove he was selling items that incorporated all the stuff that was in his house," Egan explains. Unlabeled bottles sat by the sink, and bizarrely, more than a dozen bottles lay on his treadmill. There was no cellar, but the house was unreasonably cold: "The whole house was climate controlled. The thermostat was set very low. And, in fact, in this beautiful, almost million-dollar house, they used space heaters in the two bedrooms. So the entire house was a wine cellar, wine factory," now-retired FBI Special Agent Jim Wynne, who investigated the Kurniawan case, told the court.[6]

The day Kurniawan became America's first wine scammer to be jailed was sweet victory for Bill Koch, who had been a victim of fraudsters before Kurniawan entered the scene. He had filled his cellars with the best wines that money could buy. In 2005, he successfully bid on 2,600 bottles of wine from the cellar of Californian businessman Eric

Greenberg. The lot included historic bottles that purported to be Château Lafite Rothschild 1811, Chateau Latour 1864 and 1865, as well as a magnum of Petrus from 1921. His new delivery, however, included two dozen bottles that after some intense investigation were determined not to be genuine. Koch had a thirst for justice, and almost eight years after buying Greenberg's wines—and several years after the Jefferson cases finally came to an end—a three-week trial was finally uncorked, pitting Koch against Greenberg in court. It was Michael Egan's first appearance on the stand as an expert witness—he didn't know it yet, but it would serve as a warm-up to the Kurniawan trial. "It was scary for the first time during the Greenberg case. You were in the witness box for a long time, with four lawyers on each side. The prosecution would try to discredit you or swing you over to their side, but we had done lots of dry runs in the hotel beforehand. And Eric Greenberg would try to stare you down." The evidence was stacked against Greenberg. Egan remembers, "Eric had sold a slew of fakes via Zachys and he tried to hide behind the auction house, claiming they were culpable. He claimed to be an amateur, but wine authenticator Bill Edgerton had already told Eric that a lot of his wines were duff and he went ahead and sold them anyway."

A WHIFF OF SKUNK

Far away from the cut and thrust of courtrooms, Bill Edgerton has been running his wine appraisal business for more than three decades in Norwalk, Connecticut. However, ferreting out fakes was a relatively new string to his bow. His main business involves the three Ds: damage, divorce, and death, which entails assessing insurance claims for cellars that have been water or heat damaged, and valuing cellars for disgruntled ex-wives and grieving families. It's not glamorous, but someone has to do it. He has even had the unenviable task of checking if wine has been tainted by skunk spray. "There is no training that I know of for detecting bad wines; most people who taste wine are trying to find the best one but typically they are not bad," he says. "I have probably tasted more bad wines than anyone else alive."[7]

When Koch invited Edgerton to inspect his wine collection, it wasn't to root out any skunk taint but to unearth the pretenders. Over the course of a year, Edgerton visited Koch's cellars and, deep in the underground caves that are home to rack upon rack of Bordeaux and Burgundy's finest, he spotted something on a bottle that looked all too familiar. A small sticker with a number and Edgerton's initials on it in red ink was affixed to a suspect bottle. Another stickered bottle turned up, and then another, and another with the remnants of adhesive where once had been his stickers. How had bottles bearing Edgerton's handwriting come to be in Koch's cellar? Edgerton went through his notebooks: he had assessed Eric Greenberg's cellar several years earlier, after doubt was cast over the authenticity of some of his collection. Greenberg had called in Edgerton, who stickered the bottles during his appraisal. While Greenberg claimed that he had no idea that the bottles Koch bought at the Zachys auction were fake, his argument came unstuck with Edgerton's stickers.

The jury in the Greenberg case awarded Koch the money he paid for the twenty-four dodgy bottles—$355,811—as well as $12 million in damages. Having successfully fended off a slew of stiff questions in the courtroom, Egan was approached by the FBI to be the expert witness in an upcoming case involving a man named Rudy Kurniawan. Egan soon found himself on the other side of the Atlantic, holed up in another forgettable New York hotel room for a wine fraud trial. "The Rudy case was more cut and dry because he had been caught red-handed," remembers Egan.

By the time the FBI raided Kurniawan's house in 2012, the wine-collecting community had already realized he was up to no good. As early as 2008, Egan spent ten days inspecting a collection of wines a client had purchased from Kurniawan: "About 90 percent of them were fake." What's more, weeks after the global economy had come crashing to the ground in 2008, Kurniawan had tried to sell some wine through auction house Acker Merrall & Condit, wine that he claimed was produced by Domaine Ponsot, a family-run winery in Burgundy. But the sale was thwarted: the man then at the helm of the winery, fourth-generation winemaker Laurent Ponsot, flew to New York to ensure that the lots were withdrawn from the auction. Ponsot was prompted to make the trip after seeing the Acker Merrall catalogue, which included a 1929 wine from his family's domaine. Alarm bells sounded: his grandfather didn't start estate bottling until 1934, so the wine couldn't possibly exist. Kurniawan was unapologetic: "We try our best to get it right, but it's Burgundy, and sometimes shit happens."[8]

Ponsot was not in a forgiving mood, pursuing Kurniawan for answers about the source of his fraudulent wines. Ponsot worked hard to build a relationship with Kurniawan, and after much persistence, he was able to get Kurniawan to reveal that a man called Pak Hendra—Pak meaning "Mister" in Indonesia—had sold the wines to him. Kurniawan gave Ponsot two phone numbers to call, which proved to be duds. "There was no Indonesian collector. The bottles didn't come from Indonesia. They came from Southern California. It was just another one of Kurniawan's lies. It was more of the magic," prosecutor Jason Hernandez told the court during the trial.[9] It wasn't only Ponsot who was in hot pursuit: the persistent Koch was also on Kurniawan's trail after buying some of his wines in 2005 and 2006. Other wine collectors started to make some very public accusations, including Los Angeles attorney Don Cornwell, who had first met Kurniawan in 2002. "My bullshit meter went off the scale," said Cornwell. "If you told him you'd tasted a rare Roumier [a prized Burgundy producer], he'd say, 'Oh yes, I had three rarer Roumiers at a recent tasting.' He had to dominate the conversation, and he seemed to do this with every person he met."[10] Little did Kurniawan realize that Cornwell was a bulldog who would pursue him relentlessly over the next decade, watching his every move, waiting for him to trip up, and eventually outing him in 2012 on *Wine Berserkers,* a wine enthusiast's web forum. A month after Cornwell's very public finger pointing, the FBI knocked on Kurniawan's door.

The Indonesian scammer entered a not guilty plea at his trial, but it was difficult to explain away the overwhelming evidence. Kurniawan became the first person in the United States to be convicted and jailed for selling counterfeit wines. He was handed a ten-year jail sentence and ordered to forfeit $20 million and pay more than $28 million in restitution to his victims. In a statement, the US Attorney in Manhattan, Preet Bharara, said, "Rudy Kurniawan planned and executed an intricate counterfeit wine scheme, mixing cheaper, more common wines, bottling the mixture into old bottles with fake labels, and then fraudulently selling those bottles for millions of dollars. Now, Kurniawan will trade his life of luxury for time behind bars."[11]

And that is how a Texas auction house whose normal stock in trade is whiteware and used cars came to sell some of the world's finest wines.

HOW TO COMMIT FRAUD

While Rudy had his sophisticated in-house wine factory, it turns out there are easier ways of committing luxury wine fraud: buy a lesser vintage of a wine and change the year to make the bottle more desirable, and more expensive. That's how Bill Edgerton and his daughter Annie, the other member of his wine-sleuthing team, ended up tasting fourteen magnums of fake wine with America's most famous wine critic, Robert Parker. Edgerton had broken the news to a client that his precious magnums weren't genuine, and intrigued by what might be in the bottles, waived his appraisal fee in return for the wines. "During the tasting, it turned out the 1945 Mouton [Rothschild] was more likely a 1941," he says. "It was a legitimate bottle and a capsule of the right period with the requisite amount of sediment but someone had relabeled the 1941 as 1945." The 1945 sells for about five times the price of the 1941, and someone clearly thought it was a risk worth taking. However, it didn't end too badly for Edgerton and his daughter: "Some of the fakes like the '1945' Mouton magnum were so good that we took it to the lunch table and polished it off. Afterwards Annie, who was starring on Broadway in the musical *Mamma Mia*, caught a train back to New York and performed on stage that night. She later wrote that one of the best wines she had ever had was the fake 1945 Mouton."[12]

Another method of committing luxury wine fraud is to fill an original, empty bottle with a cheaper wine. It appears from his seized emails that this was one of Kurniawan's tricks. In the past, it was thought that the finest wines couldn't be replicated convincingly: "Any attempt to fabricate Romanée-Conti [one of Burgundy's finest red wines] would not thus easily answer," claimed one of the nineteenth century's most famous wine writers, Cyrus Redding, "because the finesse, delicacy and perfume of the wine are not to be copied."[13] Yet Kurniawan and others have given it a good go and fooled many experts. In Kurniawan's house, there were recipes detailing the ingredients he used to replicate fine wines, such as a 1945 Mouton Rothschild: two parts Château Cos d'Estournel to one part Château Palmer and one part California Cabernet. It wasn't a cheap exercise, but when the end gain was in the five figures, the sum was greater than its parts.

It is thought that genuine rare-wine bottles can fetch hundreds of dollars on the black market even if they are empty, and there have been tales of restaurants and winemakers smashing their finest bottles after drinking the contents, in a bid to thwart any opportunists. Master of Wine Fiona Morrison and her husband Jacques Thienpont own the tiny estate of Le Pin in the village of Pomerol. Theirs is one of the most coveted wines from the Bordeaux region and with just 6,000 bottles made every year, each costing several thousand dollars, their wine is a prime target for fraudsters. Morrison explains, "When we go to Hong Kong or China for a tasting of our wines, we demand that we witness the destruction of those bottles."[14] This usually means the pair has to negotiate a path through restaurant kitchens to the rubbish bins out the back to smash the bottles.

Luxury wine fraud is difficult and expensive to prove beyond doubt. Although warranties are in place at auction houses that promise to refund buyers if the lot that they purchased turns out not to be authentic, the onus is on the new owner to prove its counterfeit status. At Christie's, for example, if a buyer thinks they have bought a dud, they need to find two experts in the field to corroborate that. And they have to return the bottle to the sales room in its original condition within five years. New York–based auctioneer Zachys only gives collectors ninety days to return the wine. If the wine was put it in a cellar for many years, only to be opened and called out as a fake, the buyer has no leg to stand on. Calling the bluff of wine connoisseurs is how scammers manage to pull the wool over the eyes and lips of so-called experts. Edgerton agrees: "How many people in this world have tasted a legitimate 1900 Château Margaux or 1945 Mouton Rothschild or a 19th century Yquem? Would they know what they were tasting?"

Further developments in science in the early 2000s meant it became easier to pick out the fakes. Radiocarbon dating of wine was first attempted as early as 1954, but it became useful in the 1980s to provide ballpark dates for the Jefferson bottles. Scientists tested for carbon 14 and another radioactive isotope, tritium, but test results could be imprecise, and testing necessitated opening the bottle, which was far from ideal. A less intrusive method of determining the age of the contents of a bottle came about from an unlikely collaboration between the French fraud office and the Centre for Nuclear Studies in Bordeaux. It involves testing wine for the radioactive isotope cesium-137, which does not require opening the bottle. The theory is not dissimilar to carbon 14 testing in that cesium-137 didn't exist in the atmosphere before world superpowers started threatening each other with nuclear annihilation. The fallout from testing nuclear weapons left cesium-137 in our atmosphere, vineyards, and wines. A wine couldn't possibly contain any if it were a pre-nuclear-age wine. The amount of cesium-137 in a wine can also help determine the year of production: a wine that is off the charts with the stuff is likely to be the 1963 vintage, when the isotope's levels hit all-time highs thanks to the escalation of nuclear tests worldwide. And wines made from grapes grown in 1986 offer a hint of nuclear spice because the Chernobyl disaster spewed radioactive particles into the earth's atmosphere in April of that year. Don't panic just yet, however: the bespectacled architect of this pioneering research, Philippe Hubert, stressed that a "wine imbued with Caesium-137 isn't anything to worry about."[15] He calculated that an individual would need to drink 74,000 bottles of radioactive wine from the 1963 vintage *every year* to reach the maximum dose considered safe for humans.

While this method enables owners of rare wines dating from 1952 on to verify whether the wine comes from the year stated on the label, if there is no cesium-137 in the wine, the only conclusion is that it is from a year before 1952. In this case, the bottle would have to be uncorked to conduct further tests. Since the testing costs 250 euros per bottle, this sort of experiment is beyond the budget of all but the wealthiest collector. In any case, it's highly unlikely an auction house like Christie's would take back a wine if the method used to prove the wine's authenticity was, according to their conditions of sale, "unreasonably expensive or impractical" for them to carry out; using nuclear testing to check if your wine was made before the 1950s or not seems both expensive and impractical.

There are more affordable options for top wine estates to prevent another Rudy. Le Pin is one of many French wine estates that has adopted Near Field Communication (NFC) chips—it's the same technology that shoppers use when they wave their credit cards over a payment machine at the grocery store. Smartphone users download an app and scan the chip on the bottle to determine whether or not the bottle is authentic. This technology also allows wine lovers to indulge their inner geek by sending them to a site that tells the user all sorts of wine minutiae, from crop yields to fermentation temperatures. Le Pin placed its chip under its label for a few years, but that didn't solve the problem of dodgy dealers refilling genuine bottles, so the Belgian company behind the chip, Selinko, collaborated with a packaging company to come up with a tag that sits under the capsule—the short sleeve that goes over the top of the bottle. Selinko's CEO Patrick Eischen explains, "A little piece of the chip's antennae goes on the side of the bottle so when you open the capsule you actually break a little bit of the antennae and the chip will give a different message compared to a bottle that has previously been opened."[16] By hovering a smartphone above it, it's possible to determine whether the cork has ever been removed, tampered with, or pierced since the wine was bottled.

It's not just chip-like devices that are being implemented to discourage fraud; there are QR codes on labels, hologram stickers, and individual bottle engravings on the bottles of the finest and rarest wines in the world, but they all require the buyer to make the final checks. A throw-everything-at-it approach is the tactic used by the top producers who can afford it. Châteaux Margaux, whose wines sell for thousands of dollars per case, went for a bells and whistles approach: laser-etched bottles, a vintage-specific bottle mold, individually coded bottles and cases, special ink, and a strip that runs between the capsule and bottle with a unique reference number and pattern that can be checked on its website. When the bottle is opened, the strip is broken. These measures will help in the short term, but in twenty years' time, when these bottles are at their drinking peak, will the technology seem as outdated as a VHS or MiniDisc player?

There are more rudimentary ways of checking for fakes, according to the experts. At Britain's oldest wine merchant, Berry Bros. & Rudd, the warehouse check-in team has been trained to spot anything odd, but they don't have their smartphones at the ready. Using devices as simple as flashlights, jeweler's loups, and measuring tapes, fakes can be detected by knowing eyes. But these counterfeiting measures have only been implemented since Rudy was locked up. Berry's was established in 1698, but it was only in 2013 that it saw fit to invest in the services of an "in-house wine authenticator," who admitted, "It's fair to say that the Kurniawan trial was a real shot across the bows, for a trade that for too long had buried its head in the sand on the matter of counterfeits." He continues, "Today it might strike us as odd that it took so long for the wine trade to sit up and take notice. Once again, it is the friendly, good-natured side of the business which means that people were often too embarrassed to ask the relevant questions, for fear of upsetting a long-standing supplier, who just as often was also a friend."[17]

Likewise, the Bordeaux wine council, the CIVB, woke up to the very real problem of fraud following Kurniawan's trial. The wine association implemented a counterfeit training program in both English and Mandarin to train Interpol and customs officers. It was also involved in 48 separate investigations of wine fraud in the decade from 2011, seizing more than 100,000 fake bottles and 150,000 fake wine labels. China has long been seen as the main purveyor of fake wines, with the council estimating that as many as 30,000 bottles of fake wine are sold every hour in the People's Republic. An exhaustive survey of more than 3,000 stores in 27 towns across 13 provinces found that more than 25 percent of outlets were selling wine that was visibly fake, from Benfolds (rather than Penfolds) to Chateau Lafee (not Lafite).

Unfortunately, there's no reliable data to measure the extent of fraud in China and beyond. There have been many attempts to estimate the number of fakes in circulation, but it's like a game of pinning the tail on the donkey. France's *Sud-Ouest* newspaper once claimed that 20 percent of all wines were duds,[18] and the president of the grand-sounding Chinese Academy of Inspection and Quarantine believes 50 percent of all Lafite sold in China is fake.[19] Meanwhile, Canadian Master of Wine Rhys Pender spent a year trying to get to the bottom of the counterfeit wine market but struggled to come up with an accurate figure. What he did discover was that people's perceptions of fraud differed depending on their place in the wine market. Wine producers and wine drinkers thought counterfeits were a much bigger problem than those who sold wine: producers and drinkers estimated that one in 25 bottles, or 4 percent, were counterfeit, while fine-wine traders thought fakes accounted for somewhere between 0.2 percent and 1 percent of the market.[20] With the fine-wine market estimated to be worth around $3 billion, that means that the counterfeit market could be worth as little as $6 million or, if the *Sud-Ouest* figures are accurate, $600 million. Take your pick.

AN END TO WINE FRAUD?

Kurniawan spent seven years behind bars before being deported back to Indonesia in 2021—it turned out he had outstayed his US student visa by some distance. Having claimed bankruptcy, however, he didn't pay a cent in reparations to his victims. What's more, there are certain to be Kurniawan bottles still in the market, waiting for an unsuspecting wine lover to buy and open them. Despite the increased awareness of wine fraud and innovative methods to stamp it out, the reasons for counterfeiting wine have not changed. One man may have been caught, but there remain plenty of individuals willing to try their hand. There continue to be regular reports of raids on fake wine factories, whether it's a Milan warehouse counterfeiting one of Tuscany's most prestigious wines, Sassicaia, or a Chinese gang producing knock-off versions of Australia's Penfolds. The seeming ease with which the motivated and savvy scammer can fool the experts as well as the everyman drinker, plus the often prohibitive cost of testing, mean that wine remains ripe for counterfeiting.

10

THE LAST DROP

||||||||||||||||||||||||||||||||||||||||||||||||||||||||||||||||||||||||||||||||||||||||||||||||||||||||||||||||||||||||||||||||||||||||||||||||||||||||||||||||||||||||||||||||

WHY ARE WE FASCINATED by fraud?

The violation of trust for profit is endlessly compelling. The stories of scammers' fearlessness and guile have become glamorized, and there is a part of us that secretly wonders if we could get away with it too. Hollywood has bought into this narrative: A-lister Leonardo DiCaprio played Frank Abagnale Jr. in the Steven Spielberg movie *Catch Me If You Can*, a film *very* loosely based on the exploits of the teen con man who passed himself off as a pilot, a doctor, and a lawyer and cashed checks worth millions of dollars. Meanwhile, other convicted scammers have since been offered lucrative book deals, television series, and safe jobs acting as advisers to law agencies upon release. It's hardly a severe punishment.

But what motivates a fraudster?

It's a topic academics have often pondered and, as academics like to do, they have constructed many models to explain why fraud occurs: there's a fraud triangle, a fraud diamond, and a fraud scale, but the most memorable model is MICE, created by New York–based professor Mary-Jo Kranacher and her colleagues. The acronym stands for Money, Ideology, Coercion, and Ego. The first, money, is perhaps the most obvious reason for committing fraud. From the tavern owner in Pompeii watering down his wine, to the merchant in 1930s Burgundy importing Algerian and southern Rhône wine to bolster his reds, to Rudy Kurniawan's fake wine production line, all the individuals committing wine fraud in its various guises have been motivated by greed.

While lack of money or the desire to have more of it might be considered the single biggest reason for committing wine fraud through the ages, there are many people who are motivated by money and who don't break the law. There are also plenty of people who lack a conscience but don't commit fraud, so there must be more to the mix.

The I in MICE represents ideology or belief: those who have blended wines or falsely labeled them justify their deceit to themselves, considering their misdemeanors necessary and acceptable, whether to fulfill demand in years of short supply or to make a better wine that suits the taste of a given market. During the Little Ice Age, lead-laced wine came to the aid of German merchants looking to turn sour grapes into a lovely drink; in the mid- to late nineteenth century, crop shortages caused by vine diseases, including oidium and phylloxera, were partly to blame for the creation of bogus Bordeaux, sham Sherry, and pretend port, claimed their makers. They justified the practices—not only to themselves but to others—as an acceptable means of quenching the thirst of an undemanding market. It wasn't harming wine buyers' health, but that didn't mean they weren't victims.

Then we have coercion, which means others may be drawn into the fraudsters' circle of crime unwillingly. This is less obvious, but counterfeiters typically need accomplices, willing or otherwise, to assist them with their crimes—accomplices like the family-owned printing firm in Rodenstock's hometown, Pierre Bert's employees in the Winegate affair, or the employees of the Pieroth family in Germany. Whether or not they were aware of being accessories to a crime, they wanted to work and provide for their families; could they afford not to comply with their customers' or employers' demands? In the case of the Austrian antifreeze scandal, a number of those on the right side of the law who uncovered the diethylene glycol scandal before it was made public were harassed by the transgressors, including the chief chemist at the German wine board who faced death threats and the Austrian wine inspector who took his own life in the face of pressure.

Finally, fraudsters require a certain personality, one that includes a healthy dose of egotism, the E in MICE. It seems that they are often motivated not by money alone, but by social status and entitlement. Throughout the history of wine scandals, fraudsters have been able to gain access to elite wine circles; they were often respected by their peers and were able to fool so-called experts. The sense of achievement in going undetected has long spurred wine fraudsters to perpetuate their criminality. But why does the counterfeiting of wine in particular capture our imaginations?

We have come to regard wine as a natural product, grown in bucolic vineyards in rural idylls. It is seen as pure and unadulterated and exudes a sense of authenticity that is guaranteed by its connection with these romantic places. However, our idealistic notions about the Arcadian charm of grape growing and winemaking are often misplaced. The notion of wine coming from somewhere and its taste being intrinsically linked with that place was the cornerstone of the creation of appellations in the 1930s. Appellation laws were founded on the concept of terroir, and while it is certainly true to say that wines made from grapes grown in different vineyards taste different, appellations were often crafted to suit the needs of the people they were created to protect.

Do we place too much emphasis on place as a guarantor of quality? The producers of Burgundy have certainly done a good job of convincing us that the true essence of great wine is terroir. The rest of the world's producers have followed suit. But have we become drunk on it? It could be argued that terroir is a convenient construct created by producers seeking to differentiate themselves from competing growers in a globalizing world. In short, is it simply liquid protectionism?

Drawing a border around your wine-producing village and imposing strict rules on those within its boundaries was France's attempt to prevent fraudsters from abusing regional names and unscrupulous merchants from bogus blending. Not only did the new *appellation controlée* system of the 1930s intend to stop the influx of cheaper wines from outside the more prestigious regions, it also required locals to stick to the rules on what they could plant, and it demanded that a tasting panel give the official seal of approval that the wine was a true reflection of the appellation, whether Volnay or Vouvray.

It's hardly surprising that wines from the same appellation do share similarities—they are located in a small area sharing the same weather and the same grapes and using similar techniques in the vineyard and winery. As English viticultural consultant and Master of Wine Stephen Skelton explains, "After all, if many of the winegrowers in an area are using the same clones and rootstocks (as specified in the AC regulations), adhere to the same appellation yield levels, pick at much the same time, use similar techniques in their wineries and age their wines in barrels made from French oak, their wines are likely to taste similar—especially if they are attempting to produce wines which conform to their customers' expectations."[1]

Indeed, customers have come to expect a certain style of wine when they order a glass of Sancerre or Châteauneuf-du-Pape. These now-household names provide non-expert drinkers with a reassuringly familiar name as well as an indicator of wine style. You order a glass of Sancerre? It'll be a glass of dry white wine that's fresh and fruity (for the pedants among you, I am aware that rosé and red Sancerre exist too), while the Châteauneuf will stereotypically be a ripe, full-bodied red. An appellation's tasting panel can—and does—reject wines that don't conform. This happened to Domaine Didier Dagueneau, whose vineyards sit within Pouilly Fumé but are now sold under the *vin de France* designation after one of its wines, which also happens to be one of the Loire region's most expensive whites, failed the test. Southern France's Domaine de Trevallon opted out of the appellation system long ago because it believed that a greater proportion of Cabernet Sauvignon in its red blends would make a better wine, but the local appellation rules did not permit it.

There are a growing number of disgruntled vignerons, particularly young and experimental growers, quitting the appellation system as they look at new ways of farming more sustainably and taking a low-intervention approach in the winery. The results can lead to a rather different style of wine that fails to conform to traditional expectations. Indeed, a wine may have an entirely different personality if the producer has picked his or her grapes much later than all the neighbors, and if the wine has not been manipulated with processing aids. But does this make them less authentic? Or is it merely a different human interpretation of a vineyard within an appellation's boundaries?

The apparent rigidity of the appellation system has few fans among libertarian types, including the US think tank the Cato Institute. In a lengthy policy analysis, it claims that the link "between quality and origin are often exaggerated," and that the system created in the 1930s is both outdated and inflexible: "It rewards companies who maintain old ways of doing things by making it more difficult for innovative competitors to communicate product qualities to consumers, and it directly impedes innovation and competition by privileging established firms using traditional methods."[2]

But changing with the times also causes controversy, as the expansion of the Chablis appellation demonstrates. The region's vineyard areas shrank due to phylloxera at the end of the nineteenth century, and it seemed reasonable to reestablish those pre-phylloxera vineyards as global demand for Chablis soared in the late twentieth century. In 2021, more than 5,500 hectares of vineyard were allowed to call themselves Chablis, compared with around 2,000 in the 1970s. The expansion split this area of northern France into two camps. The first—those who were already inside the existing appellation boundaries—believed true Chablis should only be produced from vines grown on the local limestone soils known as Kimmeridgian. The other side argued for market forces: the world wanted more Chablis, and it was better to plant more vines than overcrop the existing vines and dilute the wines to meet demand. Additionally, there were many vineyards that had been a part of the region but had declined and disappeared due to phylloxera and two world wars. An expansion would merely revive what had been lost. Time has been a healer in Chablis, but the expansion of other vineyards, including the Prosecco *denominazione* in northeastern Italy, in a bid to sate global demand for fun, fruity, and frothy fizz, begs the question: Are appellations designed to protect consumers or to serve the economic interests of the producers inside their boundaries? Can they do both? If appellations are to have any value in the future, they must be trusted. If they are no longer trusted—by producers and consumers—their reason for existence expires.

Perhaps the wine world has become too fixated on place. It hasn't always been the case: ancient Egyptians used place of origin to differentiate the wines they traded, but they also classified wines by the social occasion, as Roger Scruton notes in *Questions of Taste*: "Archaeologists have recovered amphorae labelled as 'wine for first-class celebrations', 'wine for tax collection day', 'wine for dancing' and so on."[3] Could this catch on?

Science has come to the rescue since the Egyptians were ordering wines to accompany paying taxes. Looking back through history, wine has been ameliorated to ensure that it fulfills its primary aim of giving pleasure. At the very least, wine should be free of faults. That might seem like a low bar, but in the nineteenth and twentieth centuries, scientists hadn't yet figured out what was going on in wine cellars, and an extraordinary amount of wine would have failed to tick the fault-free box. Sour wines produced from unripe grapes and vinegar-like liquids that had been spoiled by oxidation have long been tarted up to create more appetizing drinks. From the wine producer to wine consumers, herbs, spices, and even lead have been used liberally in the past to achieve the end goal: pleasure.

Despite the beginnings of wine connoisseurship in the nineteenth and early twentieth centuries, blended wines provided drinking pleasure at the right price. Little has changed. Research shows that general wine consumers can't distinguish an expensive wine from a cheap and cheerful one. In a study involving more than 6,000 blind tastings of wine priced from $1.65 to $150, researchers discovered that in many instances, wine drinkers preferred the less expensive wines to their more expensive counterparts.[4] However, when you reveal the prices of wines to a wine drinker, the more expensive bottles are perceived to be of higher quality.[5] It's no wonder that aspirational wine producers use environmentally unfriendly heavy bottles and luxury packaging to provide the drinker with the perception that the contents are equally high quality. Buyer beware.

Even experts struggle to make the necessary distinctions when it comes to origin and quality. Looking back at the Winegate scandal, there were a host of industry leaders standing up in court and admitting that they could not tell the difference between a rough Riviera red and a Bordeaux-grown wine. And in a vinous case of the emperor's new clothes, the man behind the Thomas Jefferson bottles lured the wine world's most decorated individuals and dazzled them with the finest and rarest bottles one could wish to taste. During Rodenstock's lavish dinners, they swooned at the wines he sourced and believed them to be the genuine article. Were they? The overwhelming body of evidence raises serious doubts about their authenticity. However, many of the guests still remember the wines and the events as once-in-a-lifetime experiences, while the collectors who spent significant amounts of money buying bottles off Rodenstock continue to have a bitter aftertaste. The differing responses to his misdemeanors suggest that wine adulteration is not only about the liquid—and its price tag—but also an individual's relationship with the liquid and the fraudster, and their own feelings of victimization.

The wine world can no longer turn a blind eye to wine fraud. From maker to merchant, those who work in the trade have long prided themselves on wine's aura of respectability and its historical associations with great philosophers, writers, nobility, and even God himself. But it's clear that wine has a distinctly murky side, a fact that has been uncorked very publicly in recent decades. Trust needs to be restored and technology may be its savior. Despite the unsavory tales of deception and villainy, the world still loves wine: more than 30 billion bottles of wine are uncorked every year, and each has a story to tell. It is a product of people and places, prosperity and privation, with the occasional protest thrown in. So the next time you open your favorite red, look further than the bottom of your glass, and you will find that there is more to your wine than meets the mouth. Toxic? Rarely. Intoxicating? Always.

Acknowledgments

Having passed the notorious Master of Wine tasting exams in 2012, there was just the dissertation to complete before those elusive MW letters would soon be mine. Armed with a degree in history and politics, how hard could it be? But one proposal after another was rejected. I needed inspiration, and it came while I was wearing my pajamas. I had chosen Don and Petie Kladstrup's *Champagne* as my bedtime reading. It is a colorful wine history book, and it summarizes the 1911 Champagne riots in one snappy chapter. I was hooked. Riots in Champagne? This was something I could get into, and it turned out that there was a paucity of information about it, particularly in English. I would do something about it.

Three years and one baby later, I was an expert on the reasons behind the Champagne riots and the world's 384th Master of Wine. Fraud was one of the major causes of the protests, and it stirred in me an unreasonable interest in the dark side of the wine world that has culminated in this book. Encouraged by my agent Mille Hoskins, whom I met thanks to my fairy wine mother, Master of

Wine and OBE Jancis Robinson, a proposal slowly took shape. The University of California Press team saw its potential, and as a pandemic engulfed the globe, I had the dawning realization that I would be writing a wide-ranging wine history book with additional challenges, including home-schooling a six-year-old. Primary school teaching is not an experience I wish to repeat.

I'd like to thank all those individuals who took the time to be interviewed on the phone or in person and have featured in the book. The book would have been lesser without these experts in their respective fields. Special thanks go to Steve Charters, Professor of Wine Marketing at the Burgundy School of Business and my Master of Wine research paper supervisor, who guided me in those early days of exploring Champagne and fraud, and who gave his time so generously. He introduced me to other academics who have kindly offered advice and guidance, in particular Jennifer Smith Maguire, professor of cultural production and consumption at Sheffield Hallam University, and Dr. Graham Harding, an expert in all things Champagne in the nineteenth century.

Librarians are some of the most helpful people you could wish to encounter as a researcher, from the team in Épernay mediatheque who opened early to let me pore over old newspapers to those at the British Library in both Boston Spa and London. I was unable to get to Austria's national library to access some documents but a sommelier friend, Daniel Stojcic, who worked in a nearby two-Michelin-starred restaurant, was returning to visit his family in his native Vienna and offered to scan and translate pages of some much-needed sources—all for the price of a cup of a tea.

I thank the Costières de Nîmes wine association, which kindly hosted me as I explored the world of Roman wine before stomping the grapes in an itchy toga. I am also grateful to the team at the Châteauneuf-du-Pape wine association and local producers in the far southeastern reaches of France for the warm welcome to their region and invaluable assistance with my research. The Austrian Wine Board was also generous in its assistance, sending me invaluable information as well as putting me in touch with experts in the field; Lenz Moser V, Josef "Pepi" Schuller, and Klaus Postmann took time out of their busy schedules to provide context, a wealth of information, and on-the-ground insight relating to the Austrian wine scandal.

I did not expect to find a Roman wine expert right at my doorstep, but life is full of surprises: Jeremy Paterson, now-retired professor of ancient history at

Newcastle University, just happens to be an expert on the Roman wine trade. He patiently answered my questions about all things Rome and wine and read through the first chapter of the book. As a token of my appreciation, I sent him a bottle of Roman-inspired wine from my grape-stomping trip to Mas des Tourelles. Having since tasted the wine, I'm not sure he would have been thanking me for it.

It was more than a little daunting to receive the contract to write this book, and there were times when I wanted to throw in the towel, but my editor Kate Marshall has acted like a captain steering a ship, guiding me forward when I threatened to go off course. She challenged me to delve more deeply while maintaining an engaging narrative, and I hope that we have succeeded together. The peer reviewers also identified its weaknesses and have made this a stronger read. I also owe a very large glass of unadulterated wine to my copy editor, Jan Spauschus, who has polished the copy and made it shine, in addition to being supportive and good natured.

I apologize profusely to my family for making them endure yet another ambitious project. Whether it's the Master of Wine qualification, a book, or long-distance swimming, they allow me the time to shut out the world and focus intently on these challenges. A thousand thanks to Ben, my mum and dad, and my sister for being the pillars of support that allow me to live this unconventional life. To my son, Mac, this book would have been written quicker if you weren't such a wonderful distraction, but I would not have missed the school pickups nor the endless games of balloon football in our lounge for any deadline. You will always be my finest achievement, and I hope that I make you proud.

Notes

INTRODUCTION

1. Lars Holmberg, "Wine Fraud," *International Journal of Wine Research*, 2010, 105–13.

2. Steve Charters, *Wine and Society: The Social and Cultural Context of a Drink* (Amsterdam: Elsevier/Butterworth-Heinemann, 2006).

3. Kent Bach, "Knowledge, Wine and Taste: What Good Is Wine Knowledge (in Enjoying Wine?)," in Barry Smith, ed., *Questions of Taste: The Philosophy of Wine* (Oxford: Signal Books, 2007), 40.

4. Noah Charney, *The Art of Forgery* (London: Phaidon Press, 2015), 119.

5. Charney, *The Art of Forgery*, 119.

6. C. Torres, F. Javier Melgosa Arcos, and Laurence Jégouzo, *Wine Law* (Estoril, Portugal: ESHTE, 2021), 399.

7. Personal correspondence, 2009.

8. Marion Demossier, *Burgundy: The Global Story of Terroir* (New York: Berghahn Books, 2018), 13.

CHAPTER 1. WHEN IN ROME

1. Marcus Porcius Cato and Marcus Terentius Varro, *On Agriculture*, trans. William Davis Hooper and H. Boyd Ash (Cambridge, MA: Harvard University Press, 1934).

2. Apicius, *The Roman Cookery Book: A Critical Translation of "The Art of Cooking" by Apicius for Use in the Study and the Kitchen* (New York: George G. Harrap, 1958).

3. Pliny, *Pliny Natural History*, trans. H. Rackham, W. H. S. Jones, and D. E. Eichholz (London: Folio Society, 2012), book 14.8.

4. Lucius Iunius Moderatus Columella, *On Agriculture I-IV*, trans. Harrison Boyd Ash (Cambridge, MA: Harvard University Press, 1941).

5. Columella 12.19, quoted in Jerome O. Nriagu, *Lead and Lead Poisoning in Antiquity* (New York: Wiley, 1983), 349.

6. Pliny, *Pliny Natural History*, 310.

7. Pliny, *Pliny Natural History*, 319–22.

8. Pliny, *Pliny Natural History*, 326.

9. Pliny, *Pliny Natural History*, 311.

10. Ilaria Gozzini Giacosa, *A Taste of Ancient Rome* (Chicago: University of Chicago Press, 1992), 11–18.

11. André Tchernia, *Le vin de l'Italie romaine: Essai d'histoire économique d'après les amphores* (Rome: École française de Rome, 1986), 23–28.

12. Martial, *Epigrams*, trans. Walter C. A. Ker (London: William Heinemann, 1919). See 9.98.

13. Plutarch, *The Parallel Lives*, trans. Bernadotte Perrin (Cambridge, MA: Harvard University Press, 1916), 307.

14. For an overview of the supply and issues regarding water in Roman times, see David Deming, "The Aqueducts and Water Supply of Ancient Rome," *Groundwater* 58, no. 1 (2019): 152–61.

15. Martial, *Epigrams*, 9.2.5, 14.103.1.

16. Pliny, *Pliny Natural History*, 322–23.

17. Jacques Jouanna, *Greek Medicine from Hippocrates to Galen* (Leiden: Brill, 2012), 173–93, https://doi.org/10.1163/9789004232549.

18. Josef Eisinger, "Lead and Wine: Eberhard Gockel and the Colica Pictonum," *Medical History* 26, no. 3 (1982): 288.

19. "The Roman Empire: Victim of Poisoning," *International Herald Tribune*, June 1, 1983.

20. Nriagu, *Lead and Lead Poisoning in Antiquity,* viii.

21. Alan Cameron, letter to the editor, *International Herald Tribune,* June 20, 1983.

CHAPTER 2. DYING FOR A DRINK

1. Josef Eisinger, "Lead and Wine: Eberhard Gockel and the Colica Pictonum," *Medical History* 26, no. 3 (1982): 294.

2. Jan Caeyers, *Beethoven: A Life,* trans. Brent Annable (Oakland: University of California Press, 2020), 538.

3. Letter dated February 22, 1827.

4. Ludwig van Beethoven, *The Letters of Beethoven,* ed. and trans. Emily Anderson (London: Macmillan, 1961), 1.

5. Tom Service, "Symphony Guide: Beethoven's Eighth," *The Guardian,* February 11, 2014, www.theguardian.com/music/tomserviceblog/2014/feb/11/symphony-guide-beethoven-eighth.

6. Esteban Buch, *Beethoven's Ninth: A Political History,* trans. Richard Miller (Chicago: University of Chicago Press, 2004), 5.

7. Russell Martin, *Beethoven's Hair* (New York: Broadway Books, 2001), 237.

8. A. K. Kubba and M. Young, "Ludwig Van Beethoven: A Medical Biography," *The Lancet* 347, no. 8995 (1996): 167–70.

9. Michael H. Stevens, Teemarie Jacobsen, and Alicia Kay Crofts, "Lead and the Deafness of Ludwig Van Beethoven," *The Laryngoscope* 123, no. 11 (2013): 2854–58.

10. Martin, *Beethoven's Hair,* 233.

11. Martin, *Beethoven's Hair,* 235.

12. Christian Reiter, "The Causes of Beethoven's Death and His Locks of Hair: A Forensic-Toxicological Investigation," trans. Michael Lorenz, *The Beethoven Journal* 22, no. 1 (2007): 2–5.

13. Bruce Newman, "Skull Fragments Most Likely Not Beethoven's," *East Bay Times,* July 23, 2015, www.eastbaytimes.com/2015/07/23/skull-fragments-most-likely-not-beethovens/?

14. Tristan James Alexander Begg et al., "Genomic Analyses of Hair from Ludwig van Beethoven," *Current Biology* (2023), https://doi.org/10.1016/j.cub.2023.02.041.

15. Martin, *Beethoven's Hair,* 237.

16. Ian Woodfield, "Johann van Beethoven's Last Hurrah," OUP blog, Oxford University Press, October 30, 2013, https://blog.oup.com/2013/11/johann-van-beethoven-fatherhood/.

17. Anton Felix Schindler, *Beethoven as I Knew Him,* ed. Donald W. MacArdle, trans. Constance S. Jolly (New York: Dover, 1996).

18. Gene V. Ball, "Two Epidemics of Gout," *Bulletin of the History of Medicine* 45, no. 5 (1971): 401–8, www.jstor.org/stable/44447458.

19. C. Marisa R. Almeida and M. Teresa S. D. Vasconcelos, "Lead Contamination in Portuguese Red Wines from the Douro Region: From the Vineyard to the Final Product," *Journal of Agricultural and Food Chemistry* 51, no. 10 (2003): 3012–23, https://doi:10.1021/jf0259664.

20. R. Mayson, *The Wines and Vineyards of Portugal* (London: Mitchell Beazley, 2003), 11.

21. A. Baring Garrod, *The Nature and Treatment of Gout and Rheumatic Gout* (London: Walton and Maberly, 1859), 60.

22. David Hunter, "Handel's Ill Health: Documents and Diagnoses," *Royal Musical Association Research Chronicle* 41, no. 1 (2008).

23. Personal interview, September 25, 2018.

24. J.-M. Desseigne, *Le plomb dans les vins: Origines et réduction des contaminations* (Paris: Institut technique de la vigne et du vin, 1993).

25. C. M. Lopez et al., "Alteration of Biochemical Parameters Related with Exposure to Lead in Heavy Alcohol Drinkers," *Pharmacological Research* 45, no. 1 (2002): 47–50.

26. Tom Stevenson and Essi Avellan, *Christie's World Encyclopaedia of Champagne and Sparkling Wine* (New York: Sterling Epicure, 2014).

27. J. H. Graziano, V. Slavkovic, and C. Blum, "Lead Crystal: An Important Potential Source of Lead Exposure," *Chemical Speciation and Bioavailability* 3, no. 3/4 (1991): 81–85.

CHAPTER 3. AN ENLIGHTENED DRINKER?

1. Recommended reading on the development of gastronomy and gastronomic writing includes Priscilla Parkhurst Ferguson, "A Cultural Field in the Making: Gastronomy in 19th-Century France," *American Journal of Sociology* 104, no. 3 (November 1998): 597–641, https://doi.org/10.1086/210082, and Jenni-

fer J. Davis, *Defining Culinary Authority: The Transformation of Cooking in France, 1650–1830* (Baton Rouge: Louisiana State University Press, 2013). See also Jane Thompson, "Gastronomic Literature, Modern Cuisine and the Development of French Bourgeois Identity from 1800 to 1850," honors paper, Connecticut College, 2011, https://digitalcommons.conncoll.edu/histhp/9.

2. Rebecca L. Spang, *The Invention of the Restaurant: Paris and Modern Gastronomic Culture* (Cambridge, MA: Harvard University Press, 2020).

3. Joachim Christoph Nemeitz, "Séjour de Paris [. . .]" [1727], Gallica, January 1, 1970, https://gallica.bnf.fr/ark:/12148/bpt6k102148f/, 58.

4. Jean-Anthelme Brillat-Savarin, *The Physiology of Taste: Or, Meditations on Transcendental Gastronomy*, trans. M. F. K. Fisher (New York: Vintage, 2011), 319.

5. Francis William Blagdon, *Paris as It Was and as It Is; or a Sketch of the French Capital Illustrative of the Effects of the Revolution* (London: C. & R. Baldwin, 1803), 442–43, https://catalogue.bnf.fr/ark:/12148/cb318218342.

6. Quoted by Emily Monaco, "If You Think You're a Decadent Fuck, Try Feasting Like a 19th-Century Parisian," VICE, May 22, 2018, www.vice.com/en/article/435xxd/paris-bourgeous-1800s-19th-century-feasmt-gourands.

7. Brillat-Savarin, *The Physiology of Taste*, 16.

8. Brillat-Savarin, *The Physiology of Taste*, 15.

9. Recommended reading on Carême's life: Ian Kelly, *Cooking for Kings: The Life of Antonin Carême, the First Celebrity Chef* (London: Short Books, 2003).

10. Antonin Carême, *L'Art de la cuisine française au dix-neuvième siècle, tome I* (Paris: self-pub., 1833), lvi.

11. André Jullien, *The Topography of All the Known Vineyards: Containing a Description of the Kind and Quality of Their Products, and a Classification* (London: Printed for G. and W. B. Whittaker, 1824), 115.

12. Cyrus Redding, *A History and Description of Modern Wines* (London: Whittaker, Treacher & Arnot, 1833), 239–52.

13. Redding, *A History and Description of Modern Wines*, xxvi.

14. Isabella Beeton, *The Book of Household Management . . . Also Sanitary, Medical and Legal Memoranda. With a History of the Origin, Properties and Uses of All Things Connected with Home Life and Comfort* (London: Ward, Lock and Co., 1888), chap. XLI, 2164.

15. Anonymous, *Dissertation sur les vins*, 1770. Cited in J. B. Gough, "Winecraft and Chemistry in 18th-Century France: Chaptal and the Invention

of Chaptalization," *Technology and Culture* 39, no. 1 (January 1998): 83, https:// doi.org/10.2307/3107004.

16. Friedrich Christian Accum, *A Treatise on Adulterations of Food, and Culinary Poisons: Exhibiting the Fraudulent Sophistications of Bread, Beer, Wine, Spiritous Liquors, Tea, Coffee . . . and Methods of Detecting Them* (London: J. Mallett, 1820), 95.

17. Accum, *Treatise*, 98.

18. Redding, *A History and Description of Modern Wines*, 324.

19. Accum, *Treatise*, 99.

20. F. C. Mills, *The Wine Guide; Being Practical Hints on the Purchase and Management of Foreign Wines, Their History and a Complete Catalogue of All Those in Present Use* (London: Groombridge and Sons, 1860), 28.

21. A Practical Liquor Manufacturer, *The Bordeaux Wine and Liquor Dealers' Guide: A Treatise on the Manufacture and Adulteration of Liquors* (New York: Dick & Fitzgerald, 1858), ix.

22. Charles Tovey, *Wine and Wine Countries; a Record and Manual for Wine Merchants and Wine Consumers* (London: Hamilton, Adams & Co., 1862), 302.

23. Charles Tovey, *Wine and Wine Countries; a Record and Manual for Wine Merchants and Wine Consumers* (London: Whittaker & Co., 1877), 4.

24. Tovey, *Wine and Wine Countries* (1862), 301.

25. B. A. Lenoir, *Traité de la vigne et de la vinification* [. . .] *avec l'indication de celles qui produisent les meilleurs vins* (Paris: Rousselon, 1828), 4.

26. Gough, "Winecraft and Chemistry," 1.

CHAPTER 4. I PREDICT A RIOT

1. "Infuriated Winegrowers: Dragoons Draw Their Sabres," *The Advertiser* (Adelaide, SA), April 14, 1911, http://nla.gov.au/nla.news-article5266465.

2. J. Nollevalle, "1911: L'Agitation dans le vignoble champenois," *La champagne viticole* (Épernay: Syndicat general des vignerons de la Champagne, 1961), 15.

3. Nollevalle, "1911: L'Agitation dans le vignoble champenois," 18.

4. Christy Campbell, *Phylloxera: How Wine Was Saved for the World* (London: Harper Perennial, 2004), 13.

5. Figure quoted in James Simpson, *Creating Wine: The Emergence of a World Industry, 1840–1914* (Princeton, NJ: Princeton University Press, 2011), 5.

6. Simpson, *Creating Wine*, 8.

7. C. Desbois-Thibault and A. Melin, *1911–2011 Du déséquilibre au consensus: Histoire et souvenirs* (Épernay: Syndicat general des vignerons de la Champagne, 2011), 4.

8. Desbois-Thibault and Melin, *1911–2011 Du déséquilibre au consensus*, 12.

9. *Le reveil de la Marne*, January 7, 1911.

10. Nollevalle, "1911: L'Agitation dans le vignoble champenois," 4.

11. Nollevalle, "1911: L'Agitation dans le vignoble champenois," 23.

12. Dominique Fradet, *1911 en Champagne: Chronique d'une révolution* (Reims: Fradet, 2011), 27.

13. Nollevalle, "L'Agitation dans le vignoble champenois," 20.

14. Fradet, *1911 en Champagne*, 155.

15. Simpson, *Creating Wine*, 147–49.

16. Figures sourced from André Simon, *The History of Champagne* (London: Ebury Press, 1962), 111.

17. *Le vigneron champenois*, November 30, 1910.

18. G. Dervin, *Six semaines en pays phylloxérés: Étude sur la défense et la reconstitution des vignobles français atteints du phylloxéra* (Reims: Dubois-Poplimont, 1896).

19. Fradet, *1911 en Champagne*, 20–21.

20. Fradet, *1911 en Champagne*, 21.

21. Fradet, *1911 en Champagne*, 17.

22. Fradet, *1911 en Champagne*, 19.

23. For further reading on the socialist interpretation of the riots, consult J. Girault, "Le rôle du socialisme dans la révolte des vignerons de l'Aube," *Le mouvement social* 67 (April–June 1969): 89–108, and P. Koukharski, "Le mouvement paysan en France en 1911," *Questions d'histoire*, no. 1 (1952): 160–77.

24. J. Saillet, "Les composantes du mouvement dans la Marne," *Le mouvement social* 67 (April–June 1969): 85.

25. Nollevalle, "1911: L'Agitation dans le vignoble champenois," 10.

26. Marcel Lachiver, *Vins, vignes et vignerons: histoire du vignoble français* (Paris: Fayard, 1988), 478.

27. Personal correspondence, November 22, 2022.

28. *Le réveil de la Marne*, June 28, 1911.

29. Desbois-Thibault and Melin, *1911–2011 Du déséquilibre au consensus*, 39.

30. Don and Petie Kladstrup, *Champagne: How the World's Most Glamorous Wine Triumphed over War and Hard Times* (New York: Harper Perennial, 2006), 215–16.

31. Tyson Stelzer, *The Champagne Guide: 2014–2015* (Richmond, Australia: Hardie Grant Books, 2013), Kindle ed., loc. 1344–58.

CHAPTER 5. APPELLATION NATION

1. Jean Bourgougneux, "On a vole le buste du baron Leroy," *Le vigneron des côtes du Rhône* 351, no. 14 (January 1993).

2. "Le retour du buste du baron Leroy," *Le provençal*, September 3, 1993.

3. Jean-Claude Portes, *Châteauneuf-du-Pape: Première AOC de France* (Châteauneuf-du-Pape: Organisme de défense et de gestion de l'AOC Châteauneuf-du-Pape, 2016), 55.

4. Robert Joly, "Hommage des vignerons du Midi, le buste de baron Leroy," *Reflets de Provence et de la Mediterranée,* photocopy, n.d.

5. Laura Levine Frader, *Peasants and Protest: Agricultural Workers, Politics, and Unions in the Aude, 1850–1914* (Berkeley: University of California Press, 1991), 141.

6. Portes, *Châteauneuf-du-Pape,* 96.

7. Portes, *Châteauneuf-du-Pape,* 95.

8. Harry Karis, *The Châteauneuf-du-Pape Wine Book* (Roermond, The Netherlands: Kavino, 2009), 6.

9. Karis, *The Châteauneuf-du-Pape Wine Book,* 21.

10. Jean-Claude Portes, *Château La Nerthe: Five Centuries of History* (Châteauneuf-du-Pape: Château La Nerthe, 2014), 39.

11. Portes, *Château La Nerthe,* 44.

12. Portes, *Châteauneuf-du-Pape,* 89.

13. J.-E. Planchon, "La question du phylloxéra en 1876," *Revue des deux mondes* 19, no. 3 (January 15, 1877): 277.

14. Jean Lavalle, Émile Delarue, and Joseph Garnier, *Histoire et statistique de la vigne et des grands vins de la côte-d'Or* (Paris: Dusacq, 1855), v.

15. Lavalle, Delarue, and Garnier, *Histoire et statistique de la vigne,* 226.

16. Lavalle, Delarue, and Garnier, *Histoire et statistique de la vigne,* 226–27.

17. Marcel Lachiver, *Vins, vignes et vignerons: Histoire du vignoble français* (Paris: Fayard, 1988), 488.

18. Germain Martin and Paul Martenot, *Contribution à l'histoire des classes rurales en France au XIXe siècle: La côte-d'Or (étude d'économie rurale)* (Dijon: Université de Dijon, 1909), 372.

19. Maurice Constantin-Weyer, *L'âme du vin* (Paris: La table ronde, 2008), 148.

20. Martin and Martenot, *Contribution à l'histoire des classes rurales*, 387.

21. Frank Schoonmaker and Tom Marvel, *The Complete Wine Book* (London: Routledge, 1935; e-book published by Barakaldo Books, 2020), Kindle ed., loc. 2766.

22. Schoonmaker and Marvel, *The Complete Wine Book*, loc. 286.

23. Schoonmaker and Marvel, *The Complete Wine Book*, loc. 237.

24. Schoonmaker and Marvel, *The Complete Wine Book*, loc. 248.

25. Schoonmaker and Marvel, *The Complete Wine Book*, loc. 248.

26. Schoonmaker and Marvel, *The Complete Wine Book*, loc. 175.

27. Schoonmaker and Marvel, *The Complete Wine Book*, loc. 585.

28. Baron Pierre Le Roy de Boiseaumarié, "Le mouvement vers la qualité," *Reflets de Provence et de la Méditerranée*, photocopy, n.d.

29. Article in *Le petit orangeois*, July 10, 1924, cited in Portes, *Châteauneuf-du-Pape*, 106.

30. Joseph Capus and Théodore Georgopoulos, *L'évolution de la législation sur les appellations d'origine: Genèse des appellations contrôlées* (Paris: Mare & Martin, 2019), 20.

31. Lachiver, *Vins, vignes et vignerons*, 486–90.

32. In 1934, France produced 78 million hectoliters and Algeria 22 million hectoliters; in 1935, France made 76 million hectoliters and Algeria 19 million hectoliters. Lachiver, *Vins, vignes et vignerons*, 487.

33. Portes, *Châteauneuf-du-Pape*, 117.

34. Capus and Georgopoulos, *L'évolution de la législation*, 41.

35. Capus and Georgopoulos, *L'évolution de la législation*, 74.

36. Capus and Georgopoulos, *L'évolution de la législation*, 86.

CHAPTER 6. WINEGATE

The *New York Times* archive, the British Library newspaper archives, *Le Monde*, and Bordeaux *négociant* Maison Sichel's archives were also extensively used as primary sources for this chapter.

1. Frank J. Prial, "Frenchmen Are Already Calling the Bordeaux Case the Trial of the Century," *New York Times,* October 26, 1974.

2. Personal correspondence.

3. Bruno Duthomas, "Des crus raffinés, des Chartrons insoupçonnables," *Le Monde,* October 28, 1974.

4. Hervé Chabalier, "Le vin amer des Chartrons," *Le nouvel observateur,* August 27, 1973.

5. Pierre Bert, *In vino veritas: L'affaire des vins de Bordeaux* (Paris: Albin Michel, 1975), 87.

6. Terry Richard, "An Oenophile's Approach to Economics," *New York Times,* September 9, 1973.

7. Maison Sichel's archives can be found online at www.sichel.fr/fr/archives-millesimes-maison-sichel.html.

8. Personal correspondence, December 15, 2021.

9. Paul Levy, "Edmund Penning-Rowsell: Obituary," *The Independent,* March 7, 2002.

10. Edmund Penning-Rowsell, *The Wines of Bordeaux* (London: Allen Lane, 1979), 179.

11. Clive Coates, *Grands Vins: The Finest Châteaux of Bordeaux and Their Wines* (Berkeley: University of California Press, 1995), 708.

12. Peter Sichel, "1971 Vintage and Market Report: Bordeaux," Sichel & Co., www.sichel.fr/medias/fichiers/vintage%20report/Vintage%20Report%20 1971.pdf.

13. Peter Sichel, "1972 Vintage and Market Report: Bordeaux," Sichel & Co., www.sichel.fr/medias/fichiers/vintage%20report/vintage%20report%201972. pdf.

14. Peter Sichel, "1974 Vintage and Market Report: Bordeaux," Sichel & Co., www.sichel.fr/medias/fichiers/vintage%20report/vintage%20report%201974. pdf.

15. Duthomas, "Des crus raffinés, des Chartrons insoupçonnables."

16. Jack-Henry Prévôt, "Les cousins Cruse plaident leur dossier et laissent à six témoins étrangers le soin de défendre leur vin," *Sud-Ouest,* October 30, 1974.

17. Robert Daley, "That Wine, Sir, May Not Be Wine at All: Sophisticators Fool Italy with Ingenious Food and Drink Swindles," *LIFE,* February 23, 1968, 70.

18. Jack-Henry Prévôt, "Lionel Cruse: Ce n'est pas dénigrer le bordeaux que de dire qu'il y a en France d'excellents vins de table," *Sud-Ouest,* October 29, 1974.

19. Jack-Henry Prévôt, "Tous les témoins ayant été entendus, les parties civiles ont la parole," *Sud-Ouest,* November 4, 1974.

20. Chabalier, "Le vin amer des Chartrons."

21. Prévôt, "Lionel Cruse."

22. Prévôt, "Tous les témoins ayant été entendus."

23. Bruno Duthomas, "Le mythe du wine tasting," *Le Monde,* November 2, 1974.

24. Victor Noce, "Sous le signe du tonneau," *Libération,* November 17, 2000, www.liberation.fr/villes/2000/11/17/sous-le-signe-du-tonneau_344579/.

25. Peter Stephens, "Vintage Vinegar Scandal," *Daily Mirror,* October 29, 1974.

26. Coates, *Grands Vins,* 713.

CHAPTER 7. YOU SAY "PROST," I SAY "FROST"!

The *New York Times* archive and British Library newspaper archives were also extensively used as primary sources for this chapter.

1. George Mayer, Sam Simon, John Swartzwelder, and John Vitti, "The Crepes of Wrath," *The Simpsons,* season 1, episode 11, Fox, April 15, 1990.

2. Thomas Schimmel, "Der Weinskandal 1985/86," diss., Universität Wien, 1994, 19.

3. Klaus Postmann, "The Wine Scandal—Genesis and Consequences," in Willi Klinger and Karl Vocelka, eds., *Wine in Austria: The History* (Vienna: Brandstätter, 2019), 193.

4. Lenz Moser, *Weinbau einmal anders: Ein Weinbaubuch für den fortschrittlichen Weinbauern* (Vienna: Österreichischer Agrarverlag, 1966).

5. Lee Allyn Davis, *Natural Disasters* (New York: Checkmark Books, 2008), 326.

6. Roman Sandgruber, "Vineyard Areas, Production, Quantities and Consumption," in Willi Klinger and Karl Vocelka, eds., *Wine in Austria: The History* (Vienna: Brandstätter, 2019), 212.

7. Statistik Austria figures quoted in Albert Stöckl, "Austrian Wine: Developments after the Wine Scandal of 1985 and Its Current Situation," paper presented at the 3rd International Wine Business Research Conference,

Montpellier, July 6–8, 2006, Academy of Wine Business, http://academy-ofwinebusiness.com/wp-content/uploads/2010/05/Stockl.pdf, 6.

8. Postmann, "The Wine Scandal," 193.

9. Reuters, "Austria Impounds Wine Laced with Poison," *New York Times*, July 23, 1985.

10. "Saure Trauben, süße Sünden," *Die Zeit*, August 2, 1985, www.zeit.de/1985/32/saure-trauben-suesse-suenden.

11. "Saure Trauben, süße Sünden."

12. "Frostschutzwein bei Omas Geburtstag—11 vergiftet," *Bild Zeitung*, July 12, 1985.

13. Peter Moser, "Der Weinskandal in Österreich und seine Folgen," *Falstaff*, December 17, 2015.

14. John Tagliabue, "Scandal over Poisoned Wine Embitters Village in Austria," *New York Times*, August 2, 1985.

15. Postmann, "The Wine Scandal," 196.

16. "Saure Trauben, süße Sünden."

17. H. Stübling and W. Bittner, "Gepantscher Wein: 'Schön rund und ölig,'" *Der Spiegel*, July 28, 1985.

18. Carol Ballentine, "Taste of Raspberries, Taste of Death: The 1937 Elixir Sulfanilamide Incident," US Food and Drug Administration, www.fda.gov/files/about%20fda/published/The-Sulfanilamide-Disaster.pdf, accessed February 23, 2022.

19. European Commission, Scientific Committee on Consumer Products, "Opinion on Diethylene Glycol," June 24, 2008.

20. Inge Cyrus, "Genauso arg wie die Reblaus," *Der Spiegel*, July 28, 1985.

21. Cyrus, "Genauso arg wie die Reblaus."

22. Cyrus, "Genauso arg wie die Reblaus."

23. "Höchste Kunst," *Der Spiegel*, August 18, 1985.

24. Verena von Wiczlinski, *Der Glykol-Skandal im Jahr 1985*, www.regionalgeschichte.net, urn:nbn:de:0291-rzd-016494-20203112-7.

25. Josef G. and Richard G., Entscheidungstext 12 Os 172/86, OGH, Rechtsinformationssystem des Bundes (RIS) (ruling 12 Os 172/86, Supreme Court of Justice of Austria, Legal Information System), June 11, 1987.

26. Fritz Hallgarten, *Wine Scandal* (London: Weidenfeld and Nicolson, 1986), 68–69.

27. *Lichfield Mercury,* October 28, 1985, 60.

28. Preeti Aroon, "Bush Confuses APEC with OPEC, Australia with Austria," ForeignPolicy.com, September 7, 2007.

29. Louis Charbonneau, "Mystery Nation Picks Aussies over Austrians at U.N.," Reuters, October 17, 2008.

30. Cayla Dengate, "CNN Blooper: Australia Is Building a Wall at Slovenian Border," Huffington Post, March 1, 2016.

31. Josef G. and Richard G., Entscheidungstext 12 Os 172/86, OGH, Rechtsinformationssystem des Bundes (RIS) (ruling 12 Os 172/86, Supreme Court of Justice of Austria, Legal Information System), June 11, 1987.

32. Schimmel, "Der Weinskandal 1985/86," 13–15.

33. Hallgarten, *Wine Scandal,* 40.

34. Josef G. and Richard G., Entscheidungstext 12 Os 172/86, OGH, Rechtsinformationssystem des Bundes (RIS) (ruling 12 Os 172/86, Supreme Court of Justice of Austria, Legal Information System), June 11, 1987.

35. Frank J. Prial, "Italian Wine: Hard-Won Image Is Shattered," *New York Times,* April 12, 1986.

36. Personal correspondence, December 16, 2021.

37. International Organisation of Vine and Wine (OIV), "State of the World Vitivinicultural Sector in 2019," April 2019, www.oiv.int/public/medias/6782/oiv-2019-statistical-report-on-world-vitiniculture.pdf, accessed September 2022.

38. Jon Paulson, "Chardonnay v Grüner Veltliner, a Knockout Contest," JancisRobinson.com, July 26, 2002.

39. Jancis Robinson, "Grüner Veltliner—Distinctly Groovy," JancisRobinson.com, November 15, 2002.

40. "Cameron Diaz Talk about Avaline Wines," August 18, 2020, www.youtube.com/watch?v=jUs8yZbyNwg&t=10s.

CHAPTER 8. INDIANA JONES AND THE GLASS CRUSADE

1. Stephan Draf, "Hardy Rodenstock: Der große Etikettenschwindel," *Stern,* November 23, 2008, www.stern.de/wirtschaft/news/hardy-rodenstock-der-grosse-etikettenschwindel-3746930.html.

2. Mark Bilbe, "An Oral History of the Wine Trade: Michael Broadbent" (audio recording), British Library Listening and Viewing Service, 2003.

3. Jancis Robinson, *Confessions of a Wine Lover* (London: Penguin, 1997), 193–94.

4. Bilbe, "An Oral History of the Wine Trade: Michael Broadbent."

5. Chris Mercer, "Wine World Great Michael Broadbent MW Dies," Decanter. com, March 18, 2020, www.decanter.com/wine-news/michael-broadbent-mw-dies-434895/.

6. Michael Broadbent, *Michael Broadbent's Vintage Wine: Fifty Years of Tasting over Three Centuries of Wine* (London: Websters, 2002), 6.

7. Bilbe, "An Oral History of the Wine Trade: Michael Broadbent."

8. Bilbe, "An Oral History of the Wine Trade: Michael Broadbent."

9. Broadbent, *Michael Broadbent's Vintage Wine*, 42, 250.

10. Broadbent, *Michael Broadbent's Vintage Wine*, 8.

11. Howard G. Goldberg, "Oldest Bordeaux? Yes; Jefferson's? Maybe," *New York Times*, October 30, 1985.

12. Lucia Goodwin, "Research Report: Château Lafite 1787, with initials 'Th. J.,'" Thomas Jefferson Foundation, December 12, 1985, 4, https://monticello-www.s3.amazonaws.com/library/pdfs/Chateau_Lafite_1787.pdf.

13. "To Thomas Jefferson from Martha Jefferson, 8 [March] 1787," Founders Online, National Archives, https://founders.archives.gov/documents/Jefferson/01–11–02–0215. (Original source: *The Papers of Thomas Jefferson*, vol. 11, *1 January–6 August 1787*, ed. Julian P. Boyd [Princeton, NJ: Princeton University Press, 1955], 203–4.)

14. "From Thomas Jefferson to Martha Jefferson, 28 March 1787," Founders Online, National Archives, https://founders.archives.gov/documents/Jefferson/01–11–02–0244. (Original source: *The Papers of Thomas Jefferson*, vol. 11, *1 January–6 August 1787*, ed. Julian P. Boyd [Princeton, NJ: Princeton University Press, 1955], 250–52.)

15. "Notes of a Tour into the Southern Parts of France, &c., 3 March–10 June 1787," Founders Online, National Archives, https://founders.archives.gov/documents/Jefferson/01–11–02–0389. (Original source: *The Papers of Thomas Jefferson*, vol. 11, *1 January–6 August 1787*, ed. Julian P. Boyd [Princeton, NJ: Princeton University Press, 1955], 415–64.)

16. "From Thomas Jefferson to John Bondfield, 22 February 1788," Founders Online, National Archives, https://founders.archives.gov/documents/Jefferson

/01–12–02–0659. (Original source: *The Papers of Thomas Jefferson*, vol. 12, *7 August 1787–31 March 1788*, ed. Julian P. Boyd [Princeton, NJ: Princeton University Press, 1955], 616.)

17. John Hailman, *Thomas Jefferson on Wine* (Jackson: University Press of Mississippi, 2006), 138.

18. Goodwin, "Research Report," 3.

19. "Vintage Investments," *Changing Times*, July 1987, 73.

20. William Sokolin, *Liquid Assets: How to Develop an Enjoyable and Profitable Wine Portfolio* (New York: Macmillan, 1987).

21. Draf, "Hardy Rodenstock: Der große Etikettenschwindel."

22. Draf, "Hardy Rodenstock: Der große Etikettenschwindel."

23. Ezra Stotland, "White Collar Criminals," *Journal of Social Issues* 33, no. 4 (1977): 179–96, https://doi.org/10.1111/j.1540–4560.1977.tb02531.x.

24. David Molyneux-Berry, "Wine Fraud," lecture presented at the Taste3 Conference, May 2007, www.youtube.com/watch?v = HFnOSx6OwIw.

25. Molyneux-Berry, "Wine Fraud."

26. Molyneux-Berry, "Wine Fraud."

27. Michael Streck and Stephan Draf, "Der große Weinschwindel," *Stern*, March 25, 2007, www.stern.de/wirtschaft/news/entkorkt—der-grosse-weinschwindel-3355208.html.

28. Patrick Radden Keefe, "The Jefferson Bottles," *New Yorker*, August 27, 2007.

29. Broadbent, *Michael Broadbent's Vintage Wine*, 11.

30. "Verborgene Keller," *Der Spiegel*, October 27, 1991, www.spiegel.de /wirtschaft/verborgene-keller-a-304c1aa3–0002–0001–0000–000013492439.

31. Koch v. Christie's International Plc., 699 F.3d 141 (2d Cir. 2012), https://casetext.com/case/koch-v-christies-intl-plc-k-pub-ltd.

32. "Verborgene Keller."

33. Jancis Robinson, "Flushing Out Wine Fraud and Fakes," JancisRobinson.com, March 17, 2007, www.jancisrobinson.com/articles/flushing-out-wine-fraud-and-fakes.

34. Mark Bilbe, "An Oral History of the Wine Trade: Serena Sutcliffe" (audio recording), British Library Listening and Viewing Service, London, 2004.

35. Koch v. Christie's International Plc., 699 F.3d 141 (2d Cir. 2012), https://casetext.com/case/koch-v-christies-intl-plc-k-pub-ltd.

36. Goodwin, "Research Report," 1.

37. Goodwin, "Research Report," 2.

38. Keefe, "The Jefferson Bottles."

39. Draf, "Hardy Rodenstock: Der große Etikettenschwindel."

40. Draf, "Hardy Rodenstock: Der große Etikettenschwindel."

41. Koch v. Christie's International Plc., 699 F.3d 141 (2d Cir. 2012), https://casetext.com/case/koch-v-christies-intl-plc-k-pub-ltd.

42. *Wine Spectator*, December 15, 1988.

43. "Counterfeit Wine: A Vintage Crime," *CBS Sunday Morning*, season 22, episode 51, December 22, 2013, www.cbsnews.com/news/counterfeit-wine-a-vintage-crime/.

44. "Counterfeit Wine: A Vintage Crime."

45. Hailman, *Thomas Jefferson on Wine*, 398.

CHAPTER 9. A MESSAGE TO YOU, RUDY

1. Serhan Cevik and Tahsin Saadi Sedik, "A Barrel of Oil or a Bottle of Wine: How Do Global Growth Dynamics Affect Commodity Prices?" IMF Working Paper no. WP/AA/1, January 2011, 7–8.

2. Corie Brown, "$75,000 a Case? He's Buying," *Los Angeles Times*, December 1, 2006, http://articles.latimes.com/2006/dec/01/entertainment/et-rudy1.

3. Jerry Rothwell and Reuben Atlas, dirs., *Sour Grapes* (London: Dogwoof, 2016).

4. Brown, "$75,000 a Case? He's Buying."

5. Jancis Robinson, "That Crazy, Single-Owner Acker Sale," JancisRobinson.com, February 9, 2007, www.jancisrobinson.com/articles/that-crazy-single-owner-acker-sale.

6. Kerry Wills, "Kurniawan House Described as 'Wine Factory,'" *Wine Searcher*, December 11, 2013, www.wine-searcher.com/m/2013/12/rudy-kurniawan-house-described-as-wine-factory.

7. Personal correspondence, November 21, 2022.

8. Peter Hellman, "Domaine Ponsot Proprietor Halts Sale of Fake Bottles," *Wine Spectator*, May 16, 2008, www.winespectator.com/articles/domaine-ponsot-proprietor-halts-sale-of-fake-bottles-4131.

9. United States of America v. Rudy Kurniawan a/k/a Dr Conti a/k/a Mr 47, S1 12 Cr. 376(RMB) (S.D.N.Y. Dec. 9, 2013), 14.

10. Dan Collins, "In Vino Veritas? Inside the Bogus World of Wine," Huffington Post, July 8, 2012.

11. Tatiana Schlossberg, "Wine Dealer Sentenced to Ten Years for Defrauding Clients," *New York Times*, August 7, 2015.

12. Personal correspondence, November 28, 2022.

13. Cyrus Redding, *A History and Description of Modern Wines* (London: Whittaker, Treacher & Arnot, 1833), 344.

14. Personal correspondence, October 22, 2017.

15. Steve Inskeep, "How Atomic Particles Helped Solve a Wine Fraud Mystery," broadcast, *Hidden Kitchens*, NPR, June 3, 2014, www.npr.org/sections /thesalt/2014/06/03/318241738/how-atomic-particles-became-the-smoking-gun-in-wine-fraud-mystery.

16. Personal correspondence, November 16, 2017.

17. Personal correspondence, December 10, 2017.

18. Dominique Richard, "Vins de Bordeaux: Le trafic de fausses étiquettes explose sur internet," *Sud-Ouest*, November 1, 2013.

19. Sophie Kevany, "Fake Bordeaux in China Being Made on Offshore Boats, Says Official," *Decanter.com*, May 7, 2014.

20. Rhys Pender, "Counterfeit Wine—Its Impact on the Business of Wine," diss., The Institute of Masters of Wine, London, March 2010.

CHAPTER 10. THE LAST DROP

1. Stephen Skelton, *Viticulture: An Introduction to Commercial Grape Growing for Those in the Wine-Trade, Students Taking the WSET Diploma and Master of Wine Candidates* (London: Stephen Skelton, 2007), 83.

2. K. William Watson, "Reign of Terroir: How to Resist Europe's Efforts to Control Common Food Names as Geographical Indications," *CATO Institute Policy Analysis* 787, February 16, 2016, 1, 7.

3. Roger Scruton, "The Philosophy of Wine," in *Questions of Taste: The Philosophy of Wine*, ed. Barry C. Smith (Oxford: Signal Books, 2007), 16.

4. Robin Goldstein et al., "Do More Expensive Wines Taste Better? Evidence from a Large Sample of Blind Tastings," American Association of Wine

Economists Working Paper, *Journal of Wine Economics* 3, no. 1 (2008), https://wine-economics.org/.

5. Roberta Veale and Pascale Quester, "Consumer Sensory Evaluations of Wine Quality: The Respective Influence of Price and Country of Origin," *Journal of Wine Economics* 3, no. 1 (2008): 10–29, https://doi.org/10.1017/S1931436100000535.

Selected Bibliography

Accum, Friedrich Christian. *A Treatise on Adulterations of Food, and Culinary Poisons: Exhibiting the Fraudulent Sophistications of Bread, Beer, Wine, Spiritous Liquors, Tea, Coffee . . . and Methods of Detecting Them.* London: J. Mallett, 1820.

Almeida, C. Marisa R., and M. Teresa S. D. Vasconcelos. "Lead Contamination in Portuguese Red Wines from the Douro Region: From the Vineyard to the Final Product." *Journal of Agricultural and Food Chemistry* 51, no. 10 (2003): 3012–23. https:// doi .org/10.1021/jf0259664.

Anderson, Kym, and Vicente Pinilla. *Wine Globalization: A New Comparative History.* Cambridge: Cambridge University Press, 2018.

Anonymous. *Wine and Spirit Adulterators Unmasked: In a Treatise, Setting Forth the Manner Employed, and the Various Ingredients Which Constitute the Adulterations and Impositions Effected with the Different Wines and Spirits Offered to the Public, through the Medium of Cheap Prices, by Many of the Advertising and Placarding Wholesale Wine and Spirit Merchants, and Gin-Shop-Keepers, of the Present Day: Also Shewing the Method by Which the Notice of the Excise Is*

Evaded, and Affording a Variety of Other Valuable Information on the Subject. London: printed for the author by J. Robins and Co., 1827.

Apicius. *The Roman Cookery Book: A Critical Translation of "The Art of Cooking" by Apicius for Use in the Study and the Kitchen.* New York: George G. Harrap, 1958.

"Argonne Researchers Confirm Lead in Beethoven's Illness." Argonne National Laboratory, December 7, 2005. www.newswise.com/articles/argonne-researchers-confirm-lead-in-beethovens-illness?section=latest&previous_id=516649.

Arnaud, Patrick, Michel Blanc, and Marie-Claude Pichery. *Les appellations viticoles: Leur histoire, leur avenir.* Clemencey: Terre en vues, 2019.

Aroon, Preeti. "Bush Confuses APEC with OPEC, Australia with Austria." ForeignPolicy.com, September 7, 2007.

Ballentine, Carol. "Taste of Raspberries, Taste of Death: The 1937 Elixir Sulfanilamide Incident." US Food and Drug Administration. www.fda.gov/files/about%20fda/published/The-Sulfanilamide-Disaster.pdf.

Bannon, Cynthia. "Fresh Water in Roman Law: Rights and Policy." *Journal of Roman Studies* 17 (November 2017): 60–89.

Battaglene, Anthony. "Politics Meets Terroir: The Story of Prosecco—Are GI's Just a Protectionist Racket?" Lecture presented at the XIII International Terroir Congress, May 12, 2022. https://ives-openscience.eu/.

Beard, Mary. *SPQR: A History of Ancient Rome.* London: Profile Books, 2016.

Beethoven, Ludwig van. *Beethoven's Letters: A Critical Edition with Explanatory Notes.* Ed. Alfred Christlieb Kalischer, trans. J. S. Shedlock. Freeport, NY: Books for Libraries Press, 1969.

———. *The Letters of Beethoven.* Ed. and trans. Emily Anderson. London: Macmillan, 1961.

Beeton, Isabella. *The Book of Household Management . . . Also Sanitary, Medical and Legal Memoranda. With a History of the Origin, Properties and Uses of All Things Connected with Home Life and Comfort.* London: Ward, Lock and Co., 1888.

Begg, Tristan James Alexander, Axel Schmidt, Arthur Kocher, Maarten H. D. Larmuseau, Göran Runfeldt, Paul Andrew Maier, John D. Wilson, et al. "Genomic Analyses of Hair from Ludwig van Beethoven." *Current Biology* (2023). https://doi.org/10.1016/ j.cub.2023.02.041.

Berget, A. *La coopération dans la viticulture européenne; Étude d'économie rurale et d'histoire agronomique.* Lille: A. Devos, 1902.

Bert, Pierre. *In vino veritas: L'affaire des vins de Bordeaux.* Paris: Albin Michel, 1975.

Bilbe, Mark. "An Oral History of the Wine Trade: Michael Broadbent." Audio recording. British Library Listening and Viewing Service. London, 2003.

———. "An Oral History of the Wine Trade: Serena Sutcliffe." Audio recording. British Library Listening and Viewing Service. London, 2004.

Blagdon, Francis William. *Paris as It Was and as It Is; or a Sketch of the French Capital Illustrative of the Effects of the Revolution.* London: C. & R. Baldwin, 1803.

Boulay, Thibaut. "Wine Appreciation in Ancient Greece." In *A Companion to Food in the Ancient World,* ed. John Wilkins and Robin Nadeau. Malden, MA: John Wiley & Sons, 2015.

Bourgeon, Jean-Marc. "Le vignoble bourguignon des origines au milieu du XXe siècle." Centre beaunois d'études historiques, October 2016. https://cbehblog.files.wordpress.com/2016/10/le-vignoble-reperes.pdf.

Briggs, Asa. *Wine for Sale: Victoria Wine and the Liquor Trade, 1864–1984.* Chicago: University of Chicago Press, 1985.

Brillat-Savarin, Jean-Anthelme. *The Physiology of Taste: Or, Meditations on Transcendental Gastronomy.* Trans. M. F. K. Fisher. New York: Vintage, 2011.

Broadbent, Michael. *Michael Broadbent's Vintage Wine: Fifty Years of Tasting over Three Centuries of Wine.* London: Websters, 2002.

Brogan, Hugh. *The Penguin History of the USA.* London: Penguin, 1999.

Brown, Corie. "$75,000 a Case? He's Buying." *Los Angeles Times,* December 1, 2006. http://articles.latimes.com/2006/dec/01/entertainment/et-rudy1.

Buch, Esteban. *Beethoven's Ninth: A Political History.* Trans. Richard Miller. Chicago: University of Chicago Press, 2004.

Burgess, R. W. Review of *The Fall of Rome and the End of Civilization,* by Bryan Ward-Perkins. *Canadian Journal of History* 42, no. 1 (2007): 83–85. https://utpjournals.press/doi/abs/10.3138/cjh.42.1.83.

Busby, James. *Journal of a Tour through Some of the Vineyards of Spain and France.* Hunters Hill, Australia: David Ell Press, 1979.

Byszewski, Elaine T. "What's in the Wine? A History of FDA's Role." *Food and Drug Law Journal* 57, no. 3 (2002): 545–72. www.jstor.org/stable/26660495.

Cameron, Alan. Letter to the editor, *International Herald Tribune,* June 20, 1983.

Campbell, Christy. *Phylloxera: How Wine was Saved for the World*. London: Harper Perennial, 2004.

Capus, Joseph, and Théodore Georgopoulos. *L'évolution de la législation sur les appellations d'origine: Genèse des appellations contrôlées*. Paris: Mare & Martin, 2019.

Carcopino, Jérôme. *Daily Life in Ancient Rome: The People and the City at the Height of the Empire*. Ed. Henry T. Rowell, trans. E. O. Lorimer. London: Routledge, 1941.

Carême, M. A. *French Cookery: Comprising "L'art de la cuisine française," "Le patissier royal," "Le cuisinier parisien."* Trans. William Hall. London: John Murray, 1836.

Cato, Marcus Porcius, and Marcus Terentius Varro. *On Agriculture*. Trans. William Davis Hooper and H. Boyd Ash. Cambridge, MA: Harvard University Press, 1934.

Cevik, Serhan, and Tahsin Saadi Sedik. "A Barrel of Oil or a Bottle of Wine: How Do Global Growth Dynamics Affect Commodity Prices?" IMF working paper no. WP/AA/1, January 2011.

Chabalier, Hervé. "Le vin amer des Chartrons." *Le nouvel observateur,* August 27, 1973.

Chappaz, G. *Le vignoble et le vin de Champagne*. Tome II. Paris: Louis Larmat, 1951.

Charbonneau, Louis. "Mystery Nation Picks Aussies over Austrians at U.N." Reuters, October 17, 2008.

Charle, C. *A Social History of France in the 19th Century*. Oxford: Berg, 1994.

Charney, Noah. *The Art of Forgery*. London: Phaidon Press, 2015.

Charters, Steve, ed. *The Business of Champagne*. Abingdon: Routledge, 2012.

———. *Wine and Society: The Social and Cultural Context of a Drink*. Amsterdam: Elsevier/Butterworth-Heinemann, 2006.

Coates, Clive. *Grands Vins: The Finest Châteaux of Bordeaux and Their Wines*. Berkeley: University of California Press, 1995.

Collins, Dan. "In Vino Veritas? Inside the Bogus World of Wine." Huffington Post, July 8, 2012.

Colman, Tyler. *Wine Politics: How Governments, Environmentalists, Mobsters, and Critics Influence the Wines We Drink*. Berkeley: University of California Press, 2010.

Columella, Lucius Iunius Moderatus. *On Agriculture I–IV*. Trans. Harrison Boyd Ash. Cambridge, MA: Harvard University Press, 1941.

———. *Res Rustica 1–4*. Vol. 1. Cambridge, MA: Harvard University Press, 1960.

Conison, Alexander. "The Organization of Rome's Wine Trade." Dissertation, University of Michigan, 2012. https://deepblue.lib.umich.edu/bitstream /handle/2027.42/91455/conison_1.pdf;sequence=1.

Constantin-Weyer, Maurice. *L'âme du vin*. Paris: La table ronde, 2008.

"Counterfeit Wine: A Vintage Crime." Broadcast. *CBS Sunday Morning*, season 22, episode 51, December 22, 2013. www.cbsnews.com/news/counterfeit-wine-a-vintage-crime/.

Daley, Robert. "That Wine, Sir, May Not Be Wine at All: Sophisticators Fool Italy with Ingenious Food and Drink Swindles." *LIFE*, February 23, 1968.

Davis, Jennifer J. *Defining Culinary Authority: The Transformation of Cooking in France, 1650–1830*. Baton Rouge: Louisiana State University Press, 2013.

Davis, Lee Allyn. *Natural Disasters*. New York: Checkmark Books, 2008.

Dean, John W., and James Robenalt. "The Legacy of Watergate." *Litigation* 38, no. 3 (2012): 19–25. www.jstor.org/stable/23239838.

Demandt, Alexander. *Der Fall Roms: Die Auflösung des römischen Reiches im Urteil der Nachwelt*. Munich: Beck, 1984.

Deming, David. "The Aqueducts and Water Supply of Ancient Rome." *Groundwater* 58, no.1 (2019): 152–61. https://doi.org/10.1111/gwat.12958.

Demossier, Marion. *Burgundy: The Global Story of Terroir*. New York: Berghahn Books, 2018.

Dengate, Cayla. "CNN Blooper: Australia Is Building a Wall at Slovenian Border." Huffington Post, March 1, 2016.

Denman, James L. *Wine and Its Counterfeits*. London: Briscoe & Co., 1860.

Desbois-Thibault, C., and A. Melin. *1911–2011 Du déséquilibre au consensus: Histoire et souvenirs*. Épernay: Syndicat general des vignerons de la Champagne, 2011.

Diart, S. *Histoire des relations interprofessionnelles champenoises*. Reims: Farman Communication, 2010.

Dizerens, Céline, Sina Lenggenhager, Mikhael Schwander, Annika Buck, and Selina Foffa. "The 1956 Cold Wave in Western Europe." In *Historical Weather Extremes in Reanalyses*, ed. Stefan Brönnimann, 101–11. Bern: University of Bern, Institute of Geography, 2017.

Draf, Stephan. "Hardy Rodenstock: Der große Etikettenschwindel." *Stern,* November 23, 2008. www.stern.de/wirtschaft/news/hardy-rodenstock-der-grosse-etikettenschwindel-3746930.html.

Duffield, Grace, and Peter Grabosky. "The Psychology of Fraud." *Crime and Criminal Justice,* March 2001, 1–6.

Dunbabin, Katherine. *The Roman Banquet: Images of Conviviality.* Cambridge: Cambridge University Press, 2010.

Duthomas, Bruno. "Des crus raffinés, des Chartrons insoupçonnables." *Le Monde,* October 28, 1974.

———. "L'autre 'scandale': 60,000 hectolitres et un colorant." *Le Monde,* August 31, 1973.

———. "Le mythe du wine tasting." *Le Monde,* November 2, 1974.

Eckert, Werner. "25.4.1985: Der Skandal um gepanschte Weine wird aufge-deckt." *SWR2 Zeitwort,* SWR2, July 24, 2019. www.swr.de/swr2/wissen/aex-avarticle-swr-62126.html.

Eisenberger, Iris, and Rostam J. Neuwirth. "Innovative Tradition: Austrian Wine Regulation between Past and Future." In *Wine Law and Policy: From National Terroirs to a Global Market,* ed. Julien Chaisse, Fernando Dias Simões, and Danny Friedman, 127–45. Leiden: Brill, 2021.

Eisinger, Josef. "Lead and Wine: Eberhard Gockel and the Colica Pictonum." *Medical History* 26, no. 3 (1982): 279–302.

———. "Lead in History and History in Lead." Review of *Lead and Lead Poisoning in Antiquity,* by Jerome O. Nriagu. *Nature* 307, no. 9 (1984): 573.

———. "Sweet Poison." *Natural History,* July 1996.

Erwin K*** and Walter D***. Entscheidungstext 9 Os 93/86, OGH, Rechtsin-formationssystem des Bundes (RIS) (ruling 9 Os 93/86, Supreme Court of Justice of Austria, Legal Information System), October 9, 1986.

European Commission, Scientific Committee on Consumer Products. "Opin-ion on Diethylene Glycol." June 24, 2008.

Faith, Nicholas. *The Winemasters of Bordeaux.* London: Carlton, 2005.

Ferguson, Priscilla Parkhurst. "A Cultural Field in the Making: Gastronomy in 19th-Century France." *American Journal of Sociology* 104, no. 3 (November 1998): 597–641. https://doi.org/10.1086/210082.

———. "Writing out of the Kitchen: Carême and the Invention of French Cui-sine." *Gastronomica* 3, no. 3 (2003): 40–51. https://doi.org/10.1525/gfc.2003.3.3.40.

Fielden, Christopher. *Is This the Wine You Ordered, Sir?* London: Christopher Helm, 1989.

Frader, Laura Levine. *Peasants and Protest: Agricultural Workers, Politics, and Unions in the Aude, 1850–1914.* Berkeley: University of California Press, 1991.

Fradet, Dominique. *1911 en Champagne: Chronique d'une révolution.* Reims: Fradet, 2011.

Freedman, Paul. "Meats That Time Forgot." *Gourmet*, June 3, 2008. www.gourmet.com/food/2008/03/dormouse.

Gabler, James M. *The Wines and Travels of Thomas Jefferson.* Baltimore: Bacchus Press, 1995.

Gallagher, Maree, and Ian Thomas. "Food Fraud: The Deliberate Adulteration and Misdescription of Foodstuffs." *European Food and Feed Law Review* 5, no. 6 (2010): 347–53. www.jstor.org/stable/24325040.

Garnotelm, J. *L'ascension d'une grande agriculture en Champagne.* Paris: Economica, 1985.

Garrier, Gilbert. *Le phylloxéra: Une guerre de trente ans, 1870–1900.* Chaintré: Œnoplurimedia, 2006.

Gautier, Jean-François. *Le vin et ses fraudes.* Paris: Presses universitaires de France, 1995.

George, Rosemary. *The Wines of Chablis and the Grand Auxerrois.* Oxford: Infinite Ideas, 2019.

Giacosa, Ilaria Gozzini. *A Taste of Ancient Rome.* Chicago: University of Chicago Press, 1992.

Gibb, Rebecca. "Were the Causes of the 1911 Champagne Riots Essentially Economic?" Research paper, The Institute of Masters of Wine, London, 2015.

Gibbon, Edward. *The Decline and Fall of the Roman Empire.* New York: P. Fenelon Collier, 1900.

Gibbon, Edward, and David Womersley. *The History of the Decline and Fall of the Roman Empire.* London: Penguin, 1996.

Gilfillan, S. C. "'Lead Poisoning and the Fall of Rome." *Journal of Occupational Medicine* 2, no. 2 (1965): 53–60.

Girault, J. "Le rôle du socialisme dans la révolte des vignerons de l'Aube." *Le mouvement social* 67 (April–June 1969): 89–108.

Goldberg, Howard G. "Oldest Bordeaux? Yes; Jefferson's? Maybe." *New York Times*, October 30, 1985.

Goldstein, Robin, Johan Almenberg, Anna Dreber, John W. Emerson, Alexis Herschkowitsch, and Jacob Katz. "Do More Expensive Wines Taste Better? Evidence from a Large Sample of Blind Tastings." American Association of Wine Economists Working Paper. *Journal of Wine Economics* 3, no. 1 (2008). https://wine-economics.org/.

Goodwin, Lucia. "Research Report: Château Lafite 1787, with Initials 'Th. J.'" Thomas Jefferson Foundation, December 12, 1985. https://monticello-www.s3.amazonaws.com/library/pdfs/Chateau_Lafite_1787.pdf.

Gough, J. B. "Winecraft and Chemistry in 18th-Century France: Chaptal and the Invention of Chaptalization." *Technology and Culture* 39, no. 1 (January 1998): 74–104. https://doi.org/10.2307/3107004.

Greenstone, Gerry. "The History of Bloodletting." *BCMJ* 51, no. 1 (2010): 12–14. www.bcmj.org/premise/history-bloodletting.

Griffiths, Antony. *The Print before Photography: An Introduction to European Printmaking, 1550–1820*. London: British Museum, 2018.

Grill brothers. Entscheidungstext 12 Os 172/86, OGH, Rechtsinformationssystem des Bundes (RIS) (ruling 12 Os 172/86, Supreme Court of Justice of Austria, Legal Information System), June 11, 1987.

Guillebaud, Jean-Claude. "Maquillages, mouillages, coupages et vinages." *Le Monde*, October 12, 1974.

Guy, K. M. *When Champagne Became French*. Baltimore: Johns Hopkins University Press, 2003.

Hailman, John. *Thomas Jefferson on Wine*. Jackson: University Press of Mississippi, 2006.

Hallgarten, Fritz. *Wine Scandal*. London: Weidenfeld and Nicolson, 1986.

Hands, Thora. *Drinking in Victorian and Edwardian Britain*. Cham, Switzerland: Palgrave Macmillan, 2018. https://doi.org/10.1007/978–3–319–92964–4_12.

Harding, Graham. "'The Stock of a Connoisseur?': The Development and Commercialization of Wine Connoisseurship in the Long Nineteenth Century." In *Connoisseurship*, ed. Christina M. Anderson and Peter Stewart. Oxford: Oxford University Press, 2023.

Harlaut, Y., and F. Perron. *Les révoltes du Champagne*. Langres: Editions Dominique Guéniot, 2010.

Hau, M. *La croissance économique de la Champagne*. Paris: Editions Ophrys, 1976.

Heather, P.J. *Empires and Barbarians: The Fall of Rome and the Birth of Europe.* New York: Oxford University Press, 2012.

Hebborn, Eric. *The Art Forger's Handbook.* Woodstock, NY: Overlook Press, 1997.

Hellman, Peter. "Domaine Ponsot Proprietor Halts Sale of Fake Bottles." *Wine Spectator,* May 16, 2008. www.winespectator.com/articles/domaine-ponsot-proprietor-halts-sale-of-fake-bottles-4131.

Héran, François. "Lost Generations: The Demographic Impact of the Great War." *Population & Societies* 510, no. 4 (2014): 1–4. https://doi.org/10.3917/popsoc.510.0001.

Holmberg, Lars. "Wine Fraud." *International Journal of Wine Research* (2010): 105–13.

Howland, Peter J. "Distinction by Proxy: The Democratization of Fine Wine." *Journal of Sociology* 49, no. 2–3 (2013): 325–40.

Hubert, Ph., F. Perrot, J. Gaye, B. Médina, and M.S. Pravikoff. "Radioactivity Measurements Applied to the Dating and Authentication of Old Wines." *Comptes Rendus Physique* 10, no. 7 (2009): 622–29. https://doi.org/10.1016/j.crhy.2009.08.007.

Hunter, David. "Handel's Ill Health: Documents and Diagnoses." *Royal Musical Association Research Chronicle* 41, no. 1 (2008): 69–92.

Inskeep, Steve. "How Atomic Particles Helped Solve a Wine Fraud Mystery." Broadcast. *Hidden Kitchens,* NPR, June 3, 2014. www.npr.org/transcripts/318241738?t=1649242719625.

"Is Bordeaux Blushing?" *TIME,* November 18, 1974.

Johnson, Hugh. *The Story of Wine.* London: Mitchell Beazley, 1989.

Jones, Colin. "The Great Chain of Buying: Medical Advertisement, the Bourgeois Public Sphere, and the Origins of the French Revolution." *American Historical Review* 101, no. 1 (February 1996): 13–40. https://doi.org/10.2307/2169222.

Jouanna, Jacques. *Greek Medicine from Hippocrates to Galen.* Leiden: Brill, 2012. https://doi.org/10.1163/9789004232549_011.

Jullien, André. *The Topography of All the Known Vineyards: Containing a Description of the Kind and Quality of Their Products, and a Classification.* London: Printed for G. and W.B. Whittaker, 1824.

Karis, Harry. *The Châteauneuf-du-Pape Wine Book.* Roermond, The Netherlands: Kavino, 2009.

Keefe, Patrick Radden. "The Jefferson Bottles." *The New Yorker,* August 27, 2007.

Keevil, Susan. "Michael Broadbent on the Golden Years." *Decanter,* March 30, 2020. www.decanter.com/features/michael-broadbent-on-the-golden-years-248680/.

Kevany, Sophie. "Fake Bordeaux in China Being Made on Offshore Boats, Says Official." *Decanter,* May 7, 2014. www.decanter.com/wine-news/fake-bordeaux-in-china-being-made-on-offshore-boats-says-official-13036/.

Kladstrup, Don and Petie. *Champagne: How the World's Most Glamorous Wine Triumphed over War and Hard Times.* New York: Harper Perennial, 2006.

Klinger, Willi, and Karl Vocelka, eds. *Wine in Austria: The History.* Vienna: Brandstätter, 2019.

Koch v. Christie's International Plc., 699 F.3d 141 (2d Cir. 2012), https://casetext .com/case/koch-v-christies-intl-plc-k-pub-ltd.

Koch v. Rodenstock, 06 Civ. 6586 (BSJ) (DF) (S.D.N.Y. May 9, 2012). https:// casetext.com/case/koch-v-rodenstock-2.

Koukharski, P. "Le mouvement paysan en France en 1911." *Questions d'histoire,* no. 1 (1952): 160–77.

Kranacher, Mary-Jo, and Richard A. Riley. *Forensic Accounting and Fraud Examination.* Hoboken, NJ: Wiley, 2010.

Kubba, A. K., and M. Young. "Ludwig Van Beethoven: A Medical Biography." *The Lancet* 347, no. 8995 (1996): 167–70.

Lachiver, Marcel. *Vins, vignes et vignerons: Histoire du vignoble français.* Paris: Fayard, 1988.

Lavalle, Jean, Émile Delarue, and Joseph Garnier. *Histoire et statistique de la vigne et des grands vins de la côte-d'Or.* Paris: Dusacq, 1855.

Lenoir, B. A. *Traité de la culture de la vigne et de la vinification, contenant des préceptes généraux de culture applicables à tous les climats, une nomenclature des espèces de vignes, avec l'indication de celles qui produisent les meilleurs vins.* Paris: Imprimerie et librairie de Mme Ve Bouchard-Huzard, 1828.

Lessard, E., and J.-L. Barbier. *Le Champagne: Agronomie, economie.* Reims: CRDP, 1981.

Levy, Paul. "Edmund Penning-Rowsell: Obituary." *The Independent,* March 7, 2002.

Lheureux, L. *Les syndicats dans le viticole champenoise.* Paris: Librarie générale de droit et de jurisprudence, 1906.

Liszek, S. *Champagne: Un siècle d'histoire sociale.* Montreuil: VO Editions, 1995.

Lopez, C. M., N. E. Vallejo, A. E. Pinero, R. Uicich, C. F. Damin, M. I. Sarchi, E. C. Villaamil Lepori, et al. "Alteration of Biochemical Parameters Related with Exposure to Lead in Heavy Alcohol Drinkers." *Pharmacological Research* 45, no. 1 (2002): 47–50.

Lucand, Christophe. *Les négociants en vins de Bourgogne: De la fin du XIXe siècle à nos jours.* Bordeaux: Editions Féret, 2011.

Lukacs, P. *Inventing Wine: A New History of One of the World's Most Ancient Pleasures.* New York: W. W. Norton, 2012.

Maguire, Jennifer Smith, and Steve Charters. "Aesthetic Logics, *Terroir* and the Lamination of Grower Champagne." *Consumption, Markets and Culture* 24, no. 1 (2022) : 75–96.

Margalit, Yair. *Concepts in Wine Chemistry.* San Francisco: Wine Appreciation Guild, 2016.

Martial. *Epigrams.* Trans. Walter C. A. Ker. London: William Heinemann, 1919.

Martin, Germain. *Essai sur la vente des vins (plus particulièrement des vins de Bourgogne).* Dijon: Imprimerie Barbier-Marilier, 1904.

Martin, Germain, and Paul Martenot. *Contribution à l'histoire des classes rurales en France au XIXe siècle: La côte-d'Or (étude d'économie rurale).* Dijon: Université de Dijon, 1909.

Martin, Russell. *Beethoven's Hair.* New York: Broadway Books, 2001.

Mauriac, François. *Préseances.* Paris: Flammarion, 1928.

Mayer, George, Sam Simon, John Swartzwelder, and John Vitti. "The Crepes of Wrath." *The Simpsons,* season 1, episode 11, Fox, April 15, 1990.

McAdam, Doug, and Yang Su. "The War at Home: Antiwar Protests and Congressional Voting, 1965 to 1973." *American Sociological Review* 67, no. 5 (2002): 696.

McClure, James P., and J. Jefferson Looney, eds. *The Papers of Thomas Jefferson Digital Edition.* University of Virginia Press, 2009. https://rotunda.upress.virginia.edu/founders/TSJN.html.

Mercer, Chris. "Wine World Great Michael Broadbent MW Dies." *Decanter,* March 18, 2020.

Molyneux-Berry, David. "Wine Fraud." Lecture presented at the Taste3 Conference, May 2007. www.youtube.com/watch?v=HFnOSx6Ow1w.

Monaco, Emily. "If You Think You're a Decadent Fuck, Try Feasting Like a 19th-Century Parisian." VICE, May 22, 2018. www.vice.com/en/article /435xxd/paris-bourgeous-1800s-19th-century-feasmt-gourands.

Moser, Lenz. *Weinbau einmal anders: Ein Weinbaubuch für den fortschrittlichen Weinbauern.* Vienna: Österreichischer Agrarverlag, 1966.

Moser, Peter. "Der Weinskandal in Österreich und seine Folgen." *Falstaff,* December 17, 2015.

Mowery, Lauren. "Pliny the Elder, the First Wine Critic and Why He Still Matters." *Wine Enthusiast,* October 10, 2019.

Nemeitz, Joachim Christoph. "Séjour de Paris [. . .]" [1727]. Gallica, January 1, 1970. https://gallica.bnf.fr/ark:/12148/bpt6k102148f/.

Noce, Victor. "Sous le signe du tonneau." *Libération,* November 17, 2000. www .liberation.fr/villes/2000/11/17/sous-le-signe-du-tonneau_344579/.

Nollevalle, J. "1911: L'agitation dans le vignoble champenois." In *La champagne viticole.* Épernay: Syndicat general des vignerons de la Champagne, 1961.

Nriagu, Jerome O. *Lead and Lead Poisoning in Antiquity.* New York: Wiley, 1983.

Oddy, D.J. "Food in Nineteenth Century England: Nutrition in the First Urban Society." *Proceedings of the Nutrition Society* 29, no. 1 (1970): 150–57. https://doi .org/10.1079/pns19700034.

Oosthoek, K. Jan. "Little Ice Age." Environmental History Resources, July 23, 2016. www.eh-resources.org/little-ice-age/.

Paulson, Jon. "Chardonnay v Grüner Veltliner, a Knockout Contest." Jancis-Robinson.com, July 26, 2002.

Paxton, Robert O. *French Peasant Fascism: Henry Dorgères' Greenshirts and the Crises of French Agriculture, 1929–1939.* New York: Oxford University Press, 1998.

Pender, Rhys. "Counterfeit Wine: Its Impact on the Business of Wine." Dissertation, The Institute of Masters of Wine, London, March 2010.

Penning-Rowsell, Edmund. *The Wines of Bordeaux.* London: Allen Lane, 1979.

Phillips, Roderick. *A Short History of Wine.* London: Allen Lane, 2000.

Pitte, Jean-Robert. *Bordeaux/Burgundy: A Vintage Rivalry.* Trans. M.B. Debevoise. Berkeley: University of California Press, 2012.

———. *Le désir du vin: À la conquête du monde.* Paris: Fayard, 2009.

———. "Naissance et expansion des restaurants." In *Histoire de l'alimentation,* ed. Jean-Louis Flandrin and Massimo Montanari, 765–78. Paris: Fayard, 2018.

Planchon, J.-E. "La question du phylloxéra en 1876." *Revue des deux mondes* 19, no. 3 (January 15, 1877): 241–77.

Pliny. *Pliny Natural History.* Trans. H. Rackham, W. H. S. Jones, and D. E. Eichholz. London: Folio Society, 2012.

Plutarch. *The Parallel Lives.* Trans. Bernadotte Perrin. Cambridge, MA: Harvard University Press, 1916.

Portes, Jean-Claude. *Château La Nerthe: Five Centuries of History.* Châteauneuf-du-Pape: Château La Nerthe, 2014.

———. *Châteauneuf-du-Pape: Première AOC de France.* Châteauneuf-du-Pape: Organisme de défense et de gestion de l'AOC Châteauneuf-du-Pape, 2016.

Postmann, Klaus Peter. *Mein Wein aus Österreich: Die soziale und wirtschaftliche Entwicklung der Weinkultur in Österreich im 20. Jahrhundert.* Linz: Universitätsverlag Rudolf Trauner, 2003.

Pouget, Richard. "Histoire 'oubliée' de Vendargues de l'antiquité à la fin du 19eme siècle." Histoire de Vendargues, January 14, 2013. http://vendargues .histoire.pagesperso-orange.fr/Histoire%20de%20Vendargues/Histoire%20 Vendargues%20texte.htm.

A Practical Liquor Manufacturer. *The Bordeaux Wine and Liquor Dealers' Guide: A Treatise on the Manufacture and Adulteration of Liquors.* New York: Dick & Fitzgerald, 1858.

Prévôt, Jack-Henry. "Les cousins Cruse plaident leur dossier et laissent à six témoins étrangers le soin de défendre leur vin." *Sud-Ouest,* October 30, 1974.

———. "Lionel Cruse: Ce n'est pas dénigrer le bordeaux que de dire qu'il y a en France d'excellents vins de table." *Sud-Ouest,* October 29, 1974.

———. "Tous les témoins ayant été entendus, les parties civiles ont la parole." *Sud-Ouest,* November 4, 1974.

———. "Un inspecteur principale des impôts: Il fallait contrôler tout ou rien." *Sud-Ouest,* November 1, 1974.

Prial, Frank J. "Frenchmen Are Already Calling the Bordeaux Case the Trial of the Century." *New York Times,* October 26, 1974.

———. "Italian Wine: Hard-Won Image Is Shattered." *New York Times,* April 12, 1986.

Raff, Katharine. "The Roman Banquet." Metmuseum.org, October 2011. www .metmuseum.org/toah/hd/banq/hd_banq.htm.

Redding, Cyrus. *A History and Description of Modern Wines*. London: Whittaker, Treacher & Arnot, 1833.

———. *History and Description of Modern Wines*. 3rd ed. London: Bohn, 1860.

Reiter, Christian. "The Causes of Beethoven's Death and His Locks of Hair: A Forensic-Toxicological Investigation." Trans. Michael Lorenz. *The Beethoven Journal* 22, no. 1 (2007): 2–5.

Reuters. "Austria Impounds Wine Laced with Poison." *New York Times*, July 23, 1985.

Robinson, Jancis. *Confessions of a Wine Lover*. Penguin: London, 1997.

———. "Grüner Veltliner—Distinctly Groovy." JancisRobinson.com, November 15, 2002.

Robinson, Jancis, and Julia Harding. *The Oxford Companion to Wine*. Oxford: Oxford University Press, 2015.

Robinson, Jancis, Julia Harding, and José F. Vouillamoz. *Wine Grapes: A Complete Guide to 1,380 Vine Varieties, Including Their Origins and Flavors*. New York: Ecco/HarperCollins, 2012.

"The Roman Empire: Victim of Poisoning." *International Herald Tribune*, June 1, 1983.

Roseman, Joe. *SWAG: Silver, Wine, Art, Gold. Alternative Investments for the Coming Decade*. Surrey: Grosvenor House, 2012.

Rossiter, J.J. "Wine and Oil Processing at Roman Farms in Italy." *Phoenix* 35, no. 4 (1981): 345–61. https://doi.org/10.2307/1087929.

Rothwell, Jerry, and Reuben Atlas, dirs. *Sour Grapes*. London: Dogwoof, 2016.

Saillet, J. "Les composantes du mouvement dans la Marne." *Le mouvement social* 67 (April–June 1969): 81–88.

"Saure Trauben, süße Sünden." *Die Zeit*. August 2, 1985. www.zeit.de/1985/32/saure-trauben-suesse-suenden.

Scheidel, Walter. "Disease and Death in the Ancient City of Rome." SSRN, February 21, 2009. https://papers.ssrn.com/sol3/papers.cfm?abstract_id=1347510.

Schimmel, Thomas. "Der Weinskandal 1985/86." Dissertation, Universität Wien, 1994.

Schindler, Anton Felix. *Beethoven as I Knew Him*. Ed. Donald W. MacArdle, trans. Constance S. Jolly. New York: Dover, 1996.

Schlossberg, Tatiana. "Wine Dealer Sentenced to Ten Years for Defrauding Clients." *New York Times,* August 7, 2015.

Schoonmaker, Frank, and Tom Marvel. *The Complete Wine Book.* London: Routledge, 1935. E-book published by Barakaldo Books, 2020.

Schrem, Max. "Defining Culinary Authority: The Transformation of Cooking in France, 1650–1830." *Reviews in History,* July 1, 2013. https://reviews.history .ac.uk/review/1454.

Schwarm, Betsy. "Moonlight Sonata." *Encyclopædia Britannica.* www.britannica.com/topic/Moonlight-Sonata.

Selin, Shannon. "The Restaurateur: Dining in Paris in the Early 19th Century." Shannon Selin, August 15, 2019. https://shannonselin.com/2019/02/restaurateur-dining-paris-19th-century/.

Service, Tom. "Symphony Guide: Beethoven's Eighth." *The Guardian,* February 11, 2014. www.theguardian.com/music/tomserviceblog/2014/feb/11/symphony-guide-beethoven-eighth.

———. "Symphony Guide: Beethoven's Ninth ('Choral')." *The Guardian,* September 9, 2014. www.theguardian.com/music/tomserviceblog/2014/sep/09 /symphony-guide-beethoven-ninth-choral-tom-service.

Shapin, Steven. "The Tastes of Wine: Towards a Cultural History." *Rivista di estetica,* no. 51 (2012): 49–94. https://doi.org/10.4000/estetica.1395.

Simon, André. *The History of Champagne.* London: Ebury Press, 1962.

———. *History of the Champagne Trade in England.* London: Wyman & Sons, 1905.

Simpson, James. *Creating Wine: The Emergence of a World Industry, 1840–1914.* Princeton, NJ: Princeton University Press, 2011.

———. "Phylloxera, Price Volatility and Institutional Innovation in France's Domestic Wine Markets, 1870–1911." Universidad Carlos III de Madrid, Economic History and Institutions Series 02, working paper 04–46, 2004.

Skelton, Stephen. *Viticulture: An Introduction to Commercial Grape Growing for Those in the Wine-Trade, Students Taking the WSET Diploma and Master of Wine Candidates.* London: Stephen Skelton, 2007.

Skovenborg, Erik. "Lead in Wine through the Ages." *Journal of Wine Research* 6, no. 1 (1995): 49–64.

Smith, Andrew W. M. *Terror and Terroir: The Winegrowers of the Languedoc and Modern France.* Manchester: Manchester University Press, 2016.

Smith, Barry. *Questions of Taste: The Philosophy of Wine.* Oxford: Signal Books, 2007.

Sowerwine, C. *France since 1870: Culture, Society and the Making of the Republic.* Basingstoke: Palgrave Macmillan, 2001.

Spang, Rebecca L. *The Invention of the Restaurant: Paris and Modern Gastronomic Culture.* Cambridge, MA: Harvard University Press, 2020.

Stanziani, A. "Une fraude agro-alimentaire: La falsification du vin en France." *Revue d'histoire moderne et contemporaine* 50, no. 2 (2003) : 154–86.

Stelzer, Tyson. *The Champagne Guide: 2014–2015.* Richmond, Australia: Hardie Grant Books, 2013. Kindle edition.

Stephens, Peter. "Vintage Vinegar Scandal." *Daily Mirror,* October 29, 1974.

Stevens, Michael H., Teemarie Jacobsen, and Alicia Kay Crofts. "Lead and the Deafness of Ludwig Van Beethoven." *The Laryngoscope* 123, no. 11 (2013): 2854–58.

Stöckl, Albert. "Austrian Wine: Developments after the Wine Scandal of 1985 and Its Current Situation." Paper presented at the 3rd International Wine Business Research Conference, Montpellier, July 6–8, 2006, Academy of Wine Business. http://academyofwinebusiness.com/wp-content/uploads/2010/05/Stockl.pdf.

Stotland, Ezra. "White Collar Criminals." *Journal of Social Issues* 33, no. 4 (1977): 179–96. https://doi.org/10.1111/j.1540-4560.1977.tb02531.x.

Stübling, H., and W. Bittner. "Gepanschter Wein: 'Schön rund und ölig.'" *Der Spiegel,* July 28, 1985.

"The Summer of Judgment." Broadcast. *The Summer of Judgment: The Watergate Hearings.* Public Broadcasting Service, 1983. https://youtu.be/tINCO6TfoPg.

Tagliabue, John. "Scandal over Poisoned Wine Embitters Village in Austria." *New York Times,* August 2, 1985.

Tchernia, André. *Le vin de l'Italie romaine: Essai d'histoire économique d'après les amphores.* Rome: École française de Rome, 1986.

Thompson, Jane. "Gastronomic Literature, Modern Cuisine and the Development of French Bourgeois Identity from 1800 to 1850." Honors paper, Connecticut College, 2011. https://digitalcommons.conncoll.edu/histhp/9.

Toutain, J.-C. "La production agricole de la France de 1810 à 1990: Départements et régions." *Économies et sociétés,* A.F. no. 17, Tome III, 1992.

Tovey, Charles. *Wine and Wine Countries; a Record and Manual for Wine Merchants and Wine Consumers.* London: Hamilton, Adams & Co., 1862.

————. *Wine and Wine Countries; a Record and Manual for Wine Merchants and Wine Consumers.* London: Whittaker & Co., 1877.

"Trying Days for French Wines." *Belfast Telegraph,* October 28, 1974.

United States of America v. Rudy Kurniawan a/k/a Dr Conti a/k/a Mr 47, S1 12 Cr. 376(RMB) (S.D.N.Y. Dec. 9, 2013).

Veale, Roberta, and Pascale Quester. "Consumer Sensory Evaluations of Wine Quality: The Respective Influence of Price and Country of Origin." *Journal of Wine Economics* 3, no. 1 (2008): 10–29. https://doi.org/10.1017/S1931436100000535.

"Vins de Bordeaux: Giscard voit rouge." *Le canard enchaîné,* August 15, 1973.

"Vintage Investments." *Changing Times,* July 1987.

Wajsman, Nathan, Carolina Arias Burgos, and Christopher Davies. "The Economic Cost of IPR Infringement in Spirits and Wine." European Union Intellectual Property Office, July 2016.

Wallace, Benjamin. *The Billionaire's Vinegar: The Mystery of the World's Most Expensive Bottle of Wine.* New York: Three Rivers Press, 2009.

Washington, George. *The Writings of George Washington from the Original Manuscript Sources, 1745–1799,* ed. John C. Fitzpatrick. Washington, DC: United States Government Printing Office, 1931.

Watson, K. William. "Reign of Terroir: How to Resist Europe's Efforts to Control Common Food Names as Geographical Indications." *CATO Institute Policy Analysis* 787 (February 16, 2016): 1–16.

Watts, Sarah. "Why Do Some People Commit Fraud? Psychologists Say It's Complicated." *Forbes,* March 21, 2019.

Weber, E. *Peasants into Frenchmen: The Modernization of Rural France.* Stanford, CA: Stanford University Press, 1976.

Wheaton, Barbara Ketcham. *Savoring the Past: The French Kitchen and Table from 1300 to 1789.* New York: Touchstone, 2015.

Wiczlinski, Verena von. "Der Glykol-Skandal im Jahr 1985." www.regionalgeschichte.net, urn:nbn:de:0291-rzd-016494-20203112-7.

Wilson, Bee. *Swindled: From Poison Sweets to Counterfeit Coffee—The Dark History of the Food Cheats.* London: John Murray, 2009.

Winder, C. *Developmental Neurotoxicity of Lead.* Lancaster: MTP Press, 1984.

Wolikow, C. "La delimitation de la Champagne viticole." *Les cahiers de Villa Bissinger,* no. 1 (2010): 139–58.

Wolikow, Serge, and Florian Humbert. *Une histoire des vins et des produits d'AOC: L'INAO, de 1935 à nos jours.* Dijon: Éditions universitaires de Dijon, 2015.

Woodfield, Ian. "Johann van Beethoven's Last Hurrah." OUP blog. Oxford University Press, October 30, 2013. https://blog.oup.com/2013/11/johann-van-beethoven-fatherhood/.

Woods, Robert. "Ancient and Early Modern Mortality: Experience and Understanding." *Economic History Review* 60, no. 2 (May 2007): 373–99. https://doi.org/10.1111/j.1468-0289.2006.00367.x.

Woodward, Guy. "What I've Learned: Michael Broadbent." Christies.com, September 13, 2016.

Zirkle, Conway. "The Death of Gaius Plinius Secundus (23–79 A.D.)." *Isis* 58, no. 4 (1967): 553–59.

Index

Abagnale, Frank, Jr., 203
Academy of Philately, 96
Accum, Friedrich, 62–64, 70
acetaminophen, 147
acetobacter, 69
acidity, 161
Acker Merrall & Condit (auction house), 195
additives, permitted, 160–61
agriculture, 12, 17
Aix-en-Provence (France), 171, 172
alcohol, 26–27
Algeria, 80, 102, 105, 114, 159
Almanach des gourmands (Grimod), 54–56
Alois Kracher Trophy, 158
Alsace region (France), 45–46
Âme du vin, L' (Constantin-Weyer), 105–6
American Express, 190
American grapes, European varieties
    grafted onto, 78, 79–80, 103

American wines, 60, 73–74
American Wines (Schoonmaker), 108
ammonia, 131
amphoras, 11–12, 13, 21, 29, 208
antifreeze, 138–39, 143, 146, 152
aphids. *See* phylloxera (vine louse)
Apicius, 14, 15, 22, 28
appellation systems, 117, 205–6. *See also*
    French appellation system
aqueducts, 13, 25
Arcachon (France), 127
Arcadia (CA; USA), 192
Argentina, 47
Armée de l'Air (France), 98
Armenier, Catherine, 115–16
Armenier, Emile, 115
Armenier, François, 102
arsenic poisoning, 39
art collectors, 5
Art de la cuisine française, L' (Carême), 58

Artinger, Heribert, 149

Art of Glass, The (Neri), 48

Art of Making Wine, The (French manual), 68

Art of Making Wine from Raisins, The (how-to guide), 79

Aube region (France), 87–89, 92

auction houses, 198. *See also* Christie's (auction house); Sotheby's (auction house); *specific auction house*

Australia, 152–53, 191

Australian wines, 202

Austria, 9; Lower (Niederösterreich), 142; Nazi control of, 141; post-WWII economic boom, 141; vineyard management methods in, 141–42; weather and harvest in, 145; wine demand in, 141, 157, 159; winegrowing regions of, 141; wine imports in, 32, 142; wine overproduction in, 142–43; wine regulations in, 140, 142

Austrian wine fraud scandal: accomplices involved in, 205; Austrian government response to, 143–44, 153–55, 156–57; cartoon portrayals of, 138–39; discovery of, 143; glycol poisoning in, 144–45; impact of, 149–51, 152–53, 156–60; media coverage of, 143, 144, 146, 148–49, 152; similar cases, in other countries, 146–48, 155–56; wine amelioration concerns as result of, 160–62

Austrian wines: defining, 140; demand for, 140–41, 142, 145, 150; German wines blended with, 45; international sales of, 157, 159; overproduction of, 142–43, 149–50; prices of, 142–43, 149–50; regulations defining, 140, 142,

151–52, 157; reputation of, 157–58, 159–60

authenticity: auction-house policies regarding, 199; evolution of meaning, 4–6; French appellation system and, 112, 132; of Jefferson-signed wine bottles, concerns about, 163–64, 169–71, 180, 181, 182, 198, 209–10; in Roman empire, 17, 18–19; social class and, 17

autoimmune hearing loss, 38

automobile emissions, 45–46

Avaline (wine brand), 160–61

Avignon (France), 99, 101, 111–12

Aÿ (France), 74, 75–76, 80–81, 82, 85, 87, 89

Bad Marienberg (Germany), 182–83

Ball, Gene V., 43

banana skins, 131

banderole, 157

ban des vendages, 95

Bangladesh, 147

bar owners, 25

barrels, 206

Barsac (France), 123

Bar-sur-Aube (France), 88, 89

Barthe, Edouard, 112

Baudouin, Raymond, 108

Beaucaire (France), 11

Beaujolais region (France), 103

Beaujolais wines, 129

Beaune (France), 78, 102, 105–6

Beauvilliers, Antoine, 53–54

Beckenbauer, Franz, 179

beef blood, 114, 131

beer, 24, 27, 63, 143, 149

Beerenauslese (Austrian sweet wine), 143

Beethoven, Johann van, 41

Beethoven, Ludwig van: deafness of, 36–37, 38, 40, 41; death of, 37, 40, 42, 49; health problems of, 37, 40; medical research on, 38–39, 40; wine drinking habit of, 35–36, 39–42, 45, 49

Beethoven Journal, 37

Beethoven's Hair (Martin), 39

Beeton, Isabella, 61–62

Belgium, 155

Bernard le Saint, Edmée, 96, 99

Bernard le Saint, Henry, 99

Berry Bros. & Rudd (wine merchant), 200–201

Bert, Pierre, 123, 129, 132, 133, 134, 136, 204–5

Bharara, Preet, 196

Bild (German tabloid), 144

Billionaire's Vinegar, The (Wallace), 164

Bisel, Sara C., 28, 29

blackcurrant juice, 114

black market, 197

Blagdon, Francis William, 53–54

blindness, 140

blind tasting, 132, 159–60

Blondel, Romauld, 84–85

blueberries, 105

Bohr, Robert, 191

Bolo, Paul, 86–87

Bonchot, Monsieur, 101

Bonn (Germany), 36

Book of Household Management (Beeton), 61–62

Bordeaux (France), 119–22, 127, 134, 172, 191

Bordeaux/Burgundy: A Vintage Rivalry (Pitte), 69

Bordeaux region (France): American vines as rootstocks in, 78; *en primeur* week in, 185–86; Jefferson's travels in, 172; Médoc region of, 60; trade routes from, 100; vine pandemic in, 78; vines from, in other countries, 60; weather and harvest in, 124–25, 126–28, 137; wine council in (CIVB), 201; Winegate scandal and, 123–24, 131–32, 134, 136–37

Bordeaux wines: as alternative investment, 187–88; blending of, 3, 117, 121, 125; Broadbent reviews of, 169; classification of, 60; *en primeur*, 185–88; fake, 64, 122–24, 129, 132, 204; international demand for, 125, 126, 128, 136–37; Jefferson and, 172, 173; prices of, 42, 124, 125–27, 137, 174, 187; rare, Kurniawan's purchases of, 190; reputation of, 134, 136–37; 2009–2010 vintages, 187–88

Bosser, Jean-Philippe, 90

Bosser, Pierre, 89–90

Bosser-Dutarque, 90

Boston Museum of Fine Arts, 180–81

bottles/bottling: additives included before, 151–52, 161–62; Bordeaux wine aristocracy and, 121; bulk, 150; destruction of, as anti-fraud measure, 21, 191, 197–98; embossed/engraved, 70, 163–64, 182 (*see also* Jefferson-signed wine bottles); of *en primeur* wine, 185; estate, 69, 101, 108, 172–73, 195; fake, 182, 191, 200–201; fraud methods involving, 196–97; fraud prevention and, 198–200; glass, 29, 69; heavy, and wine quality, 209; by local merchants, 69–70; molds for, 70, 200; natural winemaking and, 6; opening, 198–99; Roman methods, 16–17; sealed, to avoid oxidation, 16–17;

bottles/bottling *(continued)*
standardization of, 70; stickered, 194; variations in, 182; wine fraud scandals involving, 150–52, 192–93, 196–97. *See also* corks/corking; labels/labeling
Bourbon monarchy, 88
brain damage, 46
brandy, 43, 64
bread, 63
Brescia (Italy), 61
bribery, 153–54
Brillat-Savarin, Jean Anthelme, 53, 56–57, 61, 71
brine, 16
Broadbent, Daphne, 168
Broadbent, J. Michael: as Christie's auctioneer, 164, 166–68; as guest auctioneer, in USA, 168–69; Jefferson-signed wine bottles and, 164, 169–70, 178; as Master of Wine, 168, 182; notebooks kept by, 166, 169; reputation of, 184; Rodenstock and, 165, 166, 167–68
B. Schott & Sons, 36
Buda (Hungary), 41
Budai Vörös, 41
Bundestag, 150
bureaucracy, 158–59
Burgenland (Austria), 143, 149
Burg Layen (Germany), 150
Burgundy region (France): Aube region and, 92; best vineyards in, 60; capital of, 78, 102; Jefferson's travels in, 171; vine pandemic in, 77, 103; vines' position in, 20; wine writers from, 59; wine writing on, 60
Burgundy wine: Austrian wines vs., 159–60; best whites, 171–72; blending of, 3, 101–2, 108–10, 115; fake, 104–5, 106,

109, 128–30, 195, 197; rare, Kurniawan's purchases of, 190; reputation of, 103–4; terroir and, 205–6
Buschenschank (Austrian taverns), 148–49
Bush, George W., 152–53
Buzet region (France), 132

Cabernet Franc, 3
Cabernet Sauvignon, 3, 207
Cabernet wines, 197
Cadel, Georges, 84
Cadiz (Spain), 17
Cairanne (France), 94–95
calamus (sweet flag), 16
calcium carbonate, 130
calcium sulfate, 71
California wines, 197
Calvet family, 134
Cameron, Alan, 29
Canal de Bourgogne (France), 103
Canal du Midi (France), 100
Cap Ferret peninsula (France), 127
capsule, 200
Capus, Joseph, 112, 115, 133–34
carbon dating, 177, 180, 198
carbon 14, 177, 198
Carême, Marie-Antoine ("Antonin"), 58–59
car emissions, 45–46
Catch Me If You Can (film; 2002), 203
Catherine of Braganza, 44
Catholic Church, 30, 33–34, 42
Cato, Marcus Porcius, 21; as agricultural writer, 12, 16; drinking habits of, 25–26; on Roman slave wines, 18; on vineyard yields, 23; wine amelioration legitimized by, 17; on winemaking process, 16

Cato Institute, 207

cellarius (Roman slave type), 20

cena (Roman daily meal), 20

Centre for Nuclear Studies (Bordeaux, France), 198

cesium-137, 198–99

Chaban-Delmas, Jacques, 134–35, 136

Chaban-Delmas bridge (Bordeaux, France), 119, 121, 134

Chablis region (France), 207–8

Chambertin Clos de Bèze vineyard, 169

Champagne Ayala, 75

Champagne Deutz & Geldermann, 75

Champagne Drappier, 88

Champagne Gallois, 75

Champagne Gauthier, 75

Champagne Lanson, 165

Champagne Larmandier-Bernier, 93

Champagne region (France): American vines as rootstocks in, 79–80, 103; Aube as "second zone" in, 89; Aube reinstated as part of, 92; Aube wine sales in, 87–88; boundaries reconsidered, 92–93; current prosperity of, 74–75; defining, 74, 86; delimiting of, 86, 91; growers' movement in, 87; Jefferson's travels in, 171; reputation of, and wine fraud, 83; vine pandemic in, 79–80, 103; wine fraud prosecuted in, 115; wine writers and, 60; during WWI, 90–92. *See also* Champagne riots (1911)

Champagne riots (1911): described, 75–76; roots of, 76–81, 82–84, 89; wine growers/merchants arrested following, 82, 84–85

Champagne viticole, La, 83

Champagne wines: bubbles in, 48; Californian, 73–74; current produc-

tion/sales of, 74–75; defining, 74; demand for, 80; fake, 64, 66, 80–81, 83, 85; prices of, 83; reputation of, 110

Changing Times magazine, 174

Chaptal, Jean-Antoine, 59, 67, 68–69

chaptalization, 68–69

charcoal, 14, 129

Chardonnay wines, 159–60

Charles II (King of England), 44

Charles X (King of France), 88

Chartrons district (Bordeaux, France), 119, 121–22, 128, 134

Château Brane Mouton, 164, 170, 173, 180

Château Calon-Ségur, 186–87

Château Cos d'Estournel, 197

Château d'Yquem: 1784 vintage, 169–70, 178; 1787 vintage, 178; authenticity concerns, 198; Jefferson-signed bottles of, 164, 178; Jefferson's purchases of, 172–73; Rodenstock and, 165, 169–70

Château Fortia, 98, 99, 110

Château Grillet, 172

Château Haut-Brion, 3, 60, 172, 173

Château Lafite Rothschild: 1784 vintage, 175, 180; 1787 vintage, 163, 170, 175, 176, 177, 180, 184; 1811 vintage, 193; 1865 vintage, 168; 1961 vintage, 174; as alternative investment, 188; *en primeur* purchases of, 186; fake, Chinese sales of, 201; fake, Rodenstock's sales of, 175–76, 177, 180; Jefferson-signed bottles of, 163, 164; Jefferson's order for, 172, 173; prices of, 126, 174; in Rosebery wine collection, 167–68; wine literature on, 60

Château La Nerthe, 100, 101, 110

Château Lascombes, 169

Château Latour, 3, 60, 124, 186, 188, 193

Château Loudenne, 125

Château Lynch-Bages, 186–87, 188

Château Margaux, 8; 1900 vintage, 198;
authenticity concerns, 198; fraud
prevention measures of, 200; Jefferson-signed bottles of, 164; Jefferson's
order for, 172, 173; prices of, 200;
Shanken's purchase of, 178; wine
literature on, 60, 169

Château Mouton Rothschild, 3, 126, 188;
1924 vintage, 176; 1941 vintage, 196–97;
1945 vintage, 183, 196–97, 198; Jefferson-signed bottles of, 164

Châteauneuf-du-Pape region (France),
94; as first wine appellation, 112,
115–16; Le Roy honored in, 94–96, 98;
Le Roy relocates to, 96; vineyards in,
99–100; wine exports from, 100–101;
winegrowers' association formed in,
110–12, 114

Châteauneuf-du-Pape wine, 3, 99;
appellation system and expectations
of, 206–7; as blending wine, 101–2;
estate-bottled, 101; exports of, 100–101,
105; fake, 111, 114; regulations defining,
111; reputation of, 110

Château Palmer, 4, 127, 197

Chat-en-Oeuf, 115–16

cheese, 57, 63

chefs: celebrity, 50, 58–59; master cooks
(traiteurs), 52–53

Cheq, Gaston, 89

Chernobyl disaster (1986), 156, 199

Chianti wine, 131, 132

China, 152, 188, 197, 201, 202

Chinese Academy of Inspection and
Quarantine, 201

Chinese wines, 60

Chios (Greece), 21

chips, 199–200

cholera, 25

Christianity, wine symbolism in, 3

Christie's (auction house): Broadbent as
auctioneer at, 164, 166–68; fraud
policies at, 198, 199; Frericks as client
at, 175, 176; Jefferson-signed wine
bottles sold at, 163–64, 169, 175; legal
actions against, 170, 180, 184; wine
department set up at, 166–67

cider, 64, 66

cinnamon, 17

cirrhosis, 37, 40

Cité du Vin (Bordeaux, France), 121

citric acid, 130

CIVB (Bordeaux wine council), 201

civil disorder, 7, 72, 79, 88–89, 97–98. See
also Champagne riots (1911)

claret wines, 44, 65, 124–26, 172, 188

Clicquot, Madame, 81

climate change, 102, 145

clones, 206

CNN, 153

Coates, Clive, 126–27, 136–37

coercion, 204–5

coffee, 57

collective action, 85

Collot, Georges, 88

Columbia University, 29

Columella, 17, 18, 23, 24, 28

Come Travel with Me series (Schoonmaker), 107

commissatio (Roman after-dinner
drinking games), 24–25

Complete Wine Book, The (Schoonmaker),
107–8

computers, 158–59

Condrieu (France), 172

Confédération générale agricole pour la défense des produits purs, 87

Confessions of a Wine Lover (Robinson), 165

confusion, 45

connoisseurship, 57–58

Constantin-Weyer, Maurice, 105–6

consumer protection, 70–71

cookbooks, 58

Copenhagen University, 2

corks/corking: authenticity concerns, 169, 178, 182, 191; damaged, in rare wine bottles, 164–65, 184; fake, in wine fraud scandals, 192; fraud methods involving, 64; fraud prevention and, 200; improvements in, 69, 70; lead capsules protecting, 47–48

corkscrews, 70

Cornwell, Don, 195–96

cosmetics, 45

Côte de Beaune (France), 105–6

Côte d'Or (France), 20, 103, 104, 105

Côtes du Rhône region (France), 94

Côtes du Ventoux region (France), 116

counterfeit culture, 5

Coursan (France), 97

cramps, 37

cratera (mixing bowl), 25

Crepes of Wrath, The (*Simpsons* episode), 138–39

Cromwell, Oliver, 44

CRU (restaurant; New York, NY), 191, 197

Cruse, Lionel: French tax department investigation of, 121–23, 128; self-comparison to Nixon, 118–19, 136; trial/conviction of, 132–34, 136. *See also* Winegate scandal

Cruse, Yvan, 128, 132, 136

Cruse family, 121, 122, 130, 134

crystal glassware, lead in, 30, 40, 48, 49

Csóka grapes, 41

Cumières (France), 81

cumin, 13

custard, 62, 63

Custer, George Armstrong, 181

Cyrus, Inge, 148–49

Damery (France), 81, 84

d'Angerville, Sem, 108–9

Danube River, 32

dates, 17

Davis, Lee Allyn, 141–42

De agri cultura (Cato), 16

defrutum, 13, 27–28

Demossier, Marion, 9

Denmark, 121, 155

De re rustica (Columella), 17

De re rustica (Varro), 23

diammonium phosphate, 161

diarrhea, 37

Diaz, Cameron, 160–61

DiCaprio, Leonardo, 203

diethylene glycol, 139–40, 143–44, 145–48, 151, 153. *See also* Austrian wine fraud scandal

dinner parties, 19–22

dolia (earthenware jars), 12, 15

Domaine de la Romanée Conti, 197

Domaine de la Solitude, 100, 110

Domaine de Trévallon, 207

Domaine Didier Dagueneau, 207

Domaine Ponsot, 195

Domaine Zind-Humbrecht, 45

Douai (France), 82

Douro Valley, 43–44

Drappier, Michel, 88–89
drink-drive laws, 157
Dumas, Alexandre, 58
Durand, Hervé, 11, 12, 29
Düsseldorf (Germany), 165
Dutarque, Suzanne, 90
dysentery, 25

economic depression, 113
Edelfaüle (noble rot), 149
Edgerton, Annie, 196–97
Edgerton, Bill, 193–94, 196–97, 198
Edinburgh (Scotland), 167
Egan, Michael, 191–92, 193, 194
egg whites, 20, 160, 161
ego, 5, 205
Egypt, ancient, 208–9
Einstein, Albert, 33
Eischen, Patrick, 200
Eisinger, Josef, 28, 34
Elroy, Jim, 182
Encyclopédie, 69
England, 9; Austrian wine demand in, 157; Austrian wine fraud case coverage in, 152; French Champagne riots (1911) and, 76–77; French wine sales in, 44, 100; Portuguese wine sales in, 44; Roman artifacts in, 12; treaty with Portugal, 44; wine adulteration in, 62–66; wine auctions in, 168–69; wine literature in, 50–51, 60–62
Enlightenment, 59, 67
en primeur wine, 185–88
Épernay (France), 75, 76, 81, 82, 84, 88
Epigrams (Martial), 25
Eschenauer, Heinz, 178
estate bottling, 69–70, 101, 108, 172–73, 195

Eucharist, 3, 34
Europe, cold snap in (1956), 141–42
European Commission, 147
eye pain, 37, 38

face powder, 45
Fairview winery (South Africa), 116
Falernian wine, 19, 20–21, 22
famine, 31, 32
Faventia region (Italy), 23
FBI, 182, 191, 192, 194, 196
FDA Consumer Magazine, 146
Fels am Wagram (Austria), 153
fenugreek, 13, 17
fermentation, 161
Ferrari scandal (Italy), 131–32
Ferroul, Ernest, 97
fertilizers, 142
fever, 37
figs, 131
Financial Times, 126, 179, 191
Financial Times Stock Exchange, 187
Florence (Italy), 23
Fontaine sur Aÿ (France), 92
food: adulteration of, 51, 53, 62, 63, 70–71; intellectualization of, 50, 62, 71. *See also* gastronomic literature
food critics, 50
Forbes, Kip, 163, 169, 178, 184
Ford, Gerald, 136
fortified wines, 42–43
France: American Champagne and, 73–74; car emissions regulations and, 45–46; gastronomic literature in, 54–59; Griffe law in, 7, 18; Italian wine fraud scandal and, 155; Jefferson's stay in, 171–73; mass protests in, 72, 79, 88–89, 97–98 (*see also* Champagne

riots [1911]); Masters of Wine in, 46; relations with England, 44; restaurant origins in, 51–54; Roman archaeological sites in, 10–13; vine pandemic in (*see* phylloxera [vine louse]); wine adulteration in, 62–63; wine amelioration in, 2; wine as national drink of, 116; wine fraud testing in, 198–99; wine literature in, 50–51, 59–60. *See also* French appellation system; French wines; Winegate scandal; *specific wine region*

Franco-Prussian War (1870–1871), 77

Franz Ferdinand (Archduke of Austria), 90

fraud, 203–5. *See also* wine fraud

French appellation system: birth of, 7, 98, 115, 119; Champagne appellation and, 86, 88, 92–93; Châteauneuf-du-Pape region and, 111, 112, 115–16; departees from, 207; flouting of, 119, 134; foundation for, 86; as international model, 116–17; national institute (INAO), 133–34; progress toward, 111, 112, 116; as protectionist move, 7–8; supporters of, 109; terroir and, 8–9, 205–6; Winegate scandal and, 130, 132–34; wine region practices validated in, 3; WWI and, 111

French aristocracy, 53, 55, 58–59

French army, 89–92

French Empire, First (1804–1814), 54

French Revolution (1789–1799): gastronomic literature following, 50, 51; guilds and, 52, 53; land reform following, 67–68; Louis XVI execution during, 50, 56; restaurant origins following, 51

French Revolution (1830), 88

French wines: British wine writing about, 61; chaptalization and, 68–69; exports of, 103–4; legal limits on, 46–47; prices of, 124; purity of, 78. *See also specific wine*

Frericks, Hans-Peter, 175–78, 182

fungal diseases, 65

Galen, 27

Gallic Wars (58–50 BCE), 12

Gardener's Chronicle and Agricultural Gazette, 76–77

Gard River, 25

garum (fermented fish sauce), 19

gasoline, leaded, 45–46

Gaston and Sheehan (auction house), 189

gastronome, 14, 55–57

gastronomic literature, 50, 54–59

General Agricultural Confederation for the Defense of Pure Products, 87

genetic testing, 40

George IV (King of England), 44

Georgia, 159

German Research Center for Environment and Health, 177

German wines: Austrian wines blended with, 151; Beethoven's taste for, 41; lead in, 45; reputation of, 151–52; Riesling, 41–42, 45

Germany, 9; Austrian wine demand in, 142, 145, 150, 159; Austrian wine fraud case and, 150–51; Bordeaux demand in, 129; Catholic landholdings in, 33–34, 42; Italian wine fraud scandal and, 155; lead poisoning in, 30–31, 34; Little Ice Age effects in, 31–32; Riesling as signature grape of, 32;

Germany *(continued)*
Roman artifacts in, 12; during Thirty Years' War (1618–1648), 31, 32; wine adulteration in, 31–32, 34–35, 150–51, 204; wine collectors in, 164; wine laws in, 150; wine merchants from, in Bordeaux, 121; wine production in, 31
Gesellschaft für deutsche Sprache, 152
Gevrey-Chambertin, 102
Gewurztraminer grapes, 46
Giacosa, Iliaria Gozzini, 22
Giscard d'Estaing, Valéry, 134–35
Gladstone, William, 103–4
glassware. *See* bottles/bottling; crystal glassware, lead in
globalization, 86
global warming, 145
Glühwein, 14
glycerin, 145–46, 153
glycol poisoning, 144–45
Gockel, Eberhard, 33, 34–35
Goodband, Philip, 125
Görke, Meinhard. *See* Rodenstock, Hardy
Gouges, Henri, 109
gourmand, 55–56
gout, 37, 44
graffiti, 25
grands cru classés, 60, 74, 92, 93, 126, 131
grape growers. *See* wine producers
grape juice, 68, 131, 151, 153; unfermented (must), 16
grapes: full ripening of, 110–11; harvest regulations, 111; prices of, 96; Roman harvests, 29; unripe, 209
grape skins, 18
Graves, 129, 172
Great Britain: food adulteration outlawed in, 70; Masters of Wine from, 125; wine merchants from, in Bordeaux, 121
Great Depression, 113
Greece, 41; ancient, 19, 20, 59, 77–78
greed, 2, 140, 179–80, 182, 204
Greek wines, 21
Greenberg, Eric, 192–93, 194
Grenache wine, 14, 95, 116
Griffe law (France; 1889), 6–7, 18
Grill, Josef, 151, 153–55
Grill, Richard, 151, 153–55
Grimod de la Reynière, Alexandre Balthazar Laurent, 54–56, 57–58, 71
Grüner Veltliner wines, 140, 159–60
guilds, 52–53, 57
Gustavus Adolphus (King of Sweden), 31
gypsum, 70–71

Haiden, Günther, 144
Hailman, John, 173
hallucinogens, 16
Hamburg (Germany), 105, 144
Handel, George Frideric, 44–45
Hassall, Arthur Hill, 71
Hautvillers (France), 81, 89–90
headaches, 37
hepatitis B, 40
herbs, 13–14, 15, 17, 209
Hermès (luxury goods store), 190
Hernandez, Jason, 195
Heurige (Austrian taverns), 148–49
Hiller, Ferdinand, 38, 40
Hippocrates, 27
Histoire et statistique de la vigne et des grands vins de la côte-d'Or (Lavalle), 104–5
History and Description of Modern Wines, A (Redding), 60–61

Holmberg, Lars, 2
hologram stickers, 200
Holy Roman Empire, 31
Homer, 21, 24
honey, 13, 14
Hong Kong, 187, 188, 189, 197
Hope, Charles, 167
Hopetoun House (Edinburgh,
    Scotland), 167
Hubert, Philippe, 199
Humbrecht, Léonard, 45–46, 47
Humbrecht, Olivier, 46, 47
Hümer, Friedrich, 145
Hungarian wines, 41, 168
Hunter, David, 45

ideology, 204
Iliad, The (Homer), 21
INAO (French national appellation
    institute), 92, 133–34
Indonesia, 202
inflation, 137
ink, 200
Internal Revenue Service (USA), 189
International Exhibition (Paris; 1867), 77
International Herald Tribune, 28
International Office of Wine, 96
International Wine Challenge, 158
Interpol, 201
In vino veritas (Bert), 123
Ireland, 121, 155
Irish Independent, 155
irrigation, 110
isinglass, 161
Islay, 19
Italian wines, 22, 131–32, 155–56, 172
Italy, 9, 61; appellation system in, 117, 208;
    Ferrari scandal in, 131–32; Jefferson's

travels in, 172; Roman-era wine
producers in, 20; wine demand in,
23–24; wine fraud in, 155–56, 202

Jacky (wine tour guide), 12–13
James, Jesse, 181
Japan, 46, 152, 157
jaundice, 37
Jaurès, Jean, 85
Jefferson, Thomas: correspondence of,
    170; notes kept by, 171, 172; Paris stay
    of, 170, 171–73; scholarship on, 170, 172,
    181; wine bottles bearing initials of,
    163–64; wine purchases of, 170, 171,
    172–73
Jefferson-signed wine bottles: authentic-
    ity concerns, 163–64, 169–71, 180, 181,
    182, 198, 209–10; Christie's auctioning
    of, 163, 169; contents of, 184; discovery
    of, 164, 174, 175; experts and, 209–10;
    lawsuits involving, 177, 182–84. *See
    also* Rodenstock, Hardy
Johannisberg (Germany), 42
Johnson, Samuel, 44
Johnston, Nathaniel, 69
John XXII, Pope, 99, 110
joint pain, 45
Joly, Robert, 95–96
Julius Caesar, 12, 21–22
Jullien, André, 59–60, 61, 71
Juvenal, 24

Kadarka grapes, 41
Kaufman, Paul, 39
Kékfrankos grapes, 41
Kimmeridgian (limestone soils), 208
Kluth, Rudiger, 183
knowledgeability, 4

Koch, Bill: background of, 178; collection of exhibited in Boston, 180–81; Jefferson-signed wine bottles purchased by, 178–79, 180–81; Kurniawan and, 195; lawsuits initiated by, 182–84, 192–93; wine cellar of investigated for fraud, 182

Kracher, Alois, 158

Kurniawan, Rudy: arrest/trial of, 188, 189, 190, 191; deportation of, 202; evidence against, 191, 192, 193–96, 197; fake wines sold by, 194–95; family background of, 190–91; FBI raid on, 192, 194, 196; incarceration of, 192, 196, 202; lifestyle of, 189–90; wine fraud measures following arrest of, 201–2; wines of auctioned off, 189

labels/labeling: of Austrian wines, 142, 149; authenticity and, 5, 117, 176, 183, 191; estate-bottled wine and, 69; fake, in wine fraud scandals, 183, 192, 196–97, 200–201; fraud prevention and, 191, 199, 200; French wine law and, 7, 86; ingredient lists called for on, 160, 161; MICE fraud model and, 204; mislabeling, 86, 105; paper, 70; relabeling, of blended wines, 109–10; of Roman wines, 208; silly, 116; in Winegate scandal, 128–29, 130; wine merchants and, 69–70

Lachiver, Marcel, 87–88

Laliman, Leo, 78

Lamarre, René, 80–81

Lancashire (England), 166

Lancet, The, 37–38

Lançon, Florent, 100

Languedoc region (France), 79, 122, 133

Larmandier, Pierre, 93

La Tour d'Argent restaurant (Paris, France), 164

latrines, public, 26

Lavalle, Jean, 104–5

Lavoisier, Antoine, 67

Law on the prevention of fraud in the sale of goods and falsification of foodstuffs and agricultural products (France; 1905), 116

Lawton family, 134

Layton, Tommy, 166

lead acetate, 63

Lead and Lead Poisoning in Antiquity (Nriagu), 28–29

lead capsules, 47–48

lead carbonate, 35

leaded gasoline, 45–46

lead glazes, 39

lead in wine, 9; chaptalization and, 68–69; in Germany, 32, 34–35, 204; as harmful adulteration, 30, 48–49, 65; legal limits on, 46–47; papal bull regarding, 30; in ports, 43; in Roman wines, 27–29; sweetening effects of, 30, 32, 34, 48, 63, 209; wine literature exposing, 62–63. *See also* lead poisoning

lead monoxide, 34

lead oxide, 35

lead poisoning: Beethoven and, 38–39, 40; as gradual process, 35; Handel and, 45; lead amounts causing, 28; in Rome, 30; sources of, 39–40, 45; symptoms of, 34, 40, 45. *See also* lead in wine

learning disorders, 46

Lecacheur, Michel, 86

lees (dead yeast residue), 20

Lefèvre, André, 112

legitimization, 3

Lemaire, Auguste, 84

Le Monde (newspaper), 134

Lenoir, B. A., 67

Le Petit Chat, 116

Le Pin (Pomerol, France), 197, 199–200

Le Roy de Boiseaumarié, Pierre Baron, 97; background of, 96; bronze statue portraying, 94–96; as Châteauneuf-du-Pape wine grower, 99, 101; death of, 98; as International Office of Wine president, 96; Winegate scandal and, 133–34; as winegrower supporter, 96–98, 110, 115; WWI military service of, 98, 101, 110

Le Sauvage, Raymond, 132

Lesbos (Greece), 21

Libération (leftist newspaper), 135

libertarianism, 207

Liebfraumilch, 191–92

Life magazine, 131

lime, 16

limestone soils, 208

Linlithgow (Scotland), marquess of, 167

Liquid Assets (Sokolin), 174

List, Karl, 143

List Study (Austria), 142–43

litharge, 34–35

Little Ice Age, 31–32, 204

Liv-ex fine-wine trading platform (London, England), 187

logwood tree, 64

loi de repression des fraudes (1905), 86

loi Griffe (1889), 6–7, 18

Loire Valley, 80

London (England): Egan employment in, 191–92; fine-wine trading in, 187, 189;

phylloxera identified in, 76–77; wine fraud discussions in, 180; wine imports in, 100, 157; wine merchants in, 166

lora (Roman slave wine), 18

Los Angeles Times, 190

Louis XIV (King of France), 31, 44

Louis XVI (King of France), 50, 56

Louis XVIII (King of France), 53

Lur-Saluces, Alexandre de, 165, 170

Macedonia, 41

Madeira wines, 171

Mainz (Germany), 31, 36

maison de santé, 51

Maison Sichel, 119

Malbec, 3

Mamertine wine, 22

Marbella (Spain), 183

marble dust, 16

Marie Antoinette, 50

Marlborough Express, 76

Marne department (France), 80–81, 86, 87–88

Marseille (France), 100

Martial, 25, 27

Martin, Russell, 39

Marxism Today, 126

Mas des Tourelles (Provence, France), 10–13, 14, 29

Massengill Elixir Sulfanilamide incident (1937), 146–47, 148

mass production, 59

master cooks (*traiteurs*), 52–53

Masters of Wine, 4, 46, 125, 126–27, 144, 160, 165, 168, 197, 201, 206

Mauriac, François, 119–20, 121

Mayson, Richard, 44

McConaughey, Matthew, 164
McCrone, Walter, 39
mechanization, 142
medicines, 45
Mediterranean diet, 19
Mediterranean Sea, 171
menus, à la carte, 57
mercury, 38
Merlot, 3
Merrett, Christopher, 48
Messiah (Handel), 44–45
metabisulfate, 114
methanol, 155, 156
Metz (France), 81
Meursault (France), 103
MICE (fraud model), 204–5
middle class, 61
mildew, 83
milk, 161
Mitterer, Josef, 154
moderation, 56–57
Moldova, 159
Molyneux-Berry, David, 176–77, 182
money, 93, 204. *See also* greed
Montagne de Reims region (France), 92
Monte Carlo, 182–83
Monte Massico (Italy), 20
Monticello (Charlottesville, VA, USA), 170, 174, 181
Monticello Report, 170
Montpellier (France), 79, 97–98, 110, 120
Montrachet (France), 60
Moreau, Émile, 85
Morocco, 159
Morrison, Fiona, 197–98
Mosel River, 31
Moser, Lenz, 141, 142, 158
Moser, Lenz, V, 158

Müller, Theo, 146
mulsum, 14–15
Munich (Germany), 144, 176, 177, 182–83
must, 16
myrrh, 17

Nadrarsky, Otto, 153
Nahe wine region (Germany), 150
Naples (Italy), 61
Napoleon, 39, 57, 59, 68
Narbonne (France), 19, 97
narcissism, 2
National Institute for Origin and Quality (INAO), 92
Natural Disasters (Davis), 141–42
natural wine, 5–7, 162
Near Field Communication (NFC) chips, 199–200
Neckar River, 32, 35
negociants, 124; Burgundy, 102, 105; estate bottling vs. bottling by, 108, 109; French appellation system and, 88; wine fraud committed by, 80–81, 105, 133; wines sold to, 87–88, 100, 102. *See also* wine merchants
Nemeitz, Joachim, 52
Neri, Antonio, 48
Nero (Emperor of Rome), 19
Neusiedl, Lake (Neusiedlersee), 148, 149, 158
newspapers, 61
Newton, Isaac, 44
New York (NY, USA), 9, 57, 66, 157, 189, 191, 192
New Yorker (magazine), 107, 177
New York Times, 124, 143, 145, 155–56, 169–70
New Zealand, 76, 159

Nigeria, 147

Nixon, Richard, 118–19, 135–36

noble rot, 149, 158

Norwalk (CT, USA), 193

Norway, 105

nosebleeds, 37

Nostradamus, 99, 110

Nriagu, Jerome O., 28–29

nuclear weapons testing, 198–99

Nuits-Saint-Georges (France), 128–29

Obama, Barack, 73–74

obesity, 57

Observatoire du bonheur, 120–21

Oddbins (London, England), 191–92

Odyssey, The (Homer), 21, 24

oidium (fungal disease), 65, 204

oil prices, 137

Old Canary Wine, 43

Orange (France), 98, 110, 111

organic wine, 160–61

orris root, 13

Ostia (Italy), 12

otosclerosis, 38

overproduction, 85, 96, 113–14, 156

oxalic acid, 146

oxidation, 209

paint, lead-based, 29

Palferman, Thomas, 37–38

Panama, 147

paperwork, 123, 158–59

paralysis, 45

Paris (France): Bordeaux vs., as desirable place to live, 120; celebrity chefs in, 58–59; as epicurean epicenter, 50; gastronomic literature in, 50, 54–59; International Exhibition in (1867), 77;

Jefferson-signed wine bottles discovered in, 164; Jefferson's stay in, 170, 171–73; Le Roy honored in, 98; restaurants in, 51–54, 57, 59; wine fraud prosecuted in, 115; wine merchants in, 62–63, 106; wine writers in, 59

Paris-Lyon-Marseille railway, 101

Parker, Robert, 196

Pasteur, Louis, 69

Pastre, Pierre, 98

Pender, Rhys, 201–2

Penfolds, 201, 202

Penning-Rowsell, Edmund, 126

pepper, 13, 14

Pérignon, Dom, 81

Petit Orangeois, Le (newspaper), 111

Petit Verdot, 3

Petronius, 19

Petrus, 174, 175, 183, 193

Pflugerville (TX, USA), 189

Philadelphia (PA, USA), 60

phylloxera (vine louse): in Burgundy region, 103, 104–5; in Chablis region, 207; in Champagne region, 79–80; economic impact of, 71–72, 77–78, 150; foreign grape sources during, 114; French wine law and, 6–7; identification of, 77; importation of, 78; in Languedoc region, 79; vineyard replanting following, 96; wine fraud and, 71, 103, 104–5, 204; wine shortages caused by, 78–79, 103, 105, 204

Physiology of Taste, The (Brillat-Savarin), 56–57, 61

Pieroth, Elmar, 150

Pieroth family, 205

Pieroth wines, 150–51

Pinot Noir wine, 92, 102, 106, 115
piquette (low-alcohol wine), 18, 78–79
pitch, 15–16
Pitte, Jean-Robert, 69
place of origin, 62, 205–6, 207–10
plague, 31
Planchon, Jules-Émile, 103
plateware, 45
pleasure, 3–4
Pliny the Elder, 14–15; binge drinking as
    viewed by, 24; on Falernian wine,
    20–21; lead in wine recommended by,
    28; on Roman slave wines, 18; sapa
    recipe of, 28; wine amelioration
    legitimized by, 17; on wine as
    medicine, 27; on wine authenticity,
    18–19
plumbism, 40
Plutarch, 25–26
pneumonia, 40
poison gas, 91
Pomerol wine, 174, 197
Pommard (France), 105–6
Pommard wine, 102, 106
Pompeii, 21, 25, 29, 204
Ponsot, Laurent, 195
Pontallier, Paul, 8–9
Pont du Gard, 13, 25
Porto (Portugal), 43
Portugal, 44
port wine, 43–45, 48, 61, 63–64, 168, 204
posca (Roman army wine), 18
Postmann, Klaus, 143
pots, lead-lined, 28, 29
Pouilly Fumé region (France), 207
powdered acid, 130
Power, Katherine, 161
Prädikatswein, 151, 153

Préseances (Mauriac), 121
Press Association, 75, 76
Prial, Frank J., 155–56
print culture, 59
prix fixe, 57
Prohibition Era (USA), 107, 113, 125
Prosecco region (Italy), 23, 208
protectionism, 7–8, 66–67, 86
provenance, 105; authenticity and, 8; of
    Jefferson-signed wine bottles, 179, 181;
    Jefferson wine purchases and, 172, 174;
    Kurniawan wine-tasting events and,
    190; modern gastronomes and, 14;
    Romans and, 14; social class and, 17;
    wine law and, 62; wine literature and,
    51
public latrines, 26
Puligny-Montrachet, 129
purity, 14, 17, 51, 78, 152

QR codes, 200
quality, 207–10
Questions of Taste (Scruton), 208

Raharja, Hendra, 191
railroads, 101, 103
rainfall, 124
raisins, 78–79
Rambourg, Patrick, 56
Ravenscroft, George, 48
Redding, Cyrus, 60–61, 71, 197
Reims (France), 88, 90–91
restaurant critics, 51, 54–56, 57
restaurants, birth of, 51–54, 57
retsina, 15–16
Reuters, 143, 153
Réveil de la Marne, Le, 75–76
Révolution champenoise, La (Lamarre), 81

Revue du vin de France, La (magazine), 179

rhatany, 64

Rheingau region (Germany), 31, 41–42

rheumatism, 37

Rhine River, 31

Rhône River, 100, 103, 171–72

Riesling wines, 32, 41–42, 45, 140

Robinson, Jancis, 160, 165, 179, 191

Rodenstock, Hardy: accomplices of, 204–5; Broadbent and, 165, 166, 167–68; Jefferson-signed wine bottles sold by, 163–64, 173, 175–77, 178–79; lawsuits against, 177, 182–84; reaction to doubters, 179, 181; reputation of, 175, 182; residences of, 182–83; trustworthiness of, 164; as wine collector, 164–65, 167–68; wine-tasting events hosted by, 164–66, 169, 179, 209–10. *See also* Jefferson-signed wine bottles

Roman army, 18

Roman cuisine, 15

Roman elite, 17, 19, 22, 24–25

Roman empire, 9; agriculture during, 12; class differences in, 17–18; decline of, 28–29; dinner parties in, 19–22; everyday dining in, 20, 22–23; expansion of, 19; Gallic Wars (58–50 BC), 12; imperial, 19, 20, 22–23; lead-laced wine in, 27–29; lead poisoning in, 29, 30; life expectancy in, 26; Republican period (509 BC–27 BC), 16, 19, 21; slaves in, 18, 20, 78; wine amelioration in, 2, 13–19, 27–28, 48–49; wine as medicine in, 26–27; wine authenticity in, 4, 181–82; wine demand in, 23; wine dilution in, 24–26, 204; wine writing in, 17

Roman press, 12

Roman wines: aging methods, 19; demand for, 23; dilution of, 24–25; Falernian, 19, 20–21, 22; lead in, 27–29; as medicine, 26–27; quality of, 23, 161; recreating, 29; water quality and, 25–26; wine literature on, 59

Rome (Italy), 23, 26, 61

Romilius, Pollio, 14–15

Rondeau, Monsieur, 81

rootstocks, 78, 206

Roquefort cheese, 115

Roquemaure (France), 100

Rosebery, Archibald Philip Primrose, Earl of, 167–68

Rothschild, Hannah de, 167

Rothschild, Philippe de, 126, 183

Rotterdam (Netherlands), 105

Roumier, 195

Rousseau, Armand, 109

Rubicon River, 21–22

Russia, 81, 113

Russian Revolution (1917), 113

Russian wines, 60

Rust (Austria), 148–49, 158

Rutherford, David, 130, 133

saffron, 17

Saint-Cecile-les-Vignes (France), 94–96

Saint-Estèphe (France), 132

Saint-Germain-de-Grave (France), 122

Salzburg (Austria), 141

Sancerre wine, 206–7

San Francisco State University, 4

Sangiovese grapes, 117

sapa, 27–28

sarcoidosis, 37–38

Sassicaia wine, 117, 202

sauces, 15

Sauternes region (France), 60, 112–13, 165, 186

Sautner (Austrian wine company), 143

Sauvignon Blanc wine, 116

Scandinavia, 105

Schindler, Anton, 42–43

Schloss Johannisberg (Germany), 42

Schoonmaker, Frank, 106–9

Schuller, Josef, 144–45

Scientific Committee on Consumer Products (EC), 147

scientific progress, 208

Scotland, 175

Scruton, Roger, 208

seawater, 13, 15, 16, 17

Séjour de Paris (Nemeitz), 52

Selinko, 200

Service, Tom, 36

Sète (France), 100, 172

Setia (Roman town), 27

Shanken, Marvin, 178

sherry wine, 61, 65, 70–71, 204

Shroud of Turin, 39, 178

Sichel, Charles, 119

Sichel, Peter, 124, 127, 128

Sicilian wines, 22

Signine wine, 27

Simpsons, The (TV cartoon series), 138–39

Skelton, Stephen, 206

slaves, 18

Smith, Alfred, 120

smoke, 19

snow, 27

social class: connoisseurship and, 57–58; dinner parties and, 19; wine and, 4–5, 17–18; wine fraud and, 205; wine literature and, 50–51, 61

socialism, 85–86, 97

sommelier, 20

Sorgues (France), 95, 101, 102

Sorrento wine, 27

Sotheby's (auction house), 39, 175–76, 177, 182, 192

Sour Grapes (documentary film; 2016), 191

South African wines, 65, 66, 116

South America, 175

Soviet Union, 175

Spain, 105, 117

Spang, Rebecca, 51

sparkling wine, 48, 83, 110

Spätlese (late harvest), 42

spices, 13, 14, 15, 17, 19, 209

Spiegel, Der, 146, 148–49

Spielberg, Steven, 203

Stanton, Lucia ("Cinder"), 170–71, 173–74, 181

status and wine, 4–5

Steiner, Rudolf, 6

Stelzer, Tyson, 93

Stern (magazine), 175, 182–83

Stevens, Mike, 38

Stockhausen, Samuel, 34

Stotland, Ezra, 175, 205

St. Petersburg (Russia), 175

stretching, 25

strikes, 85

Sud-Ouest (newspaper), 201, 202

Suez Canal, 77

sugar, 22, 48, 66, 68, 98, 131, 151, 153, 155, 161–62, 191

sulfanilamide, 146–47

sulfur, 69

sulfur dioxide, 16–17, 160, 161

Super Tuscans wine, 117

sustainability, 207

Sutcliffe, Serena, 179–80

sweeteners, 17

sweet flag (calamus), 16–17

Switzerland, 155, 159

Symphony Number 8 (Beethoven), 36–37

Symphony Number 9 (Beethoven), 37

Symphony Number 10 (unfinished;
  Beethoven), 49

Syndicat general des vignerons, 92

syphilis, 38

Syrah wine, 95, 116

Tansil, Eddy, 191

tartaric acid, 160, 161

Taste of Ancient Rome, A (Giacosa), 22

tasting panels, 206

taxes, 141

Taylor's port, 168

Tchernia, André, 23

tea, 63

tennis ball trick, 154

Tennyson, Alfred Lord, 44

terroir, 8–9, 205–6

Texas (USA), 189

Thienpont, Jacques, 197–98

Thirty Years' War (1618–1648), 31, 32

Through Europe on Two Dollars a Day
  (Schoonmaker), 107

thyme, 14

Tiberius (Emperor of Rome), 27

Time magazine, 139

Times, The (London), 71

Tokaji wine, 168

Tokyo (Japan), 157

Top Gun (film; 1986), 156

Topographie de tous les vignobles connus
  (Jullien), 59–60

Toulouse (France), 120

Tovey, Charles, 66, 71

trade routes, 19

trade unionism, 85, 86

Traité sur la vigne (Chaptal), 67, 68

traiteurs (master cooks), 52–53

*Tramway devant les Quinconces par temps de
  pluie, Le* (painting; Smith), 120

*Treatise on Adulterations of Food, and
  Culinary Poisons* (Accum), 62–64, 70

Trier (Germany), 146

Trimalchio's Feast (Petronius), 19

tritium, 198

Troyes (France), 88–89

Tulle de Villefranche family, 101

Tunisia, 131

Tuscany (Italy), 61, 202

typhoid, 25

typicity, 132

Tyrell, Werner, 152

Ulm (Germany), 30, 31, 32, 33, 34–35

unionization, 92, 108–9

United Kingdom: French wine sales in,
  103–4, 105; wine fraud in, 115–16

United States: Austrian wine demand in,
  157; Bordeaux demand in, 125, 129, 137;
  fake French wine sales in, 66, 129; first
  wine fraud incarceration in, 192, 196;
  French wine fraud inspector in, 115;
  French wine sales in, 101, 105; Italian
  wine fraud scandal and, 155–56;
  Massengill Elixir Sulfanilamide
  incident in (1937), 146–47, 148;
  Prohibition in, 113; Prohibition
  repealed in, 107, 125; Vietnam War,
  137; Watergate scandal in, 118–19,
  135–36; wine auctions in, 168–69

United States Bureau of Alcohol, Tobacco
  and Firearms, 155–56

United States Food and Drug Administration, 47, 49, 146, 147, 151
Universal Exhibition (Paris, France), 60
University of Dijon, 104
University of Texas, 45
University of Vienna, 140
Urville (France), 88
Use of Liquids (Hippocrates), 27
US Marshals Service, 189

Varro, 23
Vendargues (France), 96, 99
Venezuela, 115, 175
Versailles, Treaty of (1919), 113
Vesuvius eruption (79 AD), 28
"V for Victory" wine label, 183
Via Domitia, 11
Victoria (Queen of England), 42
Vienna (Austria), 36, 41, 144, 145
Viet Cong, 137
Vietnam War, 137
vin chaud, 14
vin de France, 207
Vin de l'Italie romaine, Le (Tchernia), 23
vin du pape, 99
vine louse. *See* phylloxera (vine louse)
vineyards: Austrian management
   methods, 141–42; car emissions and,
   45–46; Catholic, 34; fungal diseases
   destroying, 65; replanting, after
   Thirty Years' War, 32
Vintage Wine (Broadbent), 169
vintners, 1–2. *See also* wine merchants;
   wine producers
vision loss, 45
Viticulture with a Difference (Moser), 141
Vitis vinifera, 78
Volnay (France), 106, 108

Wallace, Benjamin, 164
Wars of Religion (1562–1598), 99
Washington, George, 173
Watergate scandal, 118–19, 135–36
water pipes, lead-soldered, 40
water quality, 25–26, 29, 34, 45, 63
Wegeler, Franz, 36
Welsh rarebit, 57
Westminster Abbey, 45
Westwood, John Obadiah, 76–77
whisky, 19, 24
"White Collar Criminals" (Stotland),
   175, 205
wine, 78; authenticity of, 4–9; carbon
   dating of, 177, 180; clarifying, 14, 20,
   161; defining, 6–7, 18–19, 69, 140;
   dilution of, 24–26, 204; *en primeur*,
   185–88; fake, 5, 61; fortified, 43–45; as
   French national drink, 116; intellectualization of, 50, 62, 71; as investment,
   174, 187–88; knowledge of, 4; lead in
   (*see* lead in wine); maturing of, 16–17,
   19; as medicine, 3, 26–27, 59; natural,
   162; organic, 160–61; pH of, 16; reasons
   for drinking, 2–4, 15–16, 32, 208–9;
   respectability and, 210; restaurants
   and, 51; as status symbol, 4–5
Wine Act (Austria; 1985), 154, 158–59
wine adulteration: amelioration vs., 2, 17,
   28, 162; in England, 62–66; gastronomic
   literature and, 59; in Germany, 31–32,
   34–35; scientific advances and reasons
   for, 69; wine literature exposing,
   62–64. *See also* Austrian wine fraud
   scandal; lead in wine; wine fraud
wine amelioration: adulteration vs., 2, 17,
   28, 62–63, 162; British wine literature
   promoting, 62; as commonplace, 2–3,

209; Roman, 13–19, 27–28. *See also* wine blends/blending

wine appraisal businesses, 193–94

Wine Berserkers (web forum), 196

wine blends/blending: as acceptable amelioration, 3; Austrian, 140, 142; Bordeaux wines, 3, 117, 121, 125; Burgundy wines, 3, 101–2, 108–10, 115; Châteauneuf-du-Pape wine used in, 100, 101, 106; in England, 64–65, 116; estate bottling and, 108; French appellation system and, 205–6, 207; in Germany, 105, 150–51; Hungarian, 41; MICE fraud model and, 204; pleasurability of, 208–9; profitability of, 106; terroir and, 8; wine fraud scandals involving, 121, 123–24, 129, 132, 134

wine chemists, 59

wine cognoscenti, as wine fraud victims, 1–2

wine collectors: auction house fraud policies and, 198, 199; Broadbent and, 166, 169; counterfeit culture and, 5; German, 164–65; Koch as, 178–79; Kurniawan and, 189–90, 195; lawsuits initiated by, 170, 184; lead in wine and, 47–48; Rodenstock's tasting events attracting, 179, 182; wine fraud committed by, 1–2; as wine fraud victims, 209–10; wine prices and, 174, 188. *See also* Rodenstock, Hardy

wine fraud: amelioration and, 2–3; appellation systems and, 207–10; extent of, 201–2; first US incarceration for, 192, 196; French laws regarding, 98; harm caused by, 2; increases in, 179–80; investigation methods, 198–99; lawsuits involving, 192–93;

luxury, methods of, 196–98; prevention methods, 199–200; public perception of, 201–2; reasons for, 175, 179–80, 202, 203–5; unreported cases of, 178; victims of, 1–2, 178, 209–10; vine pandemic and, 71–72. *See also* Austrian wine fraud scandal; Jefferson-signed wine bottles; Kurniawan, Rudy; Rodenstock, Hardy; Winegate scandal

Winegate scandal, 117; accomplices involved in, 204–5; evidence in, 122–23, 128–30; experts and, 209; Ferrari scandal and, 130–32; French appellation system and, 130, 132–34; French politics and, 134–37; impact of, 123–24, 136–37; media coverage of, 119, 123, 124, 131, 134; trial/conviction in, 129, 130, 132–34; Watergate scandal and, 118–19, 135–36

winegrowers. *See* wine producers

wine industry, political involvement in, 7, 112, 134–37

wine literature: adulteration exposed through, 62–64; birth of, 59–62; intellectualization of wine in, 50–51, 71; reference books, 65; Roman, 17

wine merchants: Austrian wine fraud scandal and, 139–40, 153; Beethoven's wine tastes and, 41; blend-and-bottle, 3, 8; in Bordeaux region (France), 3, 121, 122–24, 128, 132, 134; British, 44, 64–65; Burgundy wines and, 101–2, 105, 109; Champagne riots (1911) and, 75; Châteauneuf-du-Pape wines and, 101–2, 110; during *en primeur* week, 185, 186; French appellation system and, 114–15, 205–6; German, 30–32, 204; Jefferson and, 173; Jefferson-signed

wine merchants *(continued)*
wine bottles and, 179–80; lead
poisoning caused by, 30–31; MICE
fraud model and, 204; protectionist,
66–67; Roman, 18, 25; terroir and, 8;
wine amelioration by, 3, 70; wine as
investment and, 188; wine bottled by,
69–70, 108; wine dilution by, 25; wine
fraud committed by, 1–2, 64–66,
84–85, 122–24, 128, 134; wine literature
and, 59–60, 62–63, 64–65, 66. See also
negociants; *specific merchant*
wine producers: American, 73; associations formed by, 98, 110–12, 114, 152; in
Aube region (France), 87–88; Austrian, 140–41, 144, 148–49, 151, 158–60;
in Bordeaux region (France), 127–28;
in Burgundy region (France), 108–9,
205–6; in Champagne region (France),
74–75, 81, 83, 93, 115; in Châteauneuf-
du-Pape region (France), 97–98, 102,
110–12, 114, 116; collective action by,
7–8 (*see also* Champagne riots (1911));
of *en primeur* wines, 185, 186; fraud
prevention measures of, 200; fraud
rates as estimated by, 202; French
appellation system and, 7–8, 93,
114–16, 133, 205–6, 207, 208; French
manuals for, 68; French vine pandemic and, 6–7, 72; German, 31–32,
33–34, 42, 151–62; Greek, and Roman
market, 20; honest, 2; monasteries as,
33–34, 42; of natural wine, 6; prices set
by, 127; Roman, 13, 15–17, 19, 21, 28;
taverns run by, 148–49; terroir and, 8,
205–6; unionization of, 92, 108–9;
vine pandemic and, 72, 77; wine
amelioration by, 3, 13, 15–17, 19, 28,

31–32, 208–9; wine fraud committed
by, 2, 81, 83, 97, 110, 115, 152, 153; WWI
and, 90. *See also specific château*;
domaine; *producer*
wine schools, 159
Wines of Bordeaux, The (Penning-
Rowsell), 126
Wine Spectator, 178, 179
Wintzenheim (France), 45–46
Wolf, Herbert, 154
women, 57, 61–62
Woods Hole Oceanographic Institution,
180
World Health Organization (WHO), 49
World War I: Bolo executed during, 87;
demand for French wines following,
113; French appellation system and,
111; impact of, on French vineyard
areas, 90–92, 208; Le Roy military
service during, 98
World War II: Austrian wine tastes and,
141; Bordeaux harvests following, 128;
French appellation system and, 116;
impact of, on French vineyard areas,
90, 99, 208; impact of, on German
vineyard areas, 33
Wynne, Jim, 192

Xi Jinping, 188

yeast, 162
yeast nutrients, 161

Zachys (auction house), 193, 194, 198
Zeit, Die, 144
Zhen Wang Huang. *See* Kurniawan,
Rudy
Zimmermann, Max, 125

Founded in 1893,
UNIVERSITY OF CALIFORNIA PRESS
publishes bold, progressive books and journals
on topics in the arts, humanities, social sciences,
and natural sciences—with a focus on social
justice issues—that inspire thought and action
among readers worldwide.

The UC PRESS FOUNDATION
raises funds to uphold the press's vital role
as an independent, nonprofit publisher, and
receives philanthropic support from a wide
range of individuals and institutions—and from
committed readers like you. To learn more, visit
ucpress.edu/supportus.